A HOMETOWN COLLECTION

America's Best Recipes

Oxmoor House®

©1995 by Oxmoor House, Inc.
Book Division of Southern Progress Corporation
P.O. Box 2463, Birmingham, Alabama 35201

ISBN: 0-8487-1474-1

Manufactured in the United States of America
Third Printing 1996

Editor-in-Chief: Nancy J. Fitzpatrick
Senior Foods Editor: Susan Carlisle Payne
Senior Editor, Editorial Services: Olivia Kindig Wells
Art Director: James Boone

America's Best Recipes: A Hometown Collection

Editor: Janice Krahn Hanby
Copy Editor: Donna Baldone
Editorial Assistant: Stacey Geary
Director, Test Kitchens: Kathleen Royal Phillips
Assistant Director, Test Kitchens: Gayle Hays Sadler
Test Kitchens Home Economists: Susan Hall Bellows,
   Julie Christopher, Iris Crawley, Michele Brown Fuller,
   Natalie E. King, Elizabeth Tyler Luckett,
   Christina A. Crawford, Angie Neskaug Sinclair,
   Jan A. Smith
Senior Photographer: Jim Bathie
Photographer: Ralph Anderson
Senior Photo Stylist: Kay E. Clarke
Photo Stylist: Virginia R. Cravens
Senior Production Designer: Larry Hunter
Indexer: Mary Ann Laurens
Director of Production and Distribution: Phillip Lee
Production Manager: Gail H. Morris
Associate Production Manager: Theresa L. Beste
Production Assistant: Marianne Jordan
Project Consultants: Meryle Evans, Audrey P. Stehle

Cover: *Traverse City Cherry-Berry Pie (page 223)*

Back Cover: *Louisiana Baked Shrimp (page 178), Ketchup Salad Dressing (page 272), Hot Cross Buns (page 98), Sour Cream-Spice Layer Cake (page 108)*

Contents

Introduction

What a gold mine you hold in your hands. *America's Best Recipes* showcases over 400 of the highest rated recipes from over 200 current community cookbooks representing every state across America. The recipes take you on a cook's tour of regional cuisine, family traditions, and community concerns of the people who compiled the cookbooks. All of the recipes were rigorously tested by our test kitchen home economists, and each recipe received a quality rating. Only the very best recipes were chosen for inclusion in our book.

The long history and continued appeal of certain community cookbooks led us to salute the "best of the best" by establishing *The Southern Living Community Cookbook Hall of Fame.* We've spotlighted the 20 winners of this distinction in a special section called "Cooking with the Classics" that begins on page 5. The books nominated for this program were scored by a panel of experts on the basis of recipe content and clarity, design and graphic appeal, book story line, longevity, and volume of sales. Browse through the pages of this special chapter and you'll enjoy:

- A bird's-eye view of each of the organizations that compiled one of these award-winning cookbooks
- Sample recipes from each book, many characterizing the theme of the book and reflecting the ingredients inherent to the region
- Helpful tips for producing your own community cookbook

And don't miss our "Quick and Easy" chapter (beginning on page 47) featuring recipes that beat the clock. From delectable nibbles to scrumptious finales, all of the recipes are easy to prepare, call for just a handful of commonly used ingredients, and go from countertop to tabletop in 45 minutes or less.

We're excited about this year's selection of recipes and cookbooks, and think you will be, too. You'll find an alphabetical listing of cookbooks, including mailing addresses, in the Acknowledgments (beginning on page 320) if you'd like to order copies to explore further. You'll receive great new recipes plus the satisfaction that comes with knowing you are helping the fund-raising efforts of the volunteer organizations.

The Editors

Cooking with the Classics

Double-Frosted Bourbon Brownies, page 11

Bay Leaves

The Junior Service League of Panama City, Inc.
Panama City, Florida

On its shores lined with bay trees and scattered with fishermen, Panama City, Florida, has flourished with gracious hospitality and leisurely living since it was established. *Bay Leaves*, published in 1975 by the Junior Service League of Panama City, captures the flavor of those early days. The regional and cultural heritage of this Gulf Coast city is showcased in over 800 recipes, many like the recipe below that's indicative of the wealth of seafood found in the gulf. Profits of over $100,000 have enabled the league to fund projects including a child service center; Happy Hanger, a clothing source for needy children; Kids on the Block, puppet shows teaching children about the disabled; and the United Cerebral Palsy Center.

Bertha's Crab-Stuffed Chicken Breasts

Plan on making these stuffed chicken breasts for a special occasion. They're filled with a crabmeat mixture and topped with hollandaise sauce for panache.

6 (4-ounce) skinned and boned chicken breast halves
¼ teaspoon salt
¼ teaspoon pepper
½ cup chopped onion
½ cup chopped celery
3 tablespoons butter or margarine, melted
7 ounces fresh crabmeat, drained and flaked
½ cup herb-seasoned stuffing mix
3 tablespoons dry white wine
2 tablespoons all-purpose flour
½ teaspoon paprika
2 tablespoons butter or margarine, melted
1 (.9-ounce) package hollandaise sauce mix
¾ cup milk
½ cup (2 ounces) shredded Swiss or Cheddar cheese

Place chicken between 2 sheets of heavy-duty plastic wrap, and flatten to ¼-inch thickness, using a meat mallet or rolling pin. Sprinkle with salt and pepper; set aside.

Cook onion and celery in 3 tablespoons butter in a large skillet over medium-high heat, stirring constantly, until tender; remove from heat.

Add crabmeat, stuffing mix, and wine; stir well. Spoon mixture evenly on top of chicken breasts. Roll up chicken, starting with short end; secure with wooden picks.

Combine flour and paprika. Dredge chicken rolls in flour mixture. Place in a lightly greased 13- x 9- x 2-inch baking dish. Drizzle with 2 tablespoons butter. Bake, uncovered, at 375° for 35 minutes or until chicken is done; remove and discard wooden picks.

Combine hollandaise sauce mix and milk in a medium saucepan; stir well. Bring to a boil over medium-high heat, stirring constantly. Reduce heat and simmer, stirring constantly, 1 minute or until thickened. Add cheese, and stir until cheese melts. Serve chicken with sauce. Yield: 6 servings. John Henry Sherman, Jr.

Coconut Pie

1 (3-ounce) can flaked coconut, divided
1½ cups sugar
¼ cup cornstarch
Dash of salt
2½ cups milk
4 egg yolks, lightly beaten
¼ cup butter or margarine

2 tablespoons light corn syrup
1½ teaspoons vanilla extract
1 baked 9-inch pastry shell
4 egg whites
½ teaspoon cream of tartar
¼ teaspoon salt
½ cup sugar

Sprinkle 2 tablespoons coconut on a baking sheet; reserve remaining coconut. Bake at 350° for 3 to 4 minutes or until lightly toasted. Set toasted coconut aside.

Combine 1½ cups sugar, cornstarch, and dash of salt in a large saucepan. Add untoasted coconut, milk, and next 4 ingredients; stir well. Cook over medium heat, stirring constantly, until thickened. Spoon into prepared pastry shell.

Beat egg whites, cream of tartar, and ¼ teaspoon salt at high speed of an electric mixer until foamy. Gradually add ½ cup sugar, 1 tablespoon at a time, beating until stiff peaks form and sugar dissolves (2 to 4 minutes). Spread meringue over filling, sealing to edge of pastry. Bake at 325° for 25 to 28 minutes or until golden. Sprinkle toasted coconut on top of pie. Let cool completely on a wire rack. Cover and store in refrigerator. Yield: one 9-inch pie. Mrs. Judy Waldorff

The Gasparilla Cookbook

The Junior League of Tampa, Inc.
Tampa, Florida

Gasparilla, Tampa's famous week-long pirate celebration, is the namesake for this treasure of a cookbook. Both revel in the melding of a population and the festivities of merrymaking and good food. Steeped in history, *The Gasparilla Cookbook* reflects Tampa's Cuban, Spanish, Greek, Italian, and Southern heritages. Recipes run the gamut from Bollitos-la Florida to Luscious Lime Pie to Crab Enchiladas to the Spanish saffron rice recipe below. Chapters open with historical vignettes and pen-and-ink drawings mingling Tampa's past with its present. Celebrating 34 years of longevity, *The Gasparilla Cookbook* is one of the most prosperous in The Southern Living Community Cookbook Hall of Fame. Sales got a big boost in 1963 when First Lady Jacqueline Kennedy was photographed by the New York Times, cookbook in hand, after purchasing it at the New York World's Fair. The league has donated proceeds of nearly $2 million to charitable organizations, and in the spirit of Gasparilla, has succeeded in the areas of merrymaking and good food.

Yellow Rice and Chicken

This chicken dish is similar to paella, a Spanish dish of saffron-flavored rice and chicken or seafood. The good news about this particular recipe is that there'll be enough of the rice mixture for second helpings.

1 (3-pound) broiler-fryer, quartered	1 medium-size green pepper, chopped
1 cup olive oil	1 to 2 tablespoons salt
1½ quarts water	Pinch of saffron
1 cup chopped tomato	1 bay leaf
1 medium onion, chopped	1 (8½-ounce) can tiny English
2 cloves garlic, minced	peas, drained
1 (16-ounce) package long-grain rice	1 (2-ounce) jar diced pimiento, drained

Cook chicken in hot oil in a large oven-proof skillet over medium heat 40 to 45 minutes or until done, turning often. Drain well.

Return chicken to skillet. Add water, chopped tomato, onion, and garlic; stir well. Bring to a boil; boil 5 minutes. Add rice and next 4 ingredients; stir well.

Place skillet in oven. Bake, uncovered, at 350° for 30 to 35 minutes or until liquid is absorbed and rice is tender. Remove and discard bay leaf. Add peas and pimiento, and stir gently. Serve immediately. Yield: 4 servings.   Valencia Garden Restaurant

Trout, Russian Style

½ cup butter or margarine, softened
2 large hard-cooked eggs, finely chopped
⅓ cup finely chopped fresh parsley
2 tablespoons chopped pimiento
12 (4-ounce) trout fillets

½ teaspoon salt
¼ teaspoon ground white pepper
¼ cup milk
2 large eggs, lightly beaten
1½ cups fine, dry breadcrumbs
3 tablespoons vegetable oil, divided
2 lemons, thinly sliced

Combine butter, hard-cooked egg, parsley, and pimiento in a small bowl; stir well. Set aside.

Sprinkle fillets evenly with salt and white pepper. Combine milk and beaten egg. Dip fillets in milk mixture; dredge in breadcrumbs, coating well.

Cook 4 fillets in 1 tablespoon hot oil in an electric skillet set at 300° for 5 to 6 minutes on each side or until fish flakes easily when tested with a fork. Remove fillets to a serving platter; set aside, and keep warm. Repeat procedure with remaining fillets and oil. Spread butter mixture over warm fillets; top with lemon slices. Serve immediately. Yield: 6 servings.   Valencia Garden Restaurant

To Market, To Market

The Junior League of Owensboro, Inc.
Owensboro, Kentucky

"To market, to market
to buy a fat pig
home again, home again
jiggety jig."

Where the nursery rhyme leaves off, this cookbook takes over. *To Market, To Market* is a harvest of carefully tested recipes bound in a warm and whimsical cookbook. A product of the Junior League of Owensboro, Kentucky, it combines the charm of the South with the bounty of the Midwest. It also includes some local specialties. Bourbon, for which Kentucky is famous, is used not only in beverages, but also in meats, breads, and desserts. Check out what bourbon does for brownies in the recipe on the right. Many of the over 300 pages of recipes include brief descriptions and preparation hints to help both the beginning and the experienced cook. A "Tasteful Tips" section covers menus, measurements, and substitutions. Published in 1984, *To Market, To Market* is the most recently published cookbook in The Southern Living Community Cookbook Hall of Fame, but has already sold over 45,000 copies. As a result, more than $140,000 has benefited a parent resource center, after-school enrichment activities, and an adolescent pregnancy-prevention program.

Hot Chicken Salad

Crush your favorite brand of chips to make the topping on this casserole.

4 cups chopped cooked chicken	¼ cup grated onion
4 cups thinly sliced celery	1 cup (4 ounces) shredded Cheddar cheese
2 cups mayonnaise	2 cups crushed potato chips
1 cup sliced almonds	

Combine first 5 ingredients in a large bowl; stir well. Spoon chicken mixture into an ungreased 11- x 7- x 1 ½-inch baking dish. Sprinkle evenly with cheese. Bake, uncovered, at 450° for 10 minutes. Top with crushed potato chips, and bake 10 additional minutes or until thoroughly heated. Serve immediately. Yield: 8 servings.

Double-Frosted Bourbon Brownies

¾ cup all-purpose flour
¼ teaspoon baking soda
¼ teaspoon salt
½ cup sugar
⅓ cup shortening
2 tablespoons water
1 (6-ounce) package semisweet
   chocolate morsels
1 teaspoon vanilla extract
2 large eggs
1½ cups chopped walnuts
¼ cup bourbon
White Frosting
Chocolate Glaze

Combine first 3 ingredients in a medium bowl; stir well. Set flour mixture aside.

Combine sugar, shortening, and water in a medium saucepan. Bring to a boil over medium heat, stirring constantly; remove from heat. Add chocolate morsels and vanilla, stirring until smooth. Add eggs, one at a time, stirring after each addition. Add dry ingredients and walnuts; stir well. Spoon into a greased 9-inch square pan. Bake at 325° for 30 minutes or until a wooden pick inserted in center comes out clean.

Sprinkle bourbon evenly over warm brownies. Let cool completely in pan on a wire rack. Spread White Frosting on top of brownies. Pour warm Chocolate Glaze over frosting. Let stand until set. Cut into squares. Yield: 2½ dozen.

White Frosting

½ cup butter or margarine,
   softened
1 teaspoon vanilla extract
2 cups sifted powdered sugar

Combine butter and vanilla in a large mixing bowl; beat at medium speed of an electric mixer until creamy. Gradually add powdered sugar, beating until smooth. Yield: 1¼ cups.

Chocolate Glaze

1 (6-ounce) package semisweet
   chocolate morsels
1 tablespoon shortening

Combine chocolate morsels and shortening in top of a double boiler; bring water to a boil. Reduce heat to low; cook until chocolate morsels melt, stirring occasionally. Yield: ½ cup.

Mountain Measures

The Junior League of Charleston, Inc.
Charleston, West Virginia

The Junior League of Charleston, West Virginia, guides you through the rustic Appalachian Hills in *Mountain Measures*. West Virginian photography, poetry, and prose, along with more than 800 kitchen-tested recipes, depict the lives of pioneer women. Each of the 14 recipe chapters is designated by a different traditional quilt pattern, which appears in the margins throughout the chapter to indicate a regional dish. The pioneering spirit and work ethic have prevailed in the league's efforts to raise funds for the needy. First published in 1974, *Mountain Measures* is in its ninth printing and has sold more than 100,000 copies, netting over $220,000 for community causes. Charities assisted include the Ronald McDonald House, the Sunrise Children's Museum, and a teen outreach program.

Baked Swiss Steak

Swiss steak, called smothered steak in England, is a dish that begins with round steak dredged in flour and browned. It's "smothered" with a mixture of celery, carrot, onion, green pepper, and tomato, and baked until tender.

2 **pounds top round steak** (1 inch thick)	1 **(28-ounce) can whole tomatoes, undrained and chopped**
⅓ **cup all-purpose flour**	1 **(8-ounce) can tomato sauce**
1 **tablespoon vegetable oil**	⅓ **cup ketchup**
4 **stalks celery, coarsely chopped**	1 **tablespoon Worcestershire sauce**
3 **large carrots, scraped and coarsely chopped**	2 **teaspoons prepared horseradish**
1 **large onion, coarsely chopped**	¼ **teaspoon salt**
1 **green pepper, coarsely chopped**	⅛ **teaspoon pepper**

Dredge steak in flour. Brown steak in vegetable oil in a large skillet over medium heat; drain well. Place steak in a deep 4-quart baking dish; top with chopped celery, carrot, onion, and green pepper.

Combine tomatoes, tomato sauce, ketchup, Worcestershire sauce, horseradish, salt, and pepper; stir well, and pour over vegetables. Cover and bake at 325° for 2 to 2½ hours or until meat is tender. Yield: 6 servings. Mrs. Ronald A. McKenney

Lemon Bars Deluxe

These shortbread-based bars contain just the right amount of tangy lemon filling. Try cutting them with a heart-shaped cookie cutter instead of into bars for a special touch.

2¼ cups all-purpose flour, divided
½ cup sifted powdered sugar
1 cup butter or margarine
½ teaspoon baking powder

4 large eggs, lightly beaten
2 cups sugar
⅓ cup lemon juice
Powdered sugar

Combine 2 cups flour and ½ cup powdered sugar; cut in butter with pastry blender until mixture is crumbly. Firmly press mixture in a greased 13- x 9- x 2-inch pan. Bake at 350° for 20 to 25 minutes or until lightly browned.

Combine remaining ¼ cup flour and baking powder in a small bowl; stir well. Combine eggs, 2 cups sugar, and lemon juice in a large bowl; stir in flour mixture. Pour over prepared crust. Bake at 350° for 25 minutes or until set and lightly browned. Let cool completely in pan on a wire rack. Sprinkle with additional powdered sugar; cut into bars. Yield: 2½ dozen. Julia Newhouse

The Nashville Cookbook

The Nashville Area Home Economics Association
Nashville, Tennessee

The Nashville Cookbook is a sampler of historic Nashville and the Cumberland Region. Compiled by the Nashville Area Home Economics Association in 1976, the book was ahead of its time with a special section devoted to healthy cooking, complete with dietetic exchanges and fat and sodium values. Another distinguishing section is "Specialties of the Region," featuring recipes from the historic Maxwell House Hotel. With over 100,000 copies of *The Nashville Cookbook* in print, the Nashville Area Home Economics Association has donated over $20,000 to various charities, as well as to the historic restoration and preservation of Nashville. The area is depicted throughout the book by collector prints and descriptive text, so that you're never a "waltz" away from its Tennessee roots.

Dill Pickle Rye Bread

Make your next ham sandwich memorable with this hearty rye bread. It's flavored with chopped dill pickles, dillseeds, and caraway seeds.

3 cups all-purpose flour	½ cup buttermilk
3 cups rye flour	¼ cup vegetable oil
2 packages active dry yeast	2 tablespoons sugar
1 cup finely chopped dill pickles	2 teaspoons dillseeds
1 cup water	2 teaspoons caraway seeds
½ cup liquid drained from dill pickles	1 teaspoon salt

Combine flours in a large bowl; stir well. Combine 2 cups flour mixture and yeast in a large mixing bowl; stir well.

Combine chopped dill pickle and next 8 ingredients in a medium saucepan. Heat until dill pickle mixture reaches 120° to 130°, stirring occasionally.

Gradually add liquid mixture to yeast mixture, beating at low speed of an electric mixer until blended. Beat 2 additional minutes at medium speed. Gradually stir in enough remaining flour mixture to make a soft dough.

Turn dough out onto a lightly floured surface, and knead until smooth and elastic (about 8 minutes). Place in a well-greased bowl, turning to grease top. Cover and let rise in a warm place (85°), free from drafts, 40 minutes or until doubled in bulk.

Punch dough down; turn out onto a lightly floured surface, and knead lightly 4 or 5 times. Divide dough in half. Roll one portion of dough into a 14- x 7-inch rectangle. Roll up dough, starting at short side, pressing firmly to eliminate air pockets; pinch ends to seal. Place dough, seam side down, in a well-greased 9- x 5- x 3-inch loafpan. Repeat procedure with remaining portion of dough.

Cover and let rise in a warm place, free from drafts, 40 minutes or until doubled in bulk.

Bake at 350° for 40 to 45 minutes or until loaves sound hollow when tapped. Remove bread from pans immediately; cool on wire racks. Yield: 2 loaves.   Ruth Fay Kilgore

Squash Casserole

1 pound yellow squash, sliced	¼ cup butter or margarine
1 medium onion, chopped	2 large eggs, lightly beaten
⅓ cup water	1 tablespoon sugar
¼ teaspoon salt	¼ teaspoon salt
¾ cup (3 ounces) shredded Cheddar cheese, divided	¼ teaspoon soy sauce
	⅛ teaspoon pepper
½ cup fine, dry breadcrumbs or buttery cracker crumbs, divided	⅛ teaspoon paprika

Combine squash, onion, water, and ¼ teaspoon salt in a large saucepan. Bring to a boil; reduce heat, and simmer, uncovered, 15 minutes or until vegetables are tender. Drain and mash squash mixture. Add ½ cup Cheddar cheese, ¼ cup breadcrumbs, and next 6 ingredients; stir well. Spoon into a lightly greased 1½-quart casserole.

Bake, uncovered, at 350° for 20 minutes; top with remaining ¼ cup cheese and remaining ¼ cup breadcrumbs. Sprinkle with paprika, and bake 15 additional minutes or until cheese melts and mixture is thoroughly heated. Yield: 4 servings.   Louise Barker

One of a Kind

The Junior League of Mobile, Inc.
Mobile, Alabama

Members of the Junior League of Mobile named their cookbook to reflect how they felt about the Port City—that it's *One of a Kind.* Mobile is unique in its over two and a half centuries of history. The area was occupied by the French, English, and Spanish during its first 100 years. The settlers' influences are evident in the city's architecture and culture, as well as throughout the pages of this book. The menu section offers a sampling of history and customs in its meal suggestions for Mardi Gras, garden get-togethers, and hunt parties. The book includes a chapter on "Things Your Mother Never Told You," covering microwave cooking, helpful hints for using a food processor, and tips for low-calorie cooking. Because of Mobile's proximity to the Gulf Coast, fresh seafood recipes such as the ones that follow abound in the book. The league has donated proceeds from cookbook sales to "Mobile 2000," an education task force, and Camp Rapahoke, a camp for children with cancer.

Shrimp and Crabmeat Party Spread

Fresh shrimp and crabmeat make this appetizer spread special enough to serve at your next party. Be sure you chill the mixture 8 hours to allow the flavors to blend.

5 cups water
1½ pounds unpeeled
   medium-size fresh shrimp
1 (8-ounce) package cream
   cheese, softened
1½ tablespoons mayonnaise
1 tablespoon lemon juice
½ pound fresh crabmeat,
   drained and flaked

½ cup chopped green onions
½ teaspoon Worcestershire
   sauce
¼ teaspoon salt
¼ teaspoon hot sauce
⅛ teaspoon pepper

   Bring water to a boil; add shrimp, and cook 3 to 5 minutes or until shrimp turn pink. Drain well; rinse with cold water. Chill.
   Peel shrimp, and devein, if desired. Set aside.

Combine cream cheese, mayonnaise, and lemon juice in a medium mixing bowl; beat at medium speed of an electric mixer until smooth. Add shrimp, crabmeat, and remaining ingredients, stirring gently to combine. Cover and chill 8 hours. Serve spread with assorted crackers. Yield: 3¾ cups.   Mrs. Robert A. Cloninger

Shrimp and Green Noodle Casserole

All you'll need to add are a loaf of crusty bread and a tossed green salad to make a meal of this shrimp and pasta casserole.

8 ounces spinach noodles, uncooked
½ cup finely chopped green onions
9 cups water
3 pounds unpeeled medium-size fresh shrimp
1 cup mayonnaise
1 cup sour cream
1 (10¾-ounce) can cream of mushroom soup, undiluted
2 large eggs, lightly beaten
2 tablespoons prepared mustard
1 cup (4 ounces) shredded sharp Cheddar cheese
½ cup butter or margarine, melted

Cook noodles according to package directions; drain well. Combine noodles and green onions, tossing gently. Place noodle mixture in a buttered 13- x 9- x 2-inch baking dish. Set aside.

Bring water to a boil; add shrimp, and cook 3 to 5 minutes or until shrimp turn pink. Drain well; rinse with cold water.

Peel shrimp, and devein, if desired. Place shrimp on top of noodles.

Combine mayonnaise, sour cream, soup, eggs, and mustard in a small bowl; stir well. Pour over shrimp. Sprinkle with cheese, and drizzle with butter. Bake, uncovered, at 350° for 30 minutes or until cheese melts and mixture is thoroughly heated. Serve immediately. Yield: 8 servings.   Mrs. Sam G. Ladd

Out of Our League

The Junior League of Greensboro, Inc.
Greensboro, North Carolina

Out of the Junior League of Greensboro, North Carolina, and into over 100,000 kitchens, *Out of Our League* is a hit. You'll enjoy a collection of over 350 pages of recipes perfected by leading North Carolina hostesses who, throughout the book, provide helpful recipe preparation tips and plans for entertaining. An extensive menu section, flavored with Southern elegance, details year-round entertaining. Included are menus for celebrating holidays and numerous special occasions like a Debutante Tea and a Summer Ice Cream Social. In the tireless spirit of Southern hospitality, the menu section also includes recipes for a Progressive Dinner Party, Tailgate Picnic, Cocktail Party, and Buffet. Just as well rounded as the cookbook is the league's funding of community projects. Focusing on five issues, it's made significant contributions in the areas of family support, health, public education, community revitalization, and the environment.

Chicken Curry

The unique crust in this chicken curry casserole is made of wheat bran flakes cereal with raisins.

3 cups wheat bran flakes cereal with raisins	1 to 2 tablespoons curry powder
⅓ cup butter or margarine, melted	¼ teaspoon pepper
2 teaspoons salt, divided	2½ cups chopped cooked chicken
⅓ cup butter or margarine	2 tablespoons flaked coconut
2 tablespoons all-purpose flour	2 tablespoons chutney, chopped (optional)
2 cups half-and-half	

Combine cereal, ⅓ cup melted butter, and 1 teaspoon salt; stirring gently. Spread cereal mixture on bottom and 1 inch up sides of an ungreased 11- x 7- x 1½-inch baking dish. Set aside.

Melt ⅓ cup butter in a heavy saucepan over low heat; add flour, stirring until smooth. Cook 1 minute, stirring constantly. Gradually add half-and-half; cook over medium heat, stirring constantly, until mixture is thickened and bubbly. Stir in remaining 1 teaspoon salt, curry powder, and pepper. Add chicken, coconut, and chutney, if desired. Spoon chicken mixture evenly over cereal mixture. Bake, uncovered, at 350° for 25 minutes or until thoroughly heated. Serve immediately. Yield: 6 servings.

French-Fried Green Pepper Rings

If you're a fan of fried onion rings, you'll love this crispy green pepper version. Here the green peppers are coated with a tasty blend of Italian-seasoned bread-crumbs and Parmesan cheese.

3 **large green peppers**
2 **large eggs, lightly beaten**
2 **cups milk**
⅔ **cup Italian-seasoned breadcrumbs**

½ **cup grated Parmesan cheese**
1 **cup all-purpose flour**
Vegetable oil

Slice peppers into ¼-inch rings; remove and discard seeds and membranes. Set aside.

Combine eggs and milk, stirring well. Combine breadcrumbs and cheese, stirring well. Dip pepper rings in egg mixture, and dredge in flour. Dip again into egg mixture, and dredge in breadcrumb mixture, coating well.

Pour oil to depth of 2 inches into a Dutch oven; heat to 375°. Fry green pepper rings 1 to 2 minutes or until golden, turning once. Drain on paper towels. Serve immediately. Yield: 4 servings.

Party Potpourri

The Junior League of Memphis, Inc.
Memphis, Tennessee

Just open the cheerful cover of *Party Potpourri*, and you'll see why it's a must for any entertainer. You're greeted with nearly 100 pages of spectacular menus, complete with invitations, decorations, serving suggestions, and fun game ideas. Use the bright pink divider pages to flip easily through the recipe chapters, and you'll come upon sections titled "Setting the Scene" and "Gilding the Lily," which cover table settings, garnishing, and centerpieces. Containing a wealth of entertaining information, *Party Potpourri* is a one-stop guide from which a hostess can cull tips to combine with her own imagination for an endless potpourri of party ideas. With the same energy put into the making of this cookbook, the Junior League of Memphis has raised over $2.5 million to benefit many needy causes. Among them are a Memphis children's comprehensive health-care program, family transitional shelter, and summer camp for homeless children.

Make-Ahead Cheese Soufflé

Good news! You can make this soufflé ahead of time. Just spoon the mixture into a soufflé dish; cover and chill it 8 hours. Place the soufflé in a cold oven. Turn oven to 350°, and bake for 55 to 60 minutes or until it's puffed and set.

¼ cup plus 2 tablespoons butter
  or margarine
¼ cup plus 2 tablespoons
  all-purpose flour
1½ cups milk
1 teaspoon salt
½ teaspoon paprika
¼ teaspoon Worcestershire
  sauce

⅛ teaspoon onion salt
⅛ teaspoon dry mustard
⅛ teaspoon ground red pepper
3 cups (12 ounces) shredded
  sharp Cheddar cheese
6 large eggs, separated

Melt butter in a large heavy saucepan over low heat; add flour, stirring until smooth. Cook 1 minute, stirring constantly. Gradually add milk; cook over medium heat, stirring constantly, until mixture is thickened and bubbly. Remove from heat. Stir in salt, paprika,

Worcestershire sauce, onion salt, mustard, and red pepper. Add cheese, stirring constantly until cheese melts.

Beat egg yolks until thick and pale. Gradually stir about one-fourth of hot mixture into yolks; add to remaining hot mixture, stirring constantly. Beat egg whites in a large bowl at high speed of an electric mixer until stiff peaks form; gently fold beaten egg white, one-third at a time, into cheese mixture. Spoon into a buttered 2-quart soufflé dish. Bake at 350° for 55 to 60 minutes or until puffed and set. Serve immediately. Yield: 8 servings. Mrs. Robert G. Allen

Sausage Stroganoff

Spoon this stroganoff over hot cooked noodles or biscuits for dinner, and if there's any left over, serve it as a warm dip with assorted crackers.

1 clove garlic, halved	2 tablespoons Worcestershire
2 pounds ground mild pork	sauce
sausage	2 teaspoons soy sauce
3 tablespoons all-purpose flour	½ teaspoon salt
2 cups milk	¼ teaspoon pepper
2½ cups chopped onion	¼ teaspoon paprika
¼ cup butter or margarine,	1 (16-ounce) carton sour cream
melted	Hot cooked rice
1 (8-ounce) can sliced	
mushrooms, drained	

Rub a large skillet with garlic halves; discard garlic. Brown sausage in skillet over medium heat, stirring until it crumbles; drain. Return sausage to skillet. Add flour, stirring well. Add milk, and cook over medium heat, stirring constantly, until slightly thickened. Remove sausage mixture from skillet; set aside, and keep warm.

Cook onion in melted butter in skillet over medium-high heat, stirring constantly, until tender. Add sausage mixture, sliced mushrooms, and next 5 ingredients, stirring well. Bring to a boil; remove from heat, and gently stir in sour cream. Serve stroganoff over rice. Yield: 6 servings. Mrs. Eugene R. Nobles, Jr.

Pass the Plate

Episcopal Church Women of
Christ Episcopal Church
New Bern, North Carolina

With its 518 pages, *Pass the Plate* is one of the largest cookbooks in The Southern Living Community Cookbook Hall of Fame.

Compiled by the Episcopal Church Women of Christ Episcopal Church, the book draws from the roots of New Bern, North Carolina. Its rich German and Swiss culinary heritages flavor the pages. You can stroll the streets of town through the chapter called "Church Histories and Menus," which takes you to various churches throughout New Bern while providing complete menus for special occasions. You'll also enjoy the unique "Kids Can Cook Too!" chapter with child-friendly recipes for things like Frozen Chocolate Dirt, Doggie Biscuits, and edible Peanut Butter Play Dough. After meandering through the pages, you'll understand why nearly 100,000 people have purchased *Pass the Plate*. With the proceeds, the church women have lent a helping hand to Habitat for Humanity, Prison Ministry, and the Coastal Women's Shelter.

Incredible Pimiento Cheese

Pop some of this three-cheese spread into the freezer for up to a month, and you'll still have plenty left to store in the refrigerator for tasty cheese sandwiches throughout the week.

1 (16-ounce) loaf process cheese spread, cubed	2 cups salad dressing
4 cups (16 ounces) shredded mild Cheddar cheese	2 (4-ounce) jars diced pimiento, drained
4 cups (16 ounces) shredded sharp Cheddar cheese	3 tablespoons sugar
	½ teaspoon salt
	¼ teaspoon pepper

Position knife blade in food processor bowl; add half of all ingredients, and process until cheese mixture is well blended. Remove processed cheese mixture to a large bowl. Repeat procedure with remaining half of all ingredients.

Serve with assorted crackers, or use as a sandwich spread. Store in the refrigerator. Yield: 8 cups.   Karen Hansen Norman

Totally Amazing Tomato-Spice Cake

You'll be amazed to learn that this cake is made with pureed fresh tomatoes. The tomatoes add moisture more than flavor. In the flavor department, the cinnamon, nutmeg, cloves, and walnuts take the lead.

2½ cups fresh tomato puree (about 6 medium tomatoes)
4 cups all-purpose flour
2½ teaspoons baking soda
1½ teaspoons salt
2½ cups sugar
½ cup shortening
2½ teaspoons ground cinnamon
1 teaspoon ground nutmeg
1 teaspoon ground cloves
2 teaspoons vanilla extract
½ cup chopped walnuts

Combine first 10 ingredients in a large mixing bowl. Beat at low speed of an electric mixer until well blended. Beat batter at high speed 2 minutes. Pour batter into a greased 10-inch tube pan, spreading evenly; sprinkle with walnuts.

Bake at 350° for 65 minutes or until a wooden pick inserted in center of cake comes out clean. (Cover with aluminum foil to prevent excessive browning, if necessary.) Cool in pan on a wire rack 10 to 15 minutes; remove cake from pan, and let cool completely on wire rack. Yield: one 10-inch cake.

Recipes and Reminiscences of New Orleans

The Parent's Club of Ursuline Academy, Inc.
Harahan, Louisiana

In the 1700s, Ursuline nuns brought recipes from their homeland of France and adapted them to the food sources of New Orleans, contributing to the rich makeup of Creole cuisine. In no other community cookbook is Creole food highlighted as it is in *Recipes and Reminiscences of New Orleans.* The history of the Crescent City is peppered throughout the book in text and drawings in a fashion as spicy as the recipes for gumbos and jambalayas. Chapters are prefaced by historical sketches of the various ethnic groups whose recipes have come to constitute a heritage of superb cuisine. The over 400 kitchen-tested recipes, including those that follow, hint at the local flavor. Spice and herb charts, a glossary of regional cooking terms, and suggestions on "how to be a Creole cook with flair," will heat up any kitchen with the flavor of the French Quarter ... or of the Ursuline Academy. Produced in 1971, the cookbook has netted $1 million in sales to benefit the academy.

Grillades

Grillades is a Creole dish made up of pounded round steak that's braised in a rich tomato sauce. It's traditionally served over hot cooked grits.

1 **pound boneless round steak (½ inch thick)**	1 **cup hot water**
1½ **tablespoons all-purpose flour**	1 **medium-size green pepper, minced**
2 **tablespoons shortening, melted**	1 **tablespoon chopped fresh parsley**
1 **large onion, sliced**	1 **clove garlic, minced**
1 **(16-ounce) can whole tomatoes, undrained and chopped**	1½ **teaspoons salt**
	¼ **teaspoon pepper**

Place steak between 2 sheets of heavy-duty plastic wrap, and flatten to ¼-inch thickness, using a meat mallet or rolling pin. Cut steak into

2-inch squares; dredge in flour. Brown steak in shortening in a Dutch oven over medium heat. Remove steak, reserving drippings in pan; set steak aside, and keep warm.

Cook sliced onion in drippings in pan over medium heat, stirring constantly, 5 minutes or until tender. Add chopped tomatoes and next 6 ingredients; stir well. Return steak to pan. Bring mixture to a boil; cover, reduce heat, and simmer 1 hour or until steak is tender. Yield: 4 servings.   Aline Rault Kehlor

Mardi Gras Salad

The French-style green beans, tiny English peas, and diced vegetables look like a tangle of Mardi Gras beads.

1 (16-ounce) can French-style
   green beans, drained
1 (15-ounce) can tiny English
   peas, drained
1 (2-ounce) jar diced pimiento,
   drained
1½ cups diced celery

1 cup diced green pepper
½ cup diced onion
1 cup sugar
¾ cup white vinegar
½ cup vegetable oil
1 tablespoon salt

Combine first 6 ingredients in a medium bowl; stir well. Set vegetable mixture aside.

Combine sugar and next 3 ingredients; stir well. Pour sugar mixture over vegetable mixture; toss gently. Cover and chill at least 8 hours. Serve with a slotted spoon. Yield: 6 servings.   Mary S. Parkman

Savannah Style

The Junior League of Savannah, Inc.
Savannah, Georgia

Savannah Style truly represents Southern
elegance. Within its 464 recipes, the Junior
League of Savannah, Georgia, showcases the
city's considerable social and culinary charms.
Known as "hostess city of the South," Savannah is
revered for its style of cooking and entertaining. Each chapters
opens with a lovely illustration of an old Savannah scene and a story
of days past. Recipes such as Low Country Shrimp Boil, Savannah
Red Rice, and Plantation Eggs embody the city's flavor while
withstanding the test of time. In the 15 years since its original
printing, *Savannah Style* has raised over $400,000 to aid causes that
include a senior citizens' Alzheimer's day care center and an adult
literacy program.

Plantation Eggs

*Next time you're having a few folks for brunch, try serving this hearty egg
casserole flavored with dried beef and bacon. Homemade biscuits and fresh
fruit would round out the menu nicely.*

½ **cup sliced fresh mushrooms**
1 **tablespoon butter or**
   margarine, melted
16 **large eggs, beaten**
1 **cup evaporated milk**
¼ **teaspoon salt**
½ **cup butter or margarine,**
   divided

½ **cup all-purpose flour**
4 **cups milk**
8 **slices bacon, cooked and**
   crumbled
1 **(4½-ounce) jar dried beef,**
   rinsed, drained, and diced
¼ **teaspoon pepper**

Cook sliced mushrooms in 1 tablespoon melted butter in a small
skillet over medium-high heat, stirring constantly, until tender. Set
mushrooms aside.

Combine eggs, 1 cup evaporated milk, and salt; stir well. Melt ¼ cup
butter in a large skillet over medium-low heat; add egg mixture, and
cook, without stirring, until mixture begins to set on bottom. Draw a
spatula across bottom of pan to form large curds. Continue cooking
until eggs are firm but still moist (do not stir constantly); set aside.

Melt remaining ¼ cup butter in a heavy saucepan over low heat; add flour, stirring until smooth. Cook 1 minute, stirring constantly. Gradually add 4 cups milk; cook over medium heat, stirring constantly, until mixture is thickened and bubbly. Stir in mushrooms, bacon, dried beef, and pepper.

Pour half of sauce into an ungreased 13- x 9- x 2-inch baking dish; top with eggs. Pour remaining sauce over eggs. Cover and bake at 275° for 1 hour. Serve immediately. Yield: 12 servings.

Nutty Fingers

These pecan-studded cookies are called fingers because of their slender shape. Rolling the cookies in powdered sugar makes them all the more dainty–perfect for a shower or luncheon buffet.

½ cup plus 2 tablespoons butter or margarine, softened	2 cups all-purpose flour
¾ cup sifted powdered sugar, divided	1 tablespoon ice water
	1 tablespoon vanilla extract
	1 cup pecans, finely chopped

Beat butter at medium speed of an electric mixer until creamy; gradually add ¼ cup powdered sugar, beating well. Add flour, ice water, and vanilla, beating well. (Dough will be crumbly.) Stir in finely chopped pecans.

Shape dough into 2- x ½-inch fingers; place on greased cookie sheets. Bake at 350° for 14 to 16 minutes or until lightly browned. Cool completely on wire racks. Roll cookies in remaining ½ cup powdered sugar. Yield: 4 dozen.

Southern Accent

The Junior League of Pine Bluff, Inc.
Pine Bluff, Arkansas

When originally published in 1976, this cookbook was put together by hand. Wearing white gloves to keep from smearing the ink, cookbook committee members assembled the over 300 pages per book stacked throughout the league headquarters. That's a classic example of the heart and soul league members put into this book. An excellent illustration of Southern regional cookery, *Southern Accent* features over 750 recipes triple-tested by league members. Recipes range from homey cornbread and the tried-and-true cheese spread below to sophisticated duck and quail. Each chapter is sprinkled with preparation tips and serving suggestions, making this cookbook easy to use. A menu section covers everything from a Children's Tea Party to an elegant Seated Dinner, complete with table decorating ideas. The league's devotion and wonderful recipes have proved fruitful. Proceeds of over $265,000 from over 135,000 copies sold have enriched the community of Pine Bluff through projects like hospice, the Women's Shelter, Laucach Literary Council, the Children's Performing Arts Association, and summer reading enrichment programs.

Cheese and Bacon Spread

Green onions, almonds, and bacon make this spread a sure winner. Serve it with assorted crackers. You can store it in the refrigerator–if it lasts that long!

16 slices bacon	1⅔ cups chopped green
2 (8-ounce) containers sharp	onions
process cheese spread,	1 cup slivered almonds,
softened	toasted
2 cups mayonnaise	½ to 1 teaspoon salt

Cook bacon in a large skillet until crisp; remove bacon, discarding drippings.

Crumble bacon, and place in a large bowl. Add cheese, mayonnaise, green onions, almonds, and salt; stir well. Serve spread with assorted crackers. Yield: 5 cups.   Mrs. J. Wayne Buckley

Glazed Carrots

These baby carrots glisten with a glaze of brown sugar, honey, orange juice, and lemon juice.

2 (10-ounce) packages frozen baby carrots
½ cup butter or margarine, melted
2 tablespoons brown sugar
1 tablespoon grated orange rind

2 tablespoons fresh orange juice
1 tablespoon honey
2 teaspoons lemon juice

Cook baby carrots according to package directions until crisp-tender; drain well.

Place baby carrots in an ungreased 1½-quart baking dish. Drizzle melted butter evenly over baby carrots. Sprinkle brown sugar evenly over baby carrots.

Combine orange rind, fresh orange juice, honey, and lemon juice, stirring well. Drizzle orange juice mixture over baby carrot mixture. Bake, uncovered, at 325° for 30 minutes, stirring and basting often. Yield: 6 servings.

Mrs. Henry F. Marx

Southern Sideboards

The Junior League of Jackson, Inc.
Jackson, Mississippi

Southern Sideboards takes its name from the Southern practice of serving meals from hutch-type furniture. It's a timeless collection of 950 twice-tested Southern recipes, including features on cooking basics and food as gifts. The league has sold over 300,000 books and contributed over $1 million to the community.

Barbecued Ribs

6 pounds country-style pork ribs
1 large onion, sliced
1 lemon, thinly sliced
3 cloves garlic, minced
2 tablespoons butter, melted
1½ cups water
1 cup ketchup
¾ cup chili sauce
¼ cup firmly packed brown sugar
1 tablespoon celery seeds
2 tablespoons Worcestershire sauce
2 tablespoons soy sauce
2 tablespoons prepared mustard
2 teaspoons chili powder
½ teaspoon salt
¼ teaspoon liquid smoke
¼ teaspoon hot sauce

Place ribs in a roasting pan. Cover and bake at 450° for 45 minutes; drain. Top with onion and lemon. Cook garlic in butter in a saucepan over medium heat, stirring constantly, until tender. Add water and next 11 ingredients. Bring to a boil; pour over ribs. Bake at 350° for 1 hour, basting often. Yield: 6 servings.   Mrs. John Crawford

Strawberry Holiday Trifle

3 pints fresh strawberries
3 tablespoons sugar
Sponge Cake
¾ cup strawberry wine
Custard
¾ cup sliced almonds
Powdered sugar
Whipped cream

Rinse strawberries, and dry thoroughly. Reserve 14 whole strawberries for garnish. Hull and crush remaining strawberries. Combine crushed strawberries and 3 tablespoons sugar, stirring well. Set aside.

Split cake layers in half horizontally. Place a cake layer in bottom of 12-cup trifle bowl; brush with 3 tablespoons wine. Spoon one-third strawberry mixture over layer; top with one-third Custard. Sprinkle with ¼ cup almonds. Repeat layers twice. Brush remaining cake layer on cut side with remaining 3 tablespoons wine; place, cut side down, on top. Cover and chill at least 8 hours. Sprinkle with powdered sugar. Top with whipped cream and strawberries. Yield: 15 servings.

Sponge Cake

2 large eggs	¼ teaspoon salt
1 cup sugar	½ cup milk
1 cup all-purpose flour	2 tablespoons butter
1 teaspoon baking powder	1 teaspoon vanilla extract

Beat eggs in a large mixing bowl at high speed of an electric mixer 3 minutes or until thick and pale; gradually add sugar, and beat 4 to 5 minutes. Combine flour, baking powder, and salt; gradually fold into egg mixture.

Combine milk and butter in a saucepan; cook over low heat until butter melts. Gradually stir milk mixture and vanilla into batter. Pour into 2 greased and floured 8-inch round cakepans. Bake at 350° for 20 minutes or until a wooden pick inserted in center comes out clean. Cool in pans on wire racks 10 minutes; remove from pans, and let cool completely on wire racks. Yield: 2 (8-inch) cake layers.

Custard

⅔ cup sugar	2 tablespoons butter
2 tablespoons cornstarch	1 teaspoon vanilla extract
¼ teaspoon salt	1 teaspoon almond extract
2 cups milk	1 cup whipping cream, whipped
4 egg yolks, lightly beaten	

Combine first 3 ingredients in a saucepan; gradually stir in milk. Cook over medium heat, stirring constantly, until thickened and bubbly. Gradually stir about one-fourth of hot mixture into egg yolks; add to remaining hot mixture, stirring constantly. Cook over medium heat, stirring constantly, 2 minutes. Remove from heat; add butter and flavorings, stirring until butter melts. Cover with plastic wrap, gently pressing plastic wrap onto surface; chill. Fold whipped cream into custard mixture. Yield: 3½ cups.   Mrs. Clyde Copeland, Jr.

A Taste of Aloha

The Junior League of Honolulu, Inc.
Honolulu, Hawaii

A warm and welcoming cookbook, *A Taste of Aloha* has captured the fun, flair, and fine food of the magical islands of Hawaii. Recipes draw from the unique culinary delights of the islands, including an array of delectable seafood, fresh vegetables, and luscious fruits, that result in exciting new dishes. An extensive glossary of regional cooking ingredients and methods of preparation, as well as the "Hawaiian Fish and Seafood Chart" section, help guarantee that these tastes of the tropics will become family favorites. Suggestions for creating your own Hawaiian feast are found in the section on planning a luau. Donating proceeds from sales surpassing 100,000 books, the Junior League of Honolulu has made significant contributions to family-oriented causes. By providing assistance to foster children and abused children as well as home repair for elderly and low-income adults, the league has put a little sunshine into the lives of those in need.

Crispy Wonton

These Chinese-inspired dumplings are filled with a mixture of shrimp, pork, and vegetables, and then fried into crispy nuggets. You can halve the recipe if 8 dozen seems like too many, but we warn you—they'll disappear like popcorn.

6 unpeeled large fresh shrimp
¾ pound ground pork
¼ cup finely chopped water chestnuts
¼ cup finely chopped green onions
2 large eggs, lightly beaten
2 tablespoons chopped fresh cilantro

1 small clove garlic, minced
1 teaspoon salt
1½ (16-ounce) packages wonton wrappers (96 wrappers)
3 cups vegetable oil
Hot mustard
Sweet-and-sour sauce

Peel shrimp, and devein, if desired. Finely chop shrimp.
Position knife blade in food processor bowl; add shrimp, pork, water chestnuts, green onions, eggs, cilantro, garlic, and salt. Pulse 5 times or until blended.

Spoon 1 rounded teaspoonful pork mixture into center of each wonton wrapper; moisten edges with water. Fold wonton in half to form a triangle, pressing edges together to seal.

Pour oil into a large Dutch oven; heat to 375°. Fry wontons, in batches, 1 minute or until golden, turning once. Drain on paper towels. Serve with hot mustard and sweet-and-sour sauce. Yield: 8 dozen.

Lemon Chicken

No need to go out for Chinese food when you can make this authentic Lemon Chicken at home. The egg, cornstarch, and baking powder batter that coats the fried chicken is extra light and crispy.

1 tablespoon dry sherry	2 cups vegetable oil
1 tablespoon soy sauce	1 cup chicken broth
½ teaspoon salt	⅓ cup sugar
3 pounds skinned and boned	1 tablespoon cornstarch
chicken breast halves	1 tablespoon lemon juice
2 large eggs, beaten	1 teaspoon salt
¼ cup cornstarch	2 tablespoons vegetable oil
½ teaspoon baking powder	1 lemon, thinly sliced

Combine first 3 ingredients in a large heavy duty, zip-top plastic bag. Add chicken, and seal bag securely. Marinate chicken in refrigerator 15 minutes.

Combine eggs, ¼ cup cornstarch, and baking powder in a large bowl; stir well. Dip chicken into batter, coating well.

Pour 2 cups oil into a large heavy skillet. Fry chicken in hot oil over medium-high heat until golden, turning occasionally. Drain on paper towels. Cut chicken into 1½- x 1-inch pieces, if desired; arrange on a serving platter.

Combine chicken broth and next 4 ingredients; set aside. Place 2 tablespoons oil in a large nonstick skillet; place over medium-high heat until hot. Add lemon slices, and stir-fry 30 seconds. Add broth mixture, and stir-fry 3 additional minutes or until sauce is thickened and clear. Pour over chicken; serve immediately. Yield: 12 servings.

A Taste of Georgia

The Newnan Junior Service League, Inc.
Newnan, Georgia

Explore the delights and traditions of regional cuisine with *A Taste of Georgia*. The recipes in this collection are favorites from Southern kitchens and were triple-tested by the Newnan Junior Service League, all earning a perfect score on their one-to-four rating scale. The more than 250,000 people who've purchased the book since its original publication in 1977 have a real prize of a cookbook. The over 500 pages of recipes are sprinkled with hundreds of valuable culinary tips and include a star (★) noting those recipes that are typically Southern (like the Vidalia Onion Casserole below and, if you can believe it, 10 variations of pecan pie!). A "Special Features" section includes illustrated guides to appetizer trees, cake decorating, cheese selection, frozen punch rings, garnishes, napkin folding, and table settings. Also invaluable is a section called "Kitchen Charts" that covers everything from pan sizes to equivalent measures and substitutions. Chock-full of wonderful recipes and helpful cooking information, *A Taste of Georgia* is sure to be one of your Southern favorites.

Vidalia Onion Casserole

3 large Vidalia or other sweet onions, cut into wedges
2 tablespoons butter or margarine
2 tablespoons all-purpose flour
1 cup chicken broth
1 (5-ounce) can evaporated milk
½ teaspoon salt
½ teaspoon pepper
½ cup slivered almonds
1 cup soft breadcrumbs
½ cup (2 ounces) shredded Cheddar cheese

Cook onion in boiling water to cover in a large saucepan 2 minutes; drain and set aside.

Melt butter in a medium-size heavy saucepan over low heat; add flour, stirring until smooth. Cook 1 minute, stirring constantly. Gradually add chicken broth and evaporated milk; cook over medium heat, stirring constantly, until mixture is thickened and bubbly. Stir in salt and pepper. Add onion and slivered almonds, stirring gently to combine.

Pour into a buttered 11- x 7- x 1½-inch baking dish. Sprinkle with breadcrumbs. Bake, uncovered, at 375° for 25 minutes. Sprinkle evenly with cheese; bake, uncovered, 5 additional minutes or until cheese melts. Yield: 6 servings.   Joyce Moorman

Sour Cream Coconut Cake

This cake reminds many people on our staff of the old-timey coconut cakes their grandmothers made. It's important to frost this cake while it's still warm so that the cake will absorb moisture from the frosting as it cools.

1 cup shortening	1 cup self-rising flour
2 cups sugar	1 cup milk
5 large eggs	1 teaspoon vanilla extract
1 cup all-purpose flour	Frosting

Grease three 8-inch round cakepans; line bottoms of pans with wax paper. Grease and flour wax paper; set aside.

Beat shortening at medium speed of an electric mixer until soft and creamy; gradually add sugar, beating well. Add eggs, one at a time, beating after each addition.

Combine flours; add to shortening mixture alternately with milk, beginning and ending with flour mixture. Mix at low speed after each addition until blended. Stir in vanilla.

Pour batter into prepared pans. Bake at 350° for 22 to 25 minutes or until a wooden pick inserted in center comes out clean. Cool in pans on wire racks 10 minutes. Remove from pans; peel off wax paper.

Immediately spread 1 cup Frosting between each layer; spread remaining Frosting on top and sides of cake. Let cool completely. Yield: one 3-layer cake.

Frosting

2 cups sugar	1 (8-ounce) carton sour cream
1 (12-ounce) package frozen coconut, thawed	1 teaspoon lemon extract

Combine all ingredients in a medium bowl, stirring until blended. Yield: 3½ cups.   Vora Morgan

A Taste of Oregon

The Junior League of Eugene, Inc.
Eugene, Oregon

One of the best-selling community cookbooks of all times, *A Taste of Oregon,* is as rich in history as it is in recipes. This book takes you on a tour of Oregon, from its rustic frontier days highlighted by authentic recipes, to the present day with the emphasis on meals in minutes. The over 300 pages of recipes are dotted with historic notes, preparation tips, and serving suggestions. A menu section includes a Timber Country Breakfast, an Oregon Coast Picnic, and a Pioneer Supper, while the chapter "Potpourri" covers measurements and substitutions. Though a charming hometown favorite, *A Taste of Oregon's* popularity is widespread. Tellingly, an American woman fleeing Kuwait during the Iraqi occupation wrote the league to ask it to replace the copy she left behind. Realizing over $550,000 in profits since cookbook sales began in 1980, the Junior League of Eugene has reached out to a relief nursery for at-risk children, a program to prevent teen pregnancies, a shelter for victims of spouse abuse, and substance awareness programs.

Curried Spinach Salad

This spinach salad serves 12 generously and would be an ideal recipe to make for your next buffet. Toss it with the curry-flavored dressing just before ringing the dinner bell.

2 **pounds fresh spinach**	½ **cup raisins**
3 **Golden Delicious apples, unpeeled, cored, and diced**	⅓ **cup thinly sliced green onions**
⅔ **cup salted dry roasted peanuts**	2 **tablespoons sesame seeds, toasted**
	Dressing

Remove stems from spinach; wash leaves thoroughly, and pat dry. Tear spinach into bite-sized pieces.

Combine spinach, apple, peanuts, raisins, green onions, and sesame seeds in a large bowl; toss gently. Pour Dressing over spinach mixture; toss gently to coat. Serve immediately. Yield: 12 servings.

Dressing

½ cup white wine vinegar
1 tablespoon chutney, finely
   chopped
1 teaspoon salt

1 teaspoon curry powder
1 teaspoon dry mustard
¼ teaspoon hot sauce
⅔ cup vegetable oil

Combine first 6 ingredients in a bowl. Gradually add oil, beating with a wire whisk until blended. Cover and let stand at room temperature 2 hours. Yield: 1¼ cups.

Mom's Carrot Cake

2 cups sugar
1 cup vegetable oil
4 large eggs
2 cups all-purpose flour
2 teaspoons baking soda
2 teaspoons ground cinnamon
1 teaspoon salt
3 cups finely shredded carrot
1½ cups chopped pecans or
   walnuts, divided

½ cup raisins
2 teaspoons vanilla extract
½ cup butter or margarine,
   softened
1 (8-ounce) package cream
   cheese, softened
2 cups sifted powdered sugar
Lemon juice or milk

Grease three 9-inch round cakepans; line with wax paper. Grease and flour wax paper; set aside.

Beat 2 cups sugar and vegetable oil in a large mixing bowl at medium speed of an electric mixer 2 minutes. Add eggs, one at a time, beating after each addition.

Combine flour, baking soda, cinnamon, and salt; stir well. Gradually add to sugar mixture, beating at low speed until well blended. Stir in carrot, ½ cup chopped pecans, raisins, and vanilla.

Pour batter into prepared pans. Bake at 350° for 25 to 30 minutes or until a wooden pick inserted in center comes out clean. Cool in pans on wire racks 10 minutes; remove from pans, and let cool completely on wire racks.

Beat butter and cream cheese at medium speed until creamy. Add 2 cups powdered sugar, beating well. If necessary, add lemon juice, beating until frosting is spreading consistency. Stir in remaining 1 cup chopped pecans. Spread frosting between layers and on top and sides of cake. Yield: one 3-layer cake.

The Texas Experience

The Richardson Woman's Club, Inc.
Richardson, Texas

The big taste of the great Southwest is captured in full glory in *The Texas Experience*. The "Texas Favorites" chapter is a friendly welcome to the pages of this popular cookbook, containing recipes for chili, proclaimed the state dish by the Texas Legislature in 1977, the Gazpacho Dip below, and other Lone Star State specialties. The over 300 pages of recipes are easy to read, and cover everything from soups to nuts. Historical references, recipe notes, full-page color photography, and special-occasion menus make this book informative and a pleasure to use. Whip up a Texas State Fair or Tex-Mex Taste of the Border party, and experience friendship and food, Texas style. The marketing slogan for the cookbook , "there is no experience like a Texas experience, and everyone should have one," has served the book well. Published in 1982, the Richardson Woman's Club triple-tested all the recipes included in *The Texas Experience*. The group shared the results during numerous member luncheons and later shared the proceeds from book sales totaling over $220,000 with the local YMCA, American Heart Association, and theater and arts associations.

Gazpacho Dip

Chilling this dip before serving it allows the flavors to blend. If you have it on hand, you might add a bit of chopped fresh cilantro to the mixture for an even more authentic flavor.

3 **tablespoons vegetable oil**	1 **(4½-ounce) can chopped green chiles, undrained**
1½ **tablespoons cider vinegar**	4 **ripe avocados, peeled and diced**
1 **teaspoon salt**	
1 **teaspoon garlic salt**	
¼ **teaspoon pepper**	3 **medium tomatoes, finely chopped**
1 **(4¼-ounce) can chopped ripe olives, undrained**	5 **green onions, finely chopped**

Combine oil, vinegar, salt, garlic salt, and pepper in a small jar; cover tightly, and shake vigorously. Set oil mixture aside.

Combine chopped olives, green chiles, avocado, tomato, and green onions in a large bowl; stir well. Pour oil mixture over vegetables, stirring gently to combine. Cover and chill 3 hours. Serve dip with tortilla chips. Yield: 7 cups. Pat Williams and Carole Price

Richardson Woman's Club Coffee Punch

This quick and easy coffee punch is made with the help of a jar of instant coffee. The ginger ale that's stirred in lends some spice and sparkle to the punch.

2 **quarts hot water**
1 **(2-ounce) jar instant coffee**
2 **cups sugar**
2 **quarts half-and-half**
½ **gallon French vanilla ice cream**

1 **(1-liter) bottle ginger ale, chilled**
2 **cups whipping cream, whipped**

Combine hot water, instant coffee, and sugar in a large punch bowl; stir until coffee and sugar dissolve. Let cool completely.

Add half-and-half, ice cream, and ginger ale, stirring well. Gently fold in whipped cream. Serve immediately. Yield: 8 quarts.

Three Rivers Cookbook I

The Child Health Association of Sewickley, Inc.
Sewickley, Pennsylvania

Three Rivers Cookbook I is a charming, user-friendly cookbook that will quickly become a kitchen staple. Not only did cookbook committee members test each recipe, but they also noted the preparation time and baking time, and singled out which recipes are easy, make-ahead, and freezable dishes. As a bonus, most recipes have a tip or descriptive quote from someone who has prepared it. Sections of the cookbook devoted to local "Chefs' Specialties" and "Nationality Favorites" provide insight into the culture of the city. Each section of the cookbook opens with a sketch and a historical note about a spot of interest in the city of Pittsburgh. Produced by the Child Health Association of Sewickley, the book has been so successful that it's been followed by two sequels, *Three Rivers Cookbooks II* and *III*. Combined profits from the sale of the cookbooks have topped $1.5 million, which have been used to help southwestern Pennsylvania children in need.

Shrimp Newburg

Newburg is a very rich dish of chopped shellfish in a creamy sherry-flavored sauce. Serve the entrée with a tossed green salad and crusty dinner rolls for balance.

4½ cups water	3 tablespoons chili sauce
1½ pounds unpeeled large fresh shrimp	2 tablespoons dry sherry
2 tablespoons butter or margarine	1 tablespoon Worcestershire sauce
1 tablespoon plus 2 teaspoons all-purpose flour	1 teaspoon dry mustard
1 cup half-and-half	¼ teaspoon salt
	⅛ teaspoon pepper
	Hot cooked rice

Bring water to a boil; add shrimp, and cook 3 to 5 minutes or until shrimp turn pink. Drain well; rinse with cold water.

Peel shrimp, and devein, if desired. Set aside.

Melt butter in a heavy saucepan over low heat; add flour, and stir until smooth. Cook 1 minute, stirring constantly. Gradually add half-and-half; cook over medium heat, stirring constantly, until mixture is thickened and bubbly.

Add reserved cooked shrimp, chili sauce, sherry, Worcestershire sauce, mustard, salt, and pepper; stir well. Cook mixture over low heat just until thoroughly heated. Serve immediately over rice. Yield: 3 servings.   Mrs. John G. Zimmerman, Jr.

Benz à l'Orange

This frozen vanilla ice cream concoction takes its name from the contributor. Keep a batch of it on hand and you'll have a sweet treat to serve to unexpected company.

½ **gallon vanilla ice cream,**   ½ **cup brandy**
   softened
1 **(12-ounce) can frozen orange**
   juice concentrate, partially
   thawed

Combine all ingredients in a large bowl, and stir until blended. Cover and freeze until firm.

To serve, scoop mixture into individual dessert dishes. Serve immediately. Yield: 8 cups.   Mrs. Ralph Benz, Jr.

Thru the Grapevine

The Junior League of Elmira-Corning, Inc.
Elmira, New York

It's been said that "wherever vineyards bloom, an interest in good food flourishes." From such a place comes the Junior League of Greater Elmira-Corning's *Thru the Grapevine*. Inside the rich burgundy-colored cover, pen-and-ink illustrations capture the beauty of the Finger Lakes wine region of New York, producer of acclaimed vintage wines since the early nineteenth century. A wineries touring and tasting map, glossary of wine terms, wine suggestions list, and page of helpful hints make up a mini-wine handbook within the cookbook. The recipe section begins with festive seasonal menus, including a Men's Night to Cook and a Hunter's Dinner, that are complete with wine suggestions. Following the menus are over 600 double-tested recipes, each rated on an easy/average/complicated scale. Recipes calling for wine, like the one for Keuka Lake Chicken to the right, would do nicely with a wine from the region. Good food, good wine, and good deeds are what *Thru the Grapevine* is all about. Proceeds from book sales totaling over $90,000 have helped community children's centers, foster parent programs, the local historical society, and the local performing arts center.

Hot Artichoke Dip

Lots of folks are fond of the hot dip made with mayonnaise, Parmesan cheese, and artichoke hearts. This recipe takes the popular appetizer one step further with the addition of cream cheese–yum!

1 (8-ounce) package cream
   cheese, softened
1 (14-ounce) can artichoke
   hearts, drained

2 cups mayonnaise
1¾ cups grated Parmesan
   cheese

Beat cream cheese at medium speed of an electric mixer until smooth. Mash artichoke hearts; add to cream cheese, stirring well. Stir in mayonnaise and Parmesan cheese. Spoon into a greased 11- x 7- x 1½-inch baking dish. Bake, uncovered, at 350° for 20 minutes or until thoroughly heated. Serve dip with assorted crackers. Yield: 6 cups.

Keuka Lake Chicken

1 (4- to 5-pound) roasting chicken, cut up
3 tablespoons olive oil
1 medium onion, sliced
1 (14½-ounce) can Italian-style tomatoes, undrained and chopped
1 cup chicken broth
½ cup dry white wine
2 cloves garlic, minced
2 teaspoons minced fresh parsley
1 bay leaf
½ teaspoon dried thyme
1 cup pitted ripe olives
1 pound fresh mushrooms, sliced
1 (10-ounce) jar small white onions, drained
½ cup butter or margarine, melted
¼ cup lemon juice
Hot cooked wild rice

Brown chicken in batches in olive oil in a large Dutch oven over medium-high heat. Remove chicken, reserving drippings in pan. Set chicken aside.

Cook sliced onion in drippings in pan over medium heat, stirring constantly, until tender; drain. Return chicken and onion to pan; add tomatoes and next 6 ingredients. Bring to a boil; cover, reduce heat, and simmer 1 hour or until chicken is done. Remove chicken to a deep serving platter; set aside, and keep warm.

Bring sauce in pan to a boil; boil 5 minutes or until sauce is reduced slightly. Remove from heat. Remove and discard bay leaf. Stir in olives; set aside, and keep warm.

Cook mushrooms and small white onions in butter in a large skillet over medium-high heat, stirring constantly, 2 minutes. Add lemon juice, and cook, stirring constantly, 3 additional minutes or until mushrooms are tender. Add mushroom mixture to sauce; stir well. Pour sauce over chicken. Serve chicken mixture immediately over wild rice. Yield: 6 servings.

Virginia Cookery, Past and Present

Episcopal Church Women of
Olivet Episcopal Church
Alexandria, Virginia

Originally published in 1957, *Virginia Cookery, Past and Present,* is the granddaddy of cookbooks in The Southern Living Community Cookbook Hall of Fame. And the historical value it offers our cookbook collection dates back even further. It contains the recipes and an original manuscript from the Washington and Lee families of Virginia, submitted by the great-great-granddaughter of General Robert E. Lee. Amusing and interesting excerpts from several historic Virginia cookbooks make it as at-home in a reading room as it is in the kitchen. Learn all about the great tradition of Virginia bread, qualities said to accompany a good housewife, preparing a pedigreed pot-pie, and the first can opener. All this rich past is successfully blended with a fruitful present. Having sold over 40,000 copies of *Virginia Cookery, Past and Present,* the Episcopal Church Women of Olivet Episcopal Church have funneled proceeds back into the parish.

Imperial Crab

If you don't have the scalloped baking shells called for in this recipe, you can bake the rich crabmeat mixture in 6-ounce custard cups or small gratin dishes instead.

½ cup mayonnaise
1 tablespoon capers
½ teaspoon salt
⅛ teaspoon pepper

1 pound fresh crabmeat, drained and flaked
½ cup fine, dry breadcrumbs
Paprika

Combine first 4 ingredients in a medium bowl; stir well. Add crabmeat, and stir gently.

Spoon crabmeat mixture evenly into 6 greased scalloped baking shells. Sprinkle breadcrumbs evenly over crabmeat mixture; sprinkle with paprika.

Bake, uncovered, at 350° for 25 minutes or until thoroughly heated. Serve immediately. Yield: 6 servings.   Elizabeth Lamb

Spoonbread

Spoonbread is a pudding-like cornbread that's soft enough to eat with a spoon.

3 cups milk
1 cup cornmeal
1 tablespoon butter or
   margarine

1 tablespoon sugar
1 teaspoon salt
3 large eggs, separated

Combine milk and cornmeal in top of a double boiler; bring water to a boil. Reduce heat to low; cook, stirring constantly, 10 minutes or until mixture is slightly thickened. Add butter, sugar, and salt, stirring until butter melts.

Beat egg yolks until thick and pale. Gradually stir about one-fourth of hot mixture into egg yolks; add to remaining hot mixture, stirring constantly.

Beat egg whites at high speed of an electric mixer until stiff peaks form; gently fold beaten egg white into cornmeal mixture. Spoon batter into a lightly greased 9-inch square pan. Bake at 350° for 35 to 40 minutes or until set and lightly browned. Serve immediately. Yield: 6 servings.

Mrs. William Higham

Creating Your Own Cookbook

Creating a community cookbook is much like preparing a favorite recipe–its ingredients are key to success. The following essentials can help you whip up a winner.

1. Plan ahead. It takes time to gather, sort, test, and edit your recipes. Add the printing time, and the book production process often takes up to two years.

2. Establish a cookbook committee. The old saying "too many cooks in the kitchen spoil the broth" doesn't hold true when compiling a cookbook. A hard-working, devoted group is essential.

3. Decisions, decisions. Establish at the outset what type of book you want to create, what your budget will be, and what your fund-raising goals are. Today's community cookbooks run the gamut from small spiral-bound books to hardcover volumes with full-color photography. Community cookbook publishers tell us that a book with an average printing of five to 10 thousand copies generally produces a return of three times the initial investment.

4. Collect recipes. Gather recipes from within your organization, from friends, and perhaps from local chefs and celebrities. Request in a letter that each person submit at least five original recipes, each from a different food category and each on a separate sheet of paper. Ask that they include the recipe title, list of ingredients, preparation instructions, and yield. Additional information, such as recipe origin, preparation tips, whether a dish is freezable or can be made ahead, is helpful. Ask that the contributor's name and phone number be on each recipe in case further questions arise.

5. Sort recipes. Evaluate the chapter flow of your favorite cookbooks, and group your recipes accordingly. Organize the recipes within each chapter alphabetically or by food type.

6. Test recipes. To ensure quality, test each recipe. Note details like can and package sizes, pan sizes, baking times and temperatures, and yields. Many organizations turn taste-testing into group luncheons or experimental family dinners.

7. Edit. Record recipes in a consistent manner, being accurate and concise. Proofread each recipe carefully, especially all of the numbers.

8. Plan a party! Celebrate the publication of your cookbook with a party for all who helped. You'll have a wonderful collection of delicious recipes and delightful memories bound in a cookbook to treasure forever.

Quick & Easy Recipes

10-Minute Stroganoff, page 54

Cold Buttered Rum Drink

For a frosty treat in a flash, nothing could be quicker and easier than this ice cream-rum beverage made in the blender.

1 **quart butter pecan ice cream**   ½ **cup dark rum**

Combine ingredients in container of an electric blender; cover and process until smooth, stopping once to scrape down sides. Pour into glasses; serve immediately. Yield: 3½ cups.   Penny Rogers

Tempting Southern Treasures
Riverchase Women's Club
Hoover, Alabama

Orange-Sour Cream Dip

Vanilla instant pudding provides the creamy base for this simple fruit dip.

1 **(6-ounce) can frozen orange**   1¼ **cups milk**
   juice concentrate, thawed and   ¼ **cup sour cream**
   undiluted
1 **(3¾-ounce) package vanilla**
   instant pudding mix

Combine first 3 ingredients in a medium bowl, stirring with a wire whisk until blended. Stir in sour cream. Cover and chill at least 2 hours. Serve with fresh fruit. Yield: 2½ cups.   Jean Merkle

Sweet Home Alabama Cooking
44th National Square Dance Convention
Montgomery, Alabama

Hot Cheese Dip

2 cups (8 ounces) shredded
   extra sharp Cheddar cheese

1 cup mayonnaise
1 small onion, grated

Combine all ingredients in a medium bowl, stirring well. Place mixture in an ungreased 1-quart baking dish. Bake, uncovered, at 350° for 15 minutes or until hot and bubbly. Serve with assorted crackers. Yield: 2½ cups.

Beth Yanity

Ridgefield Cooks
Women's Committee of the Ridgefield Community Center
Ridgefield, Connecticut

Sun-Dried Tomato Dip

Sun-dried tomatoes add an intense tomato flavor to this thick and creamy dip. If you prefer a thinner consistency, add a little more oil from the tomatoes.

1 (7-ounce) jar oil-packed
   sun-dried tomatoes,
   undrained

1 (8-ounce) package cream
   cheese, softened
2 or 3 cloves garlic

Drain tomatoes, reserving 1 tablespoon oil. Position knife blade in food processor bowl; add oil, tomatoes, cream cheese, and garlic. Process until well blended, stopping once to scrape down sides. Transfer dip to a serving bowl. Serve with raw vegetables or tortilla chips. Yield: 1¼ cups.

Culinary Masterpieces
Birmingham Museum of Art
Birmingham, Alabama

Linda Bath's Cocktail Cheese Muffins

These savory cheese-tidbits make great finger food for an appetizer buffet. If you have any mini-muffins left after the party, serve them with a bowl of hot soup or chili.

¾ cup butter or margarine
2 cups (8 ounces) shredded
   sharp Cheddar cheese
2 cups self-rising flour

1 (8-ounce) carton sour cream
2 tablespoons frozen chopped
   chives

Melt butter in a medium saucepan over medium heat. Add Cheddar cheese, and cook 2 minutes, stirring constantly. Stir in flour, sour cream, and chives.

Spoon batter into ungreased miniature (1¾-inch) muffin pans, filling two-thirds full. Bake at 375° for 20 to 22 minutes. Remove muffins from pans immediately. Yield: 4 dozen.
        Mary Ann Marks

Georgia Land
Medical Association of Georgia Alliance
Atlanta, Georgia

Quick 'n' Cheesy Cocktail Swirls

Looking for a warm appetizer that won't keep you in the kitchen while your guests entertain themselves? Try these Quick 'n' Cheesy Cocktail Swirls. They can be made ahead and refrigerated up to two hours before baking.

1 (8-ounce) can refrigerated
   crescent dinner rolls
5 slices bacon, cooked and
   crumbled
1 (3-ounce) package cream
   cheese, softened

2 tablespoons finely chopped
   onion
1 teaspoon milk
Grated Parmesan cheese

Separate refrigerated dough into 4 rectangles; gently press perforations to seal.

Combine bacon and next 3 ingredients in a small bowl; stirring well. Spread bacon mixture evenly over rectangles. Roll up rectangles, starting at long side; pinch seams to seal. Cut each roll into 8 slices; place slices, cut side down, on ungreased baking sheets. Sprinkle with

Parmesan cheese. Bake at 375° for 12 to 15 minutes or until golden. Serve warm. Yield: 32 appetizers.   Barb Clements

Immacolata Cookbook
Immacolata Church Ladies Society
St. Louis, Missouri

Tuna Fettuccine

If you have fresh parsley on hand, chop a little to sprinkle over this pasta dish to dress it up.

4 ounces fettuccine, uncooked
½ cup sliced celery
⅓ cup chopped onion
2 tablespoons butter or margarine, melted
1 (8-ounce) package cream cheese, cubed and softened

⅔ cup milk
½ teaspoon salt
¼ teaspoon pepper
1 (6⅛-ounce) can solid white tuna, drained and flaked
½ cup grated Parmesan cheese

Cook pasta according to package directions; drain well. Set aside, and keep warm.

Cook celery and onion in butter in a large skillet over medium-high heat, stirring constantly, until tender. Add cream cheese, milk, salt, and pepper; cook over medium heat until smooth, stirring occasionally. Stir in tuna and Parmesan cheese; cook until thoroughly heated, stirring occasionally.

Combine tuna mixture and pasta; toss well. Serve immediately. Yield: 2 servings.   Eldora Carter

Havelock Recipes and Remembrances
Havelock Centennial
Lincoln, Nebraska

Scallops in the Oven

1 pound sea scallops
⅓ cup thinly sliced fresh
  mushrooms
¼ cup dry white wine
1½ teaspoons chopped shallots
¼ teaspoon salt
¼ teaspoon pepper

1 tablespoon lemon juice
⅓ cup soft breadcrumbs,
  divided
2 tablespoons butter or
  margarine, melted and
  divided
Hot cooked rice

Combine first 7 ingredients in a bowl, and stir gently. Add 3 tablespoons breadcrumbs and 1 tablespoon butter; toss gently. Place scallop mixture in a lightly greased 11- x 7- x 1½-inch baking dish; sprinkle with remaining 2 tablespoons plus 1 teaspoon breadcrumbs, and drizzle with remaining 1 tablespoon butter. Bake, uncovered, at 475° for 15 minutes or until scallops are opaque. Serve over rice. Yield: 4 servings.

Maureen Bare

The Montauk Lighthouse Cookbook
The Montauk Lighthouse Committee
Montauk, New York

Sautéed Shrimp

You'll save time if you buy shrimp already peeled and deveined. Or substitute frozen shrimp in this simple seafood sauté.

¼ cup butter or margarine
1 (.7-ounce) envelope Italian
  salad dressing mix

1 pound peeled and deveined
  medium-size fresh shrimp
Hot cooked pasta

Melt butter in a large skillet over medium heat; stir in dressing mix. Add shrimp; cook, stirring constantly, 3 to 5 minutes or until shrimp turn pink. Serve immediately over pasta. Yield: 4 servings.

Good Food, Good Company
The Junior Service League of Thomasville, Georgia

Tangy Sirloin Steak Stir-Fry

For a quick yet balanced meal, serve this stir-fry over hot cooked rice or egg noodles accompanied by your favorite vegetable.

2 pounds sirloin steak
¼ cup plus 2 tablespoons
   butter or margarine, melted
½ cup chopped green onions
2 tablespoons lemon juice

2 tablespoons Worcestershire
   sauce
1 tablespoon prepared mustard
Garnish: chopped fresh parsley

Partially freeze steak; slice diagonally across grain into ¼-inch strips. Cook steak in butter in a large skillet over medium-high heat, stirring constantly, until browned. Remove steak, reserving drippings in skillet; set steak aside, and keep warm.

Add green onions to drippings in skillet; cook over medium heat, stirring constantly, until tender.

Combine lemon juice, Worcestershire sauce, and mustard in a small bowl. Add lemon juice mixture and steak to skillet, and cook until thoroughly heated. Garnish, if desired. Yield: 4 servings.

Still Gathering: A Centennial Celebration
Auxiliary to the American Osteopathic Association
Chicago, Illinois

Simple Salisbury Steak

1 (10¾-ounce) can cream of
   mushroom soup, undiluted
   and divided
1 pound ground beef
⅓ cup fine, dry breadcrumbs
¼ cup finely chopped onion
1 large egg, beaten
1½ cups sliced fresh
   mushrooms

Combine ¼ cup soup and next 4 ingredients in a large bowl; stir well. Shape mixture into 6 patties.

Brown patties in a large skillet over medium heat. Remove patties, discarding drippings in skillet. Combine remaining soup and mushrooms in skillet; add patties. Bring to a boil; cover, reduce heat, and simmer 20 minutes or until meat is done, turning patties occasionally. Yield: 6 servings.

Diana Pfeiler

Idalia Community Cookbook
Women's Fellowship of St. John United Church of Christ
Idalia, Colorado

10-Minute Stroganoff

This timesaving stroganoff can be spooned over rice or boiled potatoes.

1½ pounds ground beef
1 (8-ounce) package presliced
   fresh mushrooms
1 large onion, thinly sliced
1 (16-ounce) carton sour cream
1 (10¾-ounce) can cream of
   mushroom soup, undiluted
Garlic salt and pepper to taste
   (optional)
Hot cooked egg noodles

Brown ground beef in a large skillet, stirring until it crumbles; drain and set aside. Add mushrooms and onion to skillet, and cook over medium-high heat, stirring constantly, 5 minutes or until tender. Add ground beef, sour cream, and soup; cook over medium heat 5 minutes or until thoroughly heated, stirring occasionally. If desired, stir in garlic salt and pepper to taste. Serve immediately over noodles. Yield: 6 servings.

Kayla M. K. Fuentes

Hawaiian Medley, A Cookbook of Old Favorites, Volume IV
Kamehameha Band Booster Club
Kapalama Heights, Hawaii

Beef-Rice Italiano

1 pound ground chuck
1 small onion, chopped
½ green pepper, chopped
1 clove garlic, minced
1 (10¾-ounce) can beef broth, undiluted
1 (14½-ounce) can whole tomatoes, undrained and chopped
1¾ cups instant rice, uncooked

Cook first 4 ingredients in a large skillet over medium-high heat, stirring constantly, until meat is browned and vegetables are tender; drain. Return meat to skillet. Add beef broth and tomatoes; bring to a boil, and remove from heat. Stir in rice; cover and let stand 15 minutes. Serve immediately. Yield: 4 servings.   Patricia Chirichiello

Derry Community Playground Cookbook
Derry Playground Committee
East Derry, New Hampshire

Skillet Sombrero Pie

Crunchy corn chips scattered around the edge of the beef mixture in the skillet form the "brim" of this sombrero pie.

1 pound ground round
1 (10-ounce) package frozen whole kernel corn, thawed
1 (16-ounce) can whole tomatoes, undrained and chopped
1 (8-ounce) can tomato sauce
1 tablespoon minced onion
1 (1¼-ounce) envelope taco seasoning mix
1 cup (4 ounces) shredded Cheddar cheese
1 (10½-ounce) package corn chips

Brown meat in a large skillet, stirring until it crumbles. Drain, discarding drippings. Return meat to skillet. Add corn and next 4 ingredients; bring to a boil. Reduce heat; simmer, uncovered, 20 minutes, stirring occasionally. Sprinkle with cheese; cook until cheese melts. Arrange chips around edge. Serve immediately. Yield: 4 servings.

Sugar Snips & Asparagus Tips
Woman's Auxiliary of Infant Welfare Society of Chicago
Chicago, Illinois

Veal Parmesan

For a less-expensive version of this beat-the-clock recipe, substitute skinned and boned chicken breast halves for the veal cutlets.

1 pound veal cutlets	1 (15-ounce) can tomato sauce
¼ teaspoon salt	1 (8-ounce) package sliced
¼ teaspoon pepper	mozzarella cheese
¼ cup all-purpose flour	Grated Parmesan cheese
¼ cup butter or margarine,	
melted and divided	

Place veal between 2 sheets of heavy-duty plastic wrap, and flatten to ⅛-inch thickness, using a meat mallet or rolling pin. Sprinkle with salt and pepper, and dredge in flour.

Brown half of veal in 2 tablespoons butter in a large skillet over medium-high heat 3 minutes on each side. Remove veal, reserving drippings in skillet. Place veal in a greased 13- x 9- x 2-inch baking dish. Repeat procedure with remaining veal and 2 tablespoons butter, reserving drippings in skillet. Add tomato sauce to drippings in skillet; stir well. Bring to a boil over medium heat, stirring occasionally.

Place cheese slices on top of veal. Broil 5½ inches from heat (with electric oven door partially opened) 1 minute or until cheese melts.

Spoon sauce over veal. Sprinkle with Parmesan cheese. Serve immediately. Yield: 4 servings.

Donna Anderson

Carol & Friends, A Taste of North County
Carol & Friends Steering Committee of the Carol Cox Re-Entry
Women's Scholarship Fund at CSU-San Marcos
San Marcos, California

Pecan Lamb Chops

1 egg white, lightly beaten
1 tablespoon Dijon mustard
⅓ cup finely chopped pecans
¼ cup fine, dry breadcrumbs

1 small clove garlic, minced
4 (1-inch-thick) lamb loin chops
2 tablespoons vegetable oil

Combine egg white and mustard, stirring well. Set aside.

Combine pecans, breadcrumbs, and garlic; stir well. Dip lamb chops in egg white mixture, and dredge in pecan mixture, coating well.

Cook lamb chops in oil in a medium skillet over medium-low heat 7 to 10 minutes on each side or to desired degree of doneness. Yield: 4 servings.

Taste the Good Life
The Assistance League of Omaha, Nebraska

Parmesan Pork Tenderloin

3 tablespoons Italian-seasoned
  breadcrumbs
1 tablespoon grated Parmesan
  cheese
1 teaspoon salt
⅛ teaspoon pepper

1 (1-pound) pork tenderloin,
  cut into 1-inch-thick slices
1 small onion, chopped
1 clove garlic, minced
2 teaspoons vegetable oil

Combine first 4 ingredients; stir well, and set aside.

Place pork between 2 sheets of heavy-duty plastic wrap; flatten to ½-inch thickness, using a meat mallet or rolling pin.

Dredge pork in breadcrumb mixture, coating well. Cook pork, onion, and garlic in hot oil in a large skillet over medium heat about 10 minutes or until pork is done, turning pork once. Yield: 4 servings.

Fabulous Foods
St. John's Hospital and Southern Illinois
University School of Medicine
Springfield, Illinois

Ham Steak Hawaiian

You can substitute white wine vinegar for red wine vinegar in this speedy entrée. Red and white wine vinegars both have a pleasantly pungent flavor that gives the sauce a sweet-and-sour taste.

½ cup firmly packed brown sugar
¼ cup butter or margarine

¼ cup red wine vinegar
1 (½-inch-thick) slice fully cooked ham (about 1 pound)

Combine first 3 ingredients in a large skillet; cook over low heat, stirring constantly, until sugar dissolves and butter melts. Add ham slice; cook over medium heat 10 minutes on each side or until thoroughly heated. Yield: 4 servings.

Joan Davis

Recipes from the Heart I
South Suburban Humane Society Auxiliary
Chicago Heights, Illinois

Chicken Divan

2 (10-ounce) packages frozen broccoli spears
6 skinned and boned chicken breast halves
2 (10¾-ounce) cans cream of chicken soup, undiluted
½ cup (2 ounces) shredded sharp Cheddar cheese

½ cup mayonnaise
2 teaspoons lemon juice
½ teaspoon curry powder
½ cup fine, dry breadcrumbs
2 tablespoons butter or margarine, melted

Cook broccoli according to package directions; drain. Place in a greased 13- x 9- x 2-inch baking dish; top with chicken. Set aside.

Combine soup and next 4 ingredients in a medium saucepan; cook over medium heat, stirring constantly, until cheese melts. Pour over chicken and broccoli. Sprinkle with breadcrumbs; drizzle butter over breadcrumbs. Bake, uncovered, at 350° for 40 minutes or until chicken is done. Yield: 6 servings.

Patie Switzer

Kailua Cooks
Le Jardin Academy
Kailua, Hawaii

Chicken Marsala

If you don't have Marsala on hand, you can substitute 1 cup dry white wine and 1 tablespoon plus 1 teaspoon brandy.

4 skinned and boned chicken
   breast halves
1 large egg, lightly beaten
¼ cup all-purpose flour
2 tablespoons butter or
   margarine, melted

2 cups sliced fresh mushrooms
1 cup Marsala
1 tablespoon chopped fresh
   parsley
½ teaspoon salt
¼ teaspoon pepper

Dip chicken in egg, and dredge in flour. Brown chicken in butter in a large skillet over medium-high heat. Remove chicken, reserving drippings in skillet; set chicken aside.

Cook mushrooms in drippings in skillet over medium-high heat, stirring constantly, until tender. Add chicken, Marsala, and remaining ingredients. Cook until heated. Yield: 4 servings.   Denise Reeves

CAP-tivating Cooking
YWCA of Peoria, Children and Parents Support
Peoria, Illinois

Praline Chicken

2 teaspoons Creole seasoning
6 skinned and boned chicken
   breast halves
¼ cup butter, melted

1 tablespoon vegetable oil
⅓ cup maple syrup
2 tablespoons brown sugar
1 cup chopped pecans, toasted

Sprinkle Creole seasoning on both sides of chicken. Cook chicken in butter and oil in a large skillet over medium heat 4 to 5 minutes on each side or until done. Remove chicken, reserving drippings in skillet. Place chicken on a serving platter; set aside, and keep warm.

Add maple syrup and sugar to drippings in skillet; bring to a boil. Stir in pecans, and cook 1 minute or until thoroughly heated. Spoon pecan mixture over chicken. Yield: 6 servings.

Among the Lilies
Women in Missions, First Baptist Church of Atlanta
Atlanta, Georgia

Quick and Easy One-Pot Chicken Dinner

Stock a few convenience items in your pantry, and you'll have everything you need to stir up this easy entrée when you have leftover chicken in the fridge.

1 (16-ounce) can chow mein vegetables, drained
1 (10¾-ounce) can chicken and rice soup, undiluted
1 (10¾-ounce) can cream of chicken soup, undiluted
1 cup chopped cooked chicken
2 tablespoons soy sauce
1 (3-ounce) can chow mein noodles

Combine first 5 ingredients in a large bowl; stir well. Spoon into a well-greased 11- x 7- x 1½-inch baking dish. Sprinkle with chow mein noodles. Bake, uncovered, at 350° for 25 minutes or until hot and bubbly. Serve immediately. Yield: 4 servings.   Chrissy Erickson

Our Daily Bread
Women's Club of Our Lady of Mt. Carmel
Carmel, Indiana

Penne with Walnuts, Green Onions, and Goat Cheese

To save preparation time, look for freshly grated Romano cheese in the specialty cheese section of your grocery store. If you prefer, you can grate your own cheese when you have time, and then store it in the freezer.

1 (16-ounce) package penne pasta
1 cup chopped green onions
1 cup coarsely chopped walnuts
¼ cup olive oil
4 ounces goat cheese, crumbled
1 cup whipping cream
½ cup freshly grated Romano cheese
Freshly ground pepper to taste

Cook penne pasta according to package directions; drain well, and set aside.

Cook green onions and walnuts in olive oil in a large skillet over medium-high heat, stirring constantly, until green onions are tender.

Add pasta and goat cheese; reduce heat, and cook, stirring constantly, until cheese melts. Remove from heat. Stir in whipping cream, Romano cheese, and freshly ground pepper to taste; toss gently. Serve immediately. Yield: 6 servings.

California Sizzles
The Junior League of Pasadena, California

Beef-Tortellini Soup

For variety, you can substitute fresh ground turkey for the ground beef and yellow squash for the zucchini.

1 **pound ground beef**	1 **(9-ounce) package frozen cut**
3 **cups water**	**green beans**
1 **(28-ounce) can tomato puree**	1 **(9-ounce) package fresh**
1 **(10½-ounce) can French**	**cheese-filled tortellini**
onion soup, undiluted	1 **medium zucchini, chopped**

Brown ground beef in a large Dutch oven, stirring until it crumbles; drain. Return meat to pan. Stir in water and next 4 ingredients. Bring to a boil; cover, reduce heat, and simmer 10 minutes. Add zucchini, and cook, uncovered, 15 minutes. Yield: 11½ cups.   Carol Baker

Favorite Recipes
National Association of Women in Construction,
Tri-County Chapter #317
Vero Beach, Florida

Cream of Peanut Soup

1 small onion, finely chopped
⅔ cup finely chopped celery
¼ cup butter or margarine, melted
2 tablespoons all-purpose flour
2 cups chicken broth
1 cup milk
1 cup half-and-half
1 cup creamy peanut butter
Salt and pepper to taste
Paprika

Cook onion and celery in butter in a large saucepan over medium-high heat, stirring constantly, until tender. Reduce heat to low; add flour, stirring until blended. Cook 1 minute, stirring constantly. Gradually add chicken broth and milk; cook over medium heat, stirring constantly, until mixture is thickened and bubbly. Stir in half-and-half and peanut butter; cook 5 minutes, stirring constantly. Add salt and pepper to taste; sprinkle with paprika. Yield: 6 cups.

Holy Cow, Chicago's Cooking!
The Church of the Holy Comforter
Kenilworth, Illinois

Quick Baked Beans

Pork and beans get a quick make-over with the addition of a few basic flavor-boosting ingredients.

1 (21-ounce) can pork and beans
¼ cup ketchup
2 tablespoons brown sugar
1 tablespoon instant minced onion
½ teaspoon salt
½ teaspoon dry mustard

Combine all ingredients in a medium saucepan, stirring well. Bring to a boil; cover, reduce heat, and simmer 10 minutes, stirring occasionally. Yield: 4 servings.   Dorinda Miller

Candlelight and Wisteria
Lee-Scott Academy
Auburn, Alabama

Broccoli Casserole

2 (10-ounce) packages frozen
  chopped broccoli
1 (10¾-ounce) can cream of
  mushroom soup, undiluted
1 (8-ounce) can sliced water
  chestnuts, drained

1 (2.8-ounce) can French fried
  onions
¾ cup (3 ounces) shredded
  Cheddar cheese

Cook broccoli according to package directions; drain.

Combine broccoli, soup, water chestnuts, and onions in a small bowl; stir well. Spoon into a lightly greased 1½-quart baking dish. Cover and bake at 350° for 20 to 25 minutes. Uncover and sprinkle with cheese; bake 2 to 3 additional minutes or until cheese melts. Yield: 8 servings.

Today's Traditional: Jewish Cooking with a Lighter Touch
Congregation Beth Shalom
Carmichael, California

Spinach Casserole

You can serve this creamy casserole either as a side dish or a hot dip.

2 (10-ounce) packages frozen
  chopped spinach, thawed
1 (16-ounce) carton sour cream

1 (1-ounce) envelope onion
  soup mix

Drain spinach well, pressing between layers of paper towels. Combine spinach, sour cream, and soup mix, stirring well. Spoon into a lightly greased 1-quart baking dish. Bake, uncovered, at 350° for 30 minutes. Serve immediately. Yield: 6 servings.

The Best of Sunset Boulevard
University Synagogue Sisterhood
Los Angeles, California

Black-Eyed Pea Salad

2 (15½-ounce) cans black-eyed
  peas, rinsed and drained
1 ripe avocado, peeled and
  chopped
1 medium tomato, chopped
1 medium onion, chopped
½ cup Catalina salad dressing

Combine all ingredients in a large bowl; toss well. Cover and chill 8 hours. Yield: 6 servings.   Janie Ingram

Home Cookin'
Volunteer Services Council for Abilene State School
Abilene, Texas

Tortellini Salad

Try cheese-filled tortellini instead of meat-filled tortellini for a variation of this make-ahead salad.

1 (16-ounce) package frozen
  meat-filled tortellini
1 cup chopped hard salami
  (about ¼ pound)
2 medium-size green peppers,
  cut into ½-inch strips
1 large onion, chopped
1 (2¼-ounce) can sliced ripe
  olives, drained
1 tablespoon dried basil
1 cup Italian salad dressing

Cook tortellini according to package directions; drain well.
  Combine tortellini, salami, and next 4 ingredients in a large bowl; add salad dressing, and toss well. Cover and chill 8 hours. Toss gently before serving. Yield: 8 servings.   Linda Knip

Country Cupboard Collection, Treasured Recipes from AT&T
AT&T/Western Electric Council, Telephone Pioneers of America
Ballwin, Missouri

Quick Pickled Peaches

Serve these peaches as a tangy side dish or on a bed of lettuce as a light salad.

1 (29-ounce) can peach halves
  in heavy syrup, undrained
½ cup cider vinegar
¾ cup firmly packed brown
  sugar

1 teaspoon whole allspice
1 teaspoon whole cloves
Lettuce leaves

Drain peaches, reserving syrup; set peaches aside.

Combine syrup, vinegar, and next 3 ingredients in a medium saucepan. Bring to a boil; boil 5 minutes. Add peaches; reduce heat, and simmer, uncovered, 5 minutes. Let cool completely. Cover and chill 8 hours. Drain, discarding spices. Serve peaches on lettuce-lined salad plates. Yield: 4 servings.   Mary E. Bishop

First United Methodist Church Centennial Cookbook, 1993
United Methodist Women of First United Methodist Church
Casper, Wyoming

Broccoli Cornbread

1 (10-ounce) package frozen
  chopped broccoli, thawed
1 (8½-ounce) package corn
  muffin mix
4 large eggs, lightly beaten

¾ cup small-curd cottage cheese
½ cup butter or margarine,
  melted
⅓ cup chopped onion
1 teaspoon salt

Drain broccoli well, pressing between layers of paper towels.

Combine corn muffin mix and next 5 ingredients; stir well. Stir in broccoli.

Pour into a greased 13- x 9- x 2-inch baking dish. Bake at 400° for 20 to 25 minutes or until golden. Let cool slightly, and cut into squares. Yield: 12 servings.   Ruth J. Coleman

Fabulous Foods
St. John's Hospital and Southern Illinois
University School of Medicine
Springfield, Illinois

Easy Focaccia

To lend authenticity to this Italian specialty, gently press your finger into dough at 2-inch intervals to create "dimples" before brushing it with olive oil.

2 (1-pound) loaves frozen bread
   dough, thawed
2 tablespoons olive oil
1 small onion, thinly sliced and
   separated into rings

¼ cup grated Parmesan cheese
1 teaspoon dried rosemary
½ teaspoon garlic powder

Place each portion of dough on a lightly greased baking sheet; slightly flatten each portion of dough into a 12- x 8- x ½-inch rectangle. Brush with olive oil. Top with onion rings; sprinkle evenly with cheese, rosemary, and garlic powder. Bake at 375° for 25 minutes or until lightly browned. Serve warm, or cool completely on wire racks. Yield: 2 loaves.   Valerie Viglione

Celebration: St. Andrew's School 30th Anniversary
Book of Celebrated Recipes
St. Andrew's School Parents' Association
Boca Raton, Florida

Pumpkin-Raisin Muffins

2 (15.4-ounce) packages nut
   bread mix
1¼ cups golden raisins

2 large eggs, beaten
1 (30-ounce) can pumpkin pie
   filling

Combine bread mix and raisins in a large bowl; make a well in center of mixture. Combine beaten eggs and pie filling; add to dry ingredients, stirring just until moistened.

Place paper baking cups in muffin pans; spoon batter into cups, filling two-thirds full. Bake at 400° for 15 to 20 minutes. Remove from pans immediately. Yield: 3 dozen.   Patricia Moran

Angels & Friends Favorite Recipes II
Angels of Easter Seal
Youngstown, Ohio

Easy Ginger Cookies

Creamy peanut butter also works well in these spicy cake-like cookies.

1 (14-ounce) package
  gingerbread mix
⅔ cup water

½ cup chunky peanut butter
½ cup raisins

Combine gingerbread mix, water, and peanut butter in a large bowl, stirring until smooth. Add raisins; stir well. Drop by rounded teaspoonfuls onto greased cookie sheets. Bake at 350° for 10 to 12 minutes or until lightly browned. Cool 5 minutes on cookie sheets; remove to wire racks, and let cool completely. Yield: 3 dozen.

Almost Chefs, A Cookbook for Kids
The Palm Beach Guild for the Children's Home Society
Palm Beach, Florida

Caramelts

1 (14-ounce) package caramels
¼ cup milk

4 cups crisp rice cereal
1 cup salted roasted peanuts

Unwrap caramels, and place in a large saucepan. Add milk; cook over low heat until caramels melt, stirring often. Remove from heat, and stir in cereal and peanuts.

Spoon into a buttered 8-inch square pan. Firmly press mixture into pan. Cool completely in pan on a wire rack. Cut into squares. Yield: 16 squares.   Laura Johnson

Family Style Cookbook
Northern Door Child Care Center
Sister Bay, Wisconsin

Five-Minute Fudge

Got 5 minutes to cook? You can have fudge!

1⅔ cups sugar
⅔ cup evaporated milk
½ teaspoon salt
1½ cups miniature
   marshmallows

1½ cups semisweet chocolate
   morsels
½ cup chopped pecans or
   walnuts
1 teaspoon vanilla extract

Combine first 3 ingredients in a large saucepan. Bring to a boil; cook 5 minutes, stirring constantly. Remove from heat; add marshmallows and remaining ingredients, stirring until marshmallows and chocolate morsels melt. Spoon mixture into a buttered 9-inch square pan, spreading evenly. Cool completely. Cut into squares. Yield: 2 pounds.   Jonesie and Rose Marie Medeiros

A Collection of Favorite Recipes
Po'oklea Church
Makawao, Hawaii

Peanut Butter Pie

4 ounces cream cheese,
   softened
1 cup sifted powdered sugar
½ cup milk
⅓ cup creamy peanut butter

1 (8-ounce) container frozen
   whipped topping, thawed
1 (9-inch) graham cracker crust
Hot fudge topping

Beat cream cheese at high speed of an electric mixer until creamy; gradually add sugar, beating well. Add milk and peanut butter; beat until smooth. Gently fold in whipped topping. Spoon mixture into crust; cover and freeze until firm. Serve with hot fudge topping. Yield: one 9-inch pie.   Doreen M. Sapp

Mitten Bay Gourmet
Mitten Bay Girl Scout Council
Saginaw, Michigan

Appetizers & Beverages

Hot Cranberry-Apple Cider, page 82

Pumpkin Dip

To add color and to hint at its flavor, serve this dip in a small fresh pumpkin. Just cut off the top of the pumpkin, and remove the seeds and membranes.

2 (8-ounce) packages cream
   cheese, softened
1 (16-ounce) package powdered
   sugar, sifted

1 (16-ounce) can pumpkin
2 teaspoons ground cinnamon
½ teaspoon ground nutmeg

Beat cream cheese at medium speed of an electric mixer until creamy; gradually add sugar, beating well. Stir in pumpkin, cinnamon, and nutmeg. Serve immediately, or cover and chill. Serve dip with gingersnaps. Yield: 5 cups.

Lori Drelles

Food for Family, Friends and Fellowship
Covenant Women Ministries of Forest Park Covenant Church
Muskegon, Michigan

Dill Dip

2 cups mayonnaise
1 (16-ounce) carton sour cream
3 tablespoons grated onion
3 tablespoons minced fresh dill

3 tablespoons minced fresh
   parsley
1 to 1½ tablespoons seasoned
   salt

Combine all ingredients in a bowl; stir well. Cover and chill. Serve with assorted fresh vegetables. Yield: 4 cups.

Corky Adams

The Montauk Lighthouse Cookbook
The Montauk Lighthouse Committee
Montauk, New York

Vidalia Onion-Cheese Dip

3 large Vidalia onions or other sweet onions, coarsely chopped
2 tablespoons unsalted butter or margarine, melted
2 cups (8 ounces) shredded sharp Cheddar cheese
1 cup mayonnaise
½ teaspoon hot sauce
1 clove garlic, minced

Cook onion in butter in a large skillet over medium-high heat, stirring constantly, until tender.

Combine onion, cheese, mayonnaise, hot sauce, and garlic; stir well. Pour into a lightly buttered 1½-quart casserole. Bake, uncovered, at 375° for 20 to 25 minutes or until bubbly and golden. Serve dip with tortilla chips or assorted crackers. Yield: 4 cups.

Come On In!
The Junior League of Jackson, Mississippi

Black-Eyed Pea and Pepper Caviar

If you'd like to "lighten" this colorful dip, substitute a fat-free Italian salad dressing for the regular salad dressing.

2 (15-ounce) cans black-eyed peas, rinsed and drained
1 (15-ounce) can black-eyed peas with jalapeño peppers, rinsed and drained
2 medium tomatoes, seeded and chopped
1 cup Italian salad dressing
¾ cup chopped onion
½ cup chopped sweet yellow pepper
½ cup chopped green pepper
¼ to ¾ cup seeded, chopped jalapeño pepper
1 (2-ounce) jar diced pimiento, drained
1½ teaspoons minced garlic
½ teaspoon ground cumin
½ teaspoon pepper

Combine all ingredients in a large bowl, stirring well. Cover and chill at least 2 hours. Serve dip with large corn chips or tortilla chips. Yield: 8 cups.

Still Gathering: A Centennial Celebration
Auxiliary to the American Osteopathic Association
Chicago, Illinois

Egg Salad Canapés

Top crackers with this egg salad spread to create simple yet delicious canapés for your next gathering.

1 envelope unflavored gelatin
¼ cup cold water
½ cup boiling water
1 cup mayonnaise or salad
    dressing
10 large hard-cooked eggs,
    chopped
½ cup minced onion

½ cup chopped celery
¼ cup chopped green pepper
¼ cup minced pimiento,
    drained
1 to 1½ teaspoons salt
2 teaspoons sweet pickle
    relish
2 teaspoons lemon juice

Sprinkle gelatin over ¼ cup cold water; stir and let stand 1 minute. Add ½ cup boiling water; stir until gelatin dissolves. Stir in mayonnaise. Let cool.

Combine chopped egg and next 7 ingredients. Add egg mixture to mayonnaise mixture, stirring well. Pour into a lightly oiled 6-cup mold; cover and chill until firm. Unmold onto a serving plate. Serve with assorted crackers. Yield: 6 cups.   Helen May Doolittle

A Treasure of Taste
The Auxiliary to St. Joseph Hospital
Mishawaka, Indiana

Chicken-Nut Pâté

1 cup pecan halves
1 cup walnuts
2 cloves garlic
4 (4-ounce) skinned and boned
    chicken breast halves, cooked
    and coarsely chopped
1 cup mayonnaise

2 tablespoons minced
    crystallized ginger
1 tablespoon soy sauce
2 teaspoons Worcestershire
    sauce
1 teaspoon white wine vinegar
½ cup minced green onions

Position knife blade in food processor bowl; add nuts. Process until coarsely ground. Remove nuts, and set aside.

Add garlic to processor bowl; pulse 4 times or until garlic is minced. Add chicken; process until smooth, stopping once to scrape down sides. Add mayonnaise and next 4 ingredients; pulse until blended.

Stir in green onions and nuts. Remove mixture to a crock or medium bowl. Cover and chill at least 8 hours. Serve with assorted crackers or breadsticks. Yield: 3⅓ cups.

The Bess Collection
The Junior Service League of Independence, Missouri

Party Pâté

For a statelier presentation, spoon the pâté into a lightly oiled 3-cup mold. Cover and chill 3 hours, and then unmold the pâté onto a lettuce-lined serving plate.

¼ cup raisins
1 pound liverwurst
4 ounces cream cheese, softened

1 tablespoon plus 1 teaspoon dry sherry
⅛ teaspoon curry powder

Pour enough boiling water over raisins to cover; let stand 5 minutes. Drain.

Position knife blade in food processor bowl; add raisins, liverwurst, and remaining ingredients. Process until blended, stopping once to scrape down sides. Mound mixture on a serving plate. Cover and chill at least 3 hours. Serve with thin slices of French bread. Yield: about 2¾ cups.

Some Like It Hot
The Junior League of McAllen, Texas

Hot Seafood Spread

¾ cup chopped cooked shrimp
(about ½ pound unpeeled
medium-size fresh shrimp)
¼ pound fresh crabmeat,
drained and flaked
1 (8-ounce) package cream
cheese, softened
1½ cups grated Parmesan
cheese
⅔ cup finely chopped green
onions
⅔ cup sour cream
2 tablespoons chopped fresh
dill
2 tablespoons prepared
horseradish
2 tablespoons fresh lemon juice
1 tablespoon onion powder
1 tablespoon Worcestershire
sauce
1 clove garlic, minced
⅛ teaspoon ground white
pepper
½ cup grated Parmesan cheese

Position knife blade in food processor bowl; add all ingredients except ½ cup Parmesan cheese. Process until smooth, stopping once to scrape down sides. Spoon mixture into a lightly greased 1-quart baking dish; sprinkle with ½ cup Parmesan cheese. Bake, uncovered, at 400° for 15 minutes or until golden. Let stand 5 minutes. Serve spread with assorted unsalted crackers, thin slices of French bread, or sourdough bread cubes. Yield: about 4 cups.   Kay Raby

Women Cook for a Cause
Women's Resource Center of Schoolcraft College
Livonia, Michigan

Brie with Sun-Dried Tomatoes

If you love garlic, this Brie appetizer is for you. Add a special touch by garnishing with sun-dried tomatoes and fresh parsley sprigs.

1 (15-ounce) round Brie
1 (7-ounce) jar oil-packed
sun-dried tomatoes,
undrained
2 tablespoons minced fresh
parsley
2 tablespoons freshly grated
Parmesan cheese
6 cloves garlic, pressed

Remove rind from top of Brie, cutting to within ½ inch of outside edges. Place on a serving plate.

Remove 4 tomatoes and 1 tablespoon oil, reserving remaining tomatoes and oil for other uses. Combine tomatoes, oil, parsley, Parmesan cheese, and garlic; stir well. Spoon tomato mixture over top of Brie; let stand at room temperature 1 hour. Serve with assorted crackers. Yield: 8 appetizer servings.   Margaret Lawrence

The Maine Collection
Portland Museum of Art
Portland, Maine

Bacon and Onion Cheesecake

6 slices bacon, diced
1 large sweet onion, chopped
1 clove garlic, minced
1 (15-ounce) carton ricotta
   cheese
½ cup half-and-half

2 tablespoons all-purpose flour
½ teaspoon salt
¼ teaspoon ground red pepper
2 large eggs
½ cup thinly sliced green onions

Cook bacon in a large skillet until crisp; remove bacon, reserving drippings in skillet. Set bacon aside.

Cook onion and garlic in drippings in skillet over medium-high heat, stirring constantly, until tender. Drain and set aside.

Combine ricotta cheese and next 4 ingredients in a large mixing bowl; beat at medium speed of an electric mixer until smooth. Add eggs, one at a time, beating after each addition.

Reserve 3 tablespoons bacon for garnish. Add remaining bacon, reserved onion and garlic, and green onions to cheese mixture; stir well. Pour mixture into a greased 8-inch springform pan.

Bake at 350° for 35 to 40 minutes or until center is almost set. Let cheesecake cool 10 minutes in pan on a wire rack. Carefully remove sides of springform pan. Sprinkle with reserved bacon. Serve warm cheesecake with assorted crackers. Yield: one 8-inch cheesecake or 12 appetizer servings.   Arlene Hines

St. Catherine of Siena Celebration Cookbook
St. Catherine of Siena Church
DuBois, Pennsylvania

Almond-Cheese Pizza

1 clove garlic, minced
1½ teaspoons olive oil, divided
1 (12-inch) pizza crust
¾ cup ricotta cheese
½ cup (2 ounces) shredded mozzarella cheese
½ cup (2 ounces) shredded fontina cheese
¼ cup freshly grated Parmesan cheese, divided
2 ounces prosciutto, finely chopped
¼ teaspoon dried basil
¼ teaspoon dried oregano
½ cup slivered almonds, toasted

Combine garlic and ½ teaspoon oil; brush lightly over crust. Spread ricotta cheese evenly over crust; sprinkle with mozzarella cheese, fontina cheese, 2 tablespoons Parmesan cheese, prosciutto, basil, and oregano. Gently press almonds into toppings; sprinkle with remaining 2 tablespoons Parmesan cheese. Drizzle with remaining 1 teaspoon oil. Bake at 425° for 12 minutes or until crust is golden. Cut into wedges. Yield: one 12-inch pizza or 12 appetizer servings.

Family & Company
The Junior League of Binghamton, New York

Black Bean Pancakes with Salsa

2 (15-ounce) cans black beans, rinsed and drained
1 clove garlic
1 large egg
2 tablespoons all-purpose flour
1 tablespoon ground cumin
1 teaspoon ground coriander
1 teaspoon ground ginger
½ teaspoon salt
¼ teaspoon ground cinnamon
⅛ teaspoon ground red pepper
Canola or vegetable oil
1 cup salsa
½ cup plain nonfat yogurt
1 green onion, sliced

Position knife blade in food processor bowl; add first 10 ingredients. Process until smooth, stopping once to scrape down sides. Transfer bean mixture to a medium bowl; cover and chill 15 minutes.

Spoon 2 level tablespoons bean mixture for each pancake onto a hot, lightly oiled nonstick skillet or griddle. Cook over medium-low heat 5 minutes or until lightly browned; turn and cook 3 additional minutes or until done.

To serve, spoon salsa evenly onto the center of 6 individual serving plates. Arrange pancakes around salsa. Top each serving with yogurt; sprinkle with green onion slices. Yield: 6 appetizer servings.

Taste Without Waist
The Service League of Hickory, North Carolina

Garlic Puffs

A nutty, sweet garlic puree is sandwiched between bite-sized puff pastry squares, giving these appetizers a wonderful flavor that's worth the effort.

15 heads garlic, unpeeled	2 large eggs
2 tablespoons olive oil, divided	1 tablespoon water
⅓ cup water	
1 (17¼-ounce) package frozen puff pastry sheets, thawed	

Gently peel outer skins from garlic; cut off top one-fourth of each head, and discard. Brush a shallow roasting pan with 1 tablespoon oil. Place garlic, cut side up, in pan; pour remaining 1 tablespoon oil and ⅓ cup water into pan. Bake, uncovered, at 350° for 1 hour or until garlic is soft. Remove from oven; let cool completely in pan.

Spoon out soft garlic with a spoon, and place it in container of an electric blender. Cover and process until smooth, stopping once to scrape down sides. Set aside.

Cut each puff pastry sheet crosswise into 8 strips. Roll 8 strips to ⅛-inch thickness, and prick with a fork. Arrange on ungreased baking sheets. Spread pureed garlic evenly over strips. Roll remaining 8 strips to ⅛-inch thickness, and prick with a fork; place a strip on top of each garlic-topped strip. Cut each strip crosswise into 10 pieces.

Combine eggs and 1 tablespoon water; beat well. Brush pastry with egg mixture. Bake at 350° for 7 to 10 minutes or until golden. Yield: 80 appetizers.

From Generation to Generation
Sisterhood of Temple Emanu-El
Dallas, Texas

Gouda-Cashew Bouchées

Bouchée is French for "small patty" or "mouthful." Each one of these savory "mouthfuls" is crowned with a buttery cashew.

1½ cups (6 ounces) shredded
   Gouda cheese
½ cup butter or margarine,
   softened

1½ cups all-purpose flour
1 teaspoon dry mustard
⅛ teaspoon salt
24 whole cashews

Combine cheese and butter in a large mixing bowl; beat at medium speed of an electric mixer until blended.

Combine flour, mustard, and salt; add to cheese mixture, beating until dough is no longer crumbly. Shape into 24 (1-inch) balls. Place on lightly greased baking sheets; gently press a cashew on top of each ball. Bake at 375° for 16 to 18 minutes or until lightly browned. Let cool on wire racks. Yield: 2 dozen.　　Rebecca Hardaway King

The Summerhouse Sampler
Wynnton Elementary School PTA
Columbus, Georgia

Zucchini-Stuffed Mushrooms

3¼ cups shredded zucchini
¼ teaspoon salt
30 large fresh mushrooms
   (about 2 pounds)
¼ cup unsalted butter or
   margarine, melted and
   divided
1 clove garlic, minced

¾ cup part-skim ricotta cheese
⅓ cup crushed saltine crackers
¼ cup grated Parmesan cheese
4 oil-packed sun-dried
   tomatoes, finely chopped
¼ teaspoon dried oregano
⅛ teaspoon pepper

Combine zucchini and salt in a colander; let stand 30 minutes. Press zucchini between paper towels to remove excess moisture. Set aside.

Clean mushrooms with damp paper towels. Remove stems, and reserve for another use. Brush mushroom caps with 3 tablespoons butter. Place on a rack in a broiler pan. Set aside.

Cook garlic in remaining 1 tablespoon butter in a large skillet over medium-high heat 1 minute, stirring constantly. Add zucchini, and cook 2 additional minutes. Remove from heat, and let cool slightly. Stir in ricotta cheese and next 5 ingredients. Spoon mixture evenly into mushroom caps. Bake at 375° for 20 minutes. Serve immediately. Yield: 2½ dozen. Karen Farnsworth

The Kinderhaus Cookbook
Kinderhaus Children's Center
Williston, Vermont

Spicy Chicken on Pita Wedges

2 chicken breast halves, skinned
½ cup water
½ teaspoon lemon-pepper seasoning
12 ounces cream cheese, softened
1½ cups (6 ounces) shredded Cheddar or Monterey Jack cheese
¼ cup sour cream
2 cloves garlic, minced
1 teaspoon ground cumin
1 teaspoon chili powder
½ teaspoon ground coriander
¼ teaspoon salt
⅛ teaspoon pepper
3 green onions, sliced
¼ cup chopped purple onion
1 to 3 tablespoons chopped pickled jalapeño peppers
4 (6-inch) pita bread rounds
Garnishes: sliced ripe olives, sliced green onions, shredded Cheddar or Monterey Jack cheese

Combine first 3 ingredients in a large saucepan; bring to a boil. Cover, reduce heat, and simmer 30 minutes or until chicken is done. Remove chicken from broth, discarding broth. Let chicken cool; bone chicken, and finely chop meat.

Combine chicken, cream cheese, and next 8 ingredients in a large bowl; stir well. Add green onions, purple onion, and jalapeño pepper; stir well. Slice each pita round horizontally to make 2 rounds. Spread chicken mixture evenly over rough sides of pita bread rounds. Cut each round into 8 wedges; place wedges on ungreased baking sheets. Bake at 375° for 8 to 10 minutes or until bubbly. Garnish, if desired. Serve immediately. Yield: 64 appetizers.

Heart & Soul
The Junior League of Memphis, Tennessee

Elegant Shrimp Rounds

If you'd like to prepare this appetizer ahead, spread the shrimp mixture on the toasted bread rounds, and chill up to 8 hours before baking.

3 cups water
1 pound unpeeled medium-size
   fresh shrimp
30 slices sandwich bread,
   toasted
1 clove garlic, minced
2 tablespoons butter or
   margarine, melted
1 tablespoon dry white wine
1 teaspoon grated lime rind

1 teaspoon chopped fresh dill
1 cup plus 2 tablespoons
   mayonnaise
1 cup grated Gruyère cheese
1 tablespoon finely chopped
   green onions
2 teaspoons finely chopped
   fresh parsley
¼ teaspoon salt
⅛ teaspoon pepper

Bring water to a boil; add shrimp, and cook 3 to 5 minutes or until shrimp turn pink. Drain well; rinse with cold water. Chill.

Peel shrimp, and devein, if desired. Finely chop shrimp; set aside.

Cut rounds from each slice of bread, using a 2½-inch biscuit cutter; set aside.

Cook garlic in butter in a large skillet over medium-high heat 30 seconds, stirring constantly. Remove from heat; stir in shrimp, wine, lime rind, and dill. Let cool. Add mayonnaise and next 5 ingredients; stir well. Cover and chill 1 hour.

Spread 1 heaping tablespoon shrimp mixture on each bread round. Place on ungreased baking sheets; broil 3 inches from heat (with electric oven door partially opened) 3 minutes or until golden. Serve immediately. Yield: 2½ dozen.

Simply Heavenly
Woman's Synodical Union of the Associate Reformed
Presbyterian Church
Greenville, South Carolina

Sassy Shrimp

6 cups water
2 pounds unpeeled medium-size
  fresh shrimp
½ cup lemon juice
¼ cup vegetable oil
2 cloves garlic, crushed
1 bay leaf, crumbled
1 tablespoon dry mustard
1 tablespoon red wine vinegar
2 teaspoons salt
½ teaspoon paprika

Dash of ground red pepper
1 (3¼-ounce) can whole pitted
  ripe olives, drained
1 medium-size purple onion,
  thinly sliced
1 lemon, thinly sliced
1 (2-ounce) jar diced pimiento,
  drained
2 tablespoons chopped fresh
  parsley

Bring water to a boil; add shrimp, and cook 3 to 5 minutes or until shrimp turn pink. Drain well; rinse with cold water.

Peel shrimp, and devein, if desired. Set aside.

Combine lemon juice and next 8 ingredients in a large bowl; stir with a wire whisk until blended. Add olives, purple onion, lemon, pimiento, and parsley; stir well. Add shrimp; toss to coat. Cover and marinate in refrigerator 1 to 4 hours. Yield: 8 appetizer servings.

Back Home Again
The Junior League of Indianapolis, Indiana

Pineapple Cooler

4 cups pineapple juice
2 cups apple juice
½ cup fresh lemon juice

1 quart pineapple sherbet
Garnish: fresh mint sprigs

Combine juices; pour into a large shallow dish. Cover and freeze 1 hour or until a thin layer of ice forms on the surface. Scoop pineapple sherbet evenly into chilled glasses; pour juice mixture evenly into each glass. Garnish, if desired. Serve immediately. Yield: 10 cups.

Rhode Island Cooks
American Cancer Society, Rhode Island Division
Pawtucket, Rhode Island

Hot Cranberry-Apple Cider

Cut lemon into paper-thin slices so you'll have enough to float a lemon slice in each serving of cider.

2 quarts apple cider	4 (3-inch) sticks cinnamon
1½ quarts cranberry juice cocktail	1½ teaspoons whole cloves
¼ cup firmly packed brown sugar	1 lemon, thinly sliced and divided

Combine first 5 ingredients and half of lemon slices in a large Dutch oven. Bring to a boil; reduce heat, and simmer, uncovered, 15 minutes. Remove and discard cinnamon sticks, cloves, and lemon slices. Pour beverage into cups. Top each serving with 1 of the remaining lemon slices. Serve hot. Yield: 13 cups.   Angie Gauger

Door County Cooking
Bay View Lutheran Church
Sturgeon Bay, Wisconsin

Hot Mulled Cranberry Wine

4 cups dry red wine	6 whole cloves
4 cups cranberry juice cocktail	4 whole allspice
2 tablespoons brown sugar	Garnishes: lemon slices, orange slices, cinnamon sticks
2 tablespoons sugar	
2 (3-inch) sticks cinnamon	

Combine first 4 ingredients in a Dutch oven. Place 2 cinnamon sticks, cloves, and allspice on a piece of cheesecloth; tie ends of cheesecloth securely. Add to wine mixture. Bring to a boil; reduce heat, and simmer 30 minutes. Remove and discard cheesecloth bag. Garnish, if desired. Serve hot. Yield: 7½ cups.   Marcia M. Wharton

A Taste of South Central Pennsylvania
South Central Pennsylvania Food Bank
Harrisburg, Pennsylvania

Hot White Chocolate Brandy Alexander

3½ cups milk
½ teaspoon vanilla extract
⅛ teaspoon salt
6 ounces white chocolate, finely
   chopped

⅓ cup brandy
3 tablespoons white crème de
   cacao
Garnishes: whipped cream,
   white chocolate shavings

Combine first 3 ingredients in a medium saucepan; cook over medium heat until thoroughly heated (do not boil). Remove from heat; gradually stir about one-fourth of hot mixture into chocolate, stirring with a wire whisk until chocolate melts. Add to remaining hot mixture, stirring constantly. Stir in brandy and crème de cacao. Pour into glasses. Garnish, if desired. Serve immediately. Yield: 4½ cups.

Sensational Seasons: A Taste & Tour of Arkansas
The Junior League of Fort Smith, Arkansas

Spiced Coffee-Eggnog Punch

2 cups strong brewed coffee
1½ (3-inch) sticks cinnamon
6 whole allspice
6 whole cloves
2 (32-ounce) cans eggnog,
   chilled

1 tablespoon vanilla extract
1 cup whipping cream, whipped
1 quart vanilla ice cream,
   softened
Ground nutmeg

Combine first 4 ingredients in a saucepan. Bring to a boil; reduce heat, and simmer, uncovered, 15 minutes. Pour coffee mixture through a wire-mesh strainer into a bowl, discarding spices; chill. Combine coffee mixture, eggnog, and vanilla in a large bowl; fold in whipped cream.

Spoon softened ice cream into a punch bowl. Pour eggnog mixture over ice cream, and stir gently. Sprinkle punch with ground nutmeg. Yield: 11 cups.

Loretta Warner

Our Favorite Recipes, Seasoned with Love
Neighborhood Bible Studies
Friendship, Texas

Very Berry Punch

When making the ice ring for this punch, you can use ginger ale instead of the water, if desired, so the ice ring won't dilute the punch as it melts.

Fresh strawberries
Fresh mint sprigs
1 (10-ounce) package frozen
   strawberries in heavy syrup,
   thawed
1 (12-ounce) can frozen
   lemonade concentrate, thawed
   and undiluted

1 (12-ounce) can frozen
   cranberry-raspberry juice
   concentrate, thawed and
   undiluted
2 (1-liter) bottles seltzer, chilled
1 (1-liter) bottle ginger ale,
   chilled
Garnish: fresh strawberries

Arrange fresh strawberries and mint sprigs in bottom of a 4-cup ring mold. Fill mold with just enough water to cover fruit but not float it; freeze until firm. Fill remainder of mold with water; freeze until firm.

Place thawed strawberries in container of an electric blender; cover and process until smooth, stopping once to scrape down sides. Combine strawberry puree, lemonade concentrate, and cranberry-raspberry juice concentrate, stirring well. Remove ice ring from freezer; let stand at room temperature 2 to 3 minutes. Unmold ice ring in bottom of a punch bowl. Gently pour strawberry mixture over ice ring. Gently stir in seltzer and ginger ale. Garnish, if desired. Yield: about 4½ quarts.

Thymely Treasures
Hubbard Historical Society
Hubbard, Ohio

Breads

Hot Cross Buns, page 98

Macadamia Nut-Banana Bread

Macadamia nuts add a tropical flair to this banana bread, but you can substitute an equal amount of any type nut.

2¼ cups all-purpose flour
1 tablespoon plus ½ teaspoon
   baking powder
½ teaspoon salt
¾ cup firmly packed brown
   sugar
¼ cup sugar
1½ teaspoons ground
   cinnamon

1¼ cups mashed ripe banana
⅓ cup milk
3 tablespoons vegetable oil
1 large egg
1 teaspoon white vinegar
1 cup macadamia nuts, coarsely
   chopped

Combine first 6 ingredients in a large bowl; make a well in center of mixture. Combine banana, milk, oil, egg, and vinegar; beat with a wire whisk until blended. Add to dry ingredients, stirring just until moistened. Stir in macadamia nuts.

Spoon batter into a greased 9- x 5- x 3-inch loafpan. Bake at 350° for 1 hour or until a wooden pick inserted in center comes out clean. Cool in pan on a wire rack 10 minutes. Remove from pan, and let cool completely on wire rack. Yield: 1 loaf.

Perfect Endings: The Art of Desserts
Friends of the Arts of the Tampa Museum of Art
Tampa, Florida

Lemon-Chutney Bread

The texture and flavor of this quick bread are at their best after the bread has stood at room temperature at least 8 hours.

2½ cups all-purpose flour
1 tablespoon baking powder
½ teaspoon salt
½ cup sugar
½ cup firmly packed brown
    sugar
1½ tablespoons grated lemon
    rind

1¼ cups milk
1 (9-ounce) jar mango chutney,
    chopped
¼ cup vegetable oil
1 large egg, lightly beaten
1 tablespoon lemon juice
1 cup chopped walnuts
Lemon-Cheese Spread

Combine first 6 ingredients in a large bowl; make a well in center of mixture. Combine milk, chutney, oil, egg, and lemon juice; stir with a wire whisk until blended. Add to dry ingredients, stirring just until moistened. Stir in walnuts.

Spoon batter into a greased 9- x 5- x 3-inch loafpan. Bake at 350° for 1 hour and 10 minutes or until a wooden pick inserted in center comes out clean. Cool in pan on a wire rack 10 minutes. Remove from pan, and let cool completely on wire rack. Wrap loaf in plastic wrap; let stand at least 8 hours before slicing. Serve with Lemon-Cheese Spread. Yield: 1 loaf.

Lemon-Cheese Spread

1 (8-ounce) package cream
    cheese, softened
2 tablespoons powdered sugar

1 teaspoon grated lemon rind
1 tablespoon lemon juice

Combine all ingredients in a small mixing bowl; beat at medium speed of an electric mixer until smooth. Store spread in refrigerator. Yield: 1 cup.

Tropical Seasons, A Taste of Life in South Florida
Beaux Arts of the Lowe Art Museum of the University of Miami
Coral Gables, Florida

Pumpkin Swirl Bread

1 (8-ounce) package cream
   cheese, softened
¼ cup sugar
1 large egg
1¾ cups all-purpose flour
1 teaspoon baking soda
½ teaspoon salt
1½ cups sugar

1 teaspoon ground cinnamon
¼ teaspoon ground nutmeg
1 cup canned pumpkin
½ cup butter or margarine,
   melted
⅓ cup water
1 large egg, lightly beaten

Beat cream cheese at medium speed of an electric mixer until smooth; gradually add ¼ cup sugar, beating well. Add 1 egg, beating until blended. Set aside.

Combine flour and next 5 ingredients in a medium bowl; make a well in center of mixture. Combine pumpkin, melted butter, water, and lightly beaten egg; stir well. Add to dry ingredients, stirring just until moistened.

Pour half of batter into a greased 9- x 5- x 3-inch loafpan. Gently spread cream cheese mixture over batter, leaving a 1-inch border around outer edges. Spoon remaining batter over cream cheese mixture. Swirl batter gently with a knife.

Bake at 350° for 1 hour and 20 minutes or until a wooden pick inserted in center comes out clean. Cool in pan on a wire rack 10 minutes. Remove bread from pan, and let cool completely on wire rack. Yield: 1 loaf.

Cheryl Carney

Derry Community Playground Cookbook
Derry Playground Committee
East Derry, New Hampshire

Walnut Bread and Pumpkin Butter

This walnut-studded bread also makes a terrific bread for toasting.

1 cup unbleached flour	¼ cup walnut oil
¾ cup all-purpose flour	1 large egg
2 teaspoons baking powder	1 tablespoon lemon juice
½ teaspoon salt	1 teaspoon vanilla extract
¾ cup sugar	½ cup chopped walnuts
¾ cup milk	Pumpkin Butter

Combine first 5 ingredients in a large bowl; make a well in center of mixture. Combine milk, oil, egg, lemon juice, and vanilla; stir with a wire whisk until blended. Add to dry ingredients, stirring just until moistened. Stir in walnuts.

Spoon batter into a lightly greased 9- x 5- x 3-inch loafpan. Bake at 350° for 45 to 50 minutes or until a wooden pick inserted in center comes out clean. Cool in pan on a wire rack 10 minutes. Remove from pan, and let cool completely on wire rack. Serve with Pumpkin Butter. Yield: 1 loaf.

Pumpkin Butter

½ cup butter or margarine, softened	½ cup canned pumpkin
¼ cup sifted powdered sugar	¼ teaspoon ground cinnamon
	¼ teaspoon ground nutmeg

Beat butter at medium speed of an electric mixer until creamy; gradually add sugar, beating well. Add pumpkin, cinnamon, and nutmeg; mix well. Cover and chill at least 3 hours. Let butter stand at room temperature to soften before serving. Yield: 1¼ cups.   Gayla Plott

Tempting Southern Treasures
Riverchase Women's Club
Hoover, Alabama

Chocolate Chunk Coffee Cake

½ cup butter or margarine,
  softened
1¼ cups sugar, divided
2 large eggs
1¾ cups all-purpose flour
1 teaspoon baking soda
½ teaspoon baking powder
¼ teaspoon salt

1 (8-ounce) carton sour cream
½ teaspoon vanilla extract
1 (4-ounce) package sweet
  baking chocolate, coarsely
  chopped
½ cup chopped pecans or
  walnuts
1 teaspoon ground cinnamon

Beat butter at medium speed of an electric mixer until creamy; gradually add 1 cup sugar, beating well. Add eggs, one at a time, beating after each addition.

Combine flour, baking soda, baking powder, and salt; add to butter mixture alternately with sour cream, beginning and ending with flour mixture. Mix at low speed after each addition until blended. Stir in vanilla.

Combine remaining ¼ cup sugar, chocolate, pecans, and cinnamon in a small bowl; set aside. Pour half of batter into a greased and floured 9-inch square pan. Sprinkle with half of chocolate mixture. Top with remaining batter, and sprinkle with remaining chocolate mixture. Bake at 350° for 30 to 35 minutes or until a wooden pick inserted in center comes out clean. Let cool completely in pan on a wire rack. Yield: 12 servings.   Missy Lucier

Cookin' with Fire
Milford Permanent Firefighters Association
Milford, Massachusetts

Raspberry Crumble Coffee Cake

If you prefer one large coffee cake, use a greased 13- x 9- x 2-inch pan, and bake as directed below.

⅔ cup sugar
¼ cup cornstarch
¾ cup cold water
2 cups frozen unsweetened whole raspberries
1 tablespoon lemon juice
3 cups all-purpose flour
1 tablespoon baking powder
1 teaspoon salt
1 cup sugar

1 teaspoon ground cinnamon
¼ teaspoon ground mace
1 cup butter or margarine
2 large eggs, lightly beaten
1 cup milk
1 teaspoon vanilla extract
½ cup all-purpose flour
½ cup sugar
¼ cup butter or margarine
¼ cup sliced almonds

Combine ⅔ cup sugar, cornstarch, and water in a medium saucepan, stirring until smooth; add raspberries. Cook over medium heat, stirring constantly, until mixture thickens and comes to a boil. Boil 1 minute, stirring constantly. Remove from heat, and stir in lemon juice; let cool.

Combine 3 cups flour and next 5 ingredients; cut in 1 cup butter with pastry blender until mixture is crumbly. Add eggs, milk, and vanilla; stir well.

Spoon one-fourth of batter into each of 2 greased 8-inch round cakepans. Spread raspberry mixture over batter in pans, dividing evenly. Top evenly with remaining batter.

Combine ½ cup flour and ½ cup sugar in a small bowl; stir well. Cut in ¼ cup butter with pastry blender until mixture is crumbly. Stir in sliced almonds. Sprinkle almond mixture evenly over batter in pans. Bake at 350° for 40 to 45 minutes or until a wooden pick inserted in center of cakes comes out clean. Cool in pans on wire racks 10 minutes; remove cakes from pans, if desired, and let cool completely on wire racks. Yield: two 8-inch coffee cakes.   Kristen Lindsten

Essence of Kansas: 4-H Cookbook, Taste Two
Kansas 4-H Foundation
Manhattan, Kansas

Custard-Filled Cornbread

1 cup all-purpose flour
¾ cup yellow cornmeal
1 teaspoon baking powder
½ teaspoon baking soda
½ teaspoon salt
3 tablespoons sugar

2 large eggs
2 cups milk
3 tablespoons butter or
  margarine, melted
1½ tablespoons white vinegar
1 cup whipping cream

Combine first 6 ingredients in a large bowl; make a well in center of mixture. Combine eggs, milk, butter, and vinegar; beat with a wire whisk until blended. Add to dry ingredients, stirring just until blended.

Place a well-buttered 8-inch square baking dish in a 350° oven for 10 minutes or until hot. Remove from oven; pour batter into hot dish. Pour whipping cream into center of batter. (Do not stir.) Bake at 350° for 1 hour or until golden. Serve warm. Yield: 8 servings.

Culinary Arts, Volume II
Society of the Arts of Allentown Art Museum
Allentown, Pennsylvania

Beer and Tomato Hush Puppies

1½ cups self-rising yellow
  cornmeal
¼ cup self-rising flour
⅛ teaspoon salt
2 onions, finely chopped
1 medium-size green pepper,
  finely chopped

1 tomato, finely chopped
1 large egg, lightly beaten
1½ teaspoons Worcestershire
  sauce
⅛ teaspoon hot sauce
½ cup beer
Vegetable oil

Combine first 3 ingredients in a large bowl; stir well. Add onion, pepper, and tomato. Stir in egg, Worcestershire sauce, and hot sauce. Add beer, stirring well. Pour oil to depth of 2 inches into a small Dutch oven; heat to 375°. Carefully drop batter by rounded tablespoonfuls into oil; fry hush puppies, a few at a time, 1 to 2 minutes or until golden, turning once. Drain well on paper towels. Yield: 3½ dozen.

By Special Request, Our Favorite Recipes
Piggly Wiggly Carolina Employees
Charleston, South Carolina

Double Corn and Chile Pancakes

Try topping these corn and chile pancakes with your favorite salsa.

1½ cups yellow cornmeal
½ cup all-purpose flour
2 tablespoons baking powder
½ teaspoon salt
¼ teaspoon freshly ground
  pepper
6 large eggs, lightly beaten
2 cups milk

½ cup unsalted butter or
  margarine, melted
4 cups frozen whole kernel
  corn, thawed
½ cup coarsely chopped roasted
  red pepper
1 (4½-ounce) can chopped
  green chiles, drained

Combine first 5 ingredients in a bowl. Stir in eggs, milk, and butter (batter will be thin). Stir in corn, roasted pepper, and chiles.

Pour ¼ cup batter for each pancake onto a hot, lightly greased griddle or skillet. Cook until tops are covered with bubbles and edges look cooked; turn and cook other side. Yield: 32 (4-inch) pancakes.

Quilted Quisine
Paoli Memorial Hospital Auxiliary
Paoli, Pennsylvania

Americana Drop Biscuits

2 cups all-purpose flour
2½ teaspoons baking
  powder
½ teaspoon salt
2 tablespoons sugar
¼ cup butter

1 cup peeled, finely chopped
  cooking apple
½ cup chopped raisins
1½ teaspoons grated orange
  rind
⅔ cup milk

Combine first 4 ingredients in a bowl; stir well. Cut in butter with pastry blender until mixture is crumbly. Stir in apple, raisins, and orange rind. Add milk, stirring just until dry ingredients are moistened. Drop by rounded tablespoonfuls onto ungreased baking sheets. Bake at 450° for 10 minutes or until browned. Yield: 1½ dozen.

Cranbrook Reflections: A Culinary Collection
Cranbrook House and Gardens Auxiliary
Bloomfield Hills, Michigan

Chive-Parmesan Scones

1½ cups all-purpose flour
1 tablespoon baking powder
¼ teaspoon salt
¼ teaspoon black pepper
¼ cup butter or margarine
1 cup grated Parmesan cheese
3 tablespoons chopped chives

2 cloves garlic, pressed
½ cup whipping cream
1 large egg, lightly beaten
2 tablespoons olive oil
2 tablespoons honey
⅛ teaspoon ground red pepper

Combine first 4 ingredients in a large bowl; stir well. Cut in butter with pastry blender until mixture is crumbly. Stir in cheese, chives, and garlic. Combine whipping cream, egg, oil, and honey; add to dry ingredients, stirring just until moistened.

Drop dough by 3 tablespoonfuls, 1 inch apart, onto a greased baking sheet. Sprinkle scones evenly with red pepper. Bake at 350° for 12 minutes or until lightly browned. Serve warm. Yield: 10 scones.

Culinary Masterpieces
Birmingham Museum of Art
Birmingham, Alabama

Chocolate-Pumpkin Muffins

1½ cups all-purpose flour
2 teaspoons baking powder
½ teaspoon salt
½ cup sugar
½ teaspoon ground cinnamon
1 cup milk
½ cup canned pumpkin

¼ cup butter or margarine, melted
1 large egg, lightly beaten
1 (6-ounce) package semisweet chocolate morsels
¼ cup finely chopped pecans or walnuts

Combine first 5 ingredients in a large bowl; make a well in center of mixture. Combine milk, pumpkin, butter, and egg; add to dry ingredients, stirring just until moistened. Stir in chocolate morsels.

Spoon batter into greased muffin pans, filling three-fourths full. Sprinkle pecans over batter. Bake at 400° for 20 minutes. Remove from pans immediately. Yield: 1 dozen.   Laurie Fleming

Appalachian Appetites
The Service League of Boone, North Carolina

Swiss Cheese-Mustard Bread

Try pairing this hearty Swiss cheese- and mustard-flavored bread with sliced ham for an extra special sandwich.

¾ cup milk
½ cup water
¼ cup vegetable oil
5½ to 6 cups all-purpose flour
2 tablespoons sugar
2 teaspoons salt

2 packages active dry yeast
3 large eggs
2 cups (8 ounces) shredded Swiss cheese
2 tablespoons prepared mustard
Melted butter or margarine

Combine first 3 ingredients in a small saucepan; heat until warm (120° to 130°).

Combine 2 cups flour, sugar, salt, and yeast in a large mixing bowl. Gradually add liquid mixture to flour mixture, beating at high speed of an electric mixer. Beat 2 additional minutes at medium speed. Add eggs, cheese, and mustard, beating just until blended. Gradually stir in enough remaining flour to make a soft dough.

Turn dough out onto a lightly floured surface, and knead until smooth and elastic (about 10 minutes). Cover and let rest 30 minutes. Punch dough down; turn out onto a lightly floured surface, and knead lightly 4 or 5 times. Divide dough in half. Let dough rest 10 minutes. Shape each portion into a ball; place balls in 2 well-greased 1½-quart round baking dishes, turning to grease tops.

Cover and let rise in a warm place (85°), free from drafts, 1 hour or until doubled in bulk.

Bake at 375° for 35 to 40 minutes or until loaves sound hollow when tapped. (Cover with aluminum foil the last 15 minutes of baking to prevent excessive browning, if necessary.) Remove bread from dishes immediately; brush with melted butter. Let cool completely on wire racks. Yield: 2 loaves.

Betty Corredera

Newcomers' Favorites, International and Regional Recipes
Aiken Newcomers' Club
Aiken, South Carolina

Garlic and Pepper Baguettes

1¾ cups water
1 tablespoon unsalted butter or
  margarine
3¾ to 4¼ cups all-purpose flour
2 packages active dry yeast
1 tablespoon sugar
1 tablespoon garlic powder
2 teaspoons salt

1 teaspoon coarsely ground
  pepper
1 teaspoon dried thyme
1 tablespoon cornmeal
Vegetable cooking spray
1 egg white, lightly beaten
1 tablespoon water

Combine 1¾ cups water and butter in a saucepan; heat until butter melts, stirring occasionally. Cool to 120° to 130°.

Combine 1½ cups flour and next 6 ingredients in a large mixing bowl. Gradually add liquid mixture to flour mixture, beating at medium speed of an electric mixer. Beat 2 additional minutes at medium speed. Gradually stir in enough remaining flour to make a soft dough. (Dough will be sticky.)

Turn dough out onto a well-floured surface, and knead until smooth and elastic (about 5 minutes). Cover and let rest 20 minutes.

Lightly grease 2 large baking sheets; sprinkle with cornmeal.

Divide dough in half. Roll one portion of dough into a 15- x 10-inch rectangle. Roll up dough, starting at long side, pressing firmly to eliminate air pockets; pinch ends to seal.

Place dough, seam side down, on a prepared baking sheet. Repeat procedure with remaining portion of dough. Coat dough lightly with cooking spray. Cover and chill 2 hours. Uncover and let stand at room temperature 10 minutes.

Make ¼-inch-deep slits diagonally across baguettes. Bake at 425° for 20 minutes. Combine egg white and 1 tablespoon water; brush over loaves. Bake 5 additional minutes or until golden. Let cool completely on wire racks. Yield: 2 baguettes.

Sensational Seasons: A Taste & Tour of Arkansas
The Junior League of Fort Smith, Arkansas

Basil Batter Rolls

These pesto-flavored batter rolls couldn't be easier—no kneading!

2 packages active dry yeast
1½ cups warm water (105° to 115°)
⅓ cup shortening
4 cups unbleached flour
¼ cup sugar

1½ teaspoons salt
1 large egg
2 tablespoons pesto
2 cloves garlic, minced
Melted butter or margarine (optional)

Combine yeast and warm water in a 2-cup liquid measuring cup; let stand 5 minutes.

Combine yeast mixture, shortening, 2 cups flour, and next 3 ingredients in a large mixing bowl; beat at medium speed of an electric mixer until well blended. Stir in pesto and garlic. Gradually stir in enough remaining flour to make a soft dough. (Dough will be sticky.)

Cover and let rise in a warm place (85°), free from drafts, 50 minutes or until doubled in bulk.

Stir dough; spoon into greased muffin pans, filling half full. Cover and let rise in a warm place, free from drafts, 45 minutes.

Bake at 400° for 15 to 16 minutes or until golden. Brush with melted butter, if desired. Yield: 2 dozen.

Rogue River Rendezvous
The Junior Service League of Jackson County
Medford, Oregon

Hot Cross Buns

¾ cup milk
½ cup vegetable oil
⅓ cup sugar
¾ teaspoon salt
3½ to 4 cups all-purpose flour
2 packages active dry yeast
1 teaspoon ground cinnamon

3 large eggs
⅔ cup currants
1 egg white, lightly beaten
1½ cups sifted powdered sugar
1 tablespoon plus 1 teaspoon
  milk
¼ teaspoon vanilla extract

Combine ¾ cup milk, oil, ⅓ cup sugar, and salt in a small saucepan; heat until warm (120° to 130°). Combine 2 cups flour, yeast, and cinnamon in a large mixing bowl. Gradually add liquid mixture to flour mixture, beating at medium speed of an electric mixer until well blended. Add eggs, one at a time, beating 1½ minutes at low speed after each addition. Beat 3 additional minutes at high speed. Gradually stir in currants and enough remaining flour to make a soft dough. (Dough will be sticky.) Place in a well-greased bowl, turning to grease top.

Cover and let rise in a warm place (85°), free from drafts, 1 hour or until doubled in bulk.

Punch dough down; cover and let rest 10 minutes. Divide dough into 18 equal portions. Shape each portion into a smooth ball, tucking edge under so that it resembles a mushroom cap; place 1½ inches apart on lightly greased baking sheets. Brush with egg white. Cover and let rise in a warm place, free from drafts, 30 minutes or until doubled in bulk.

Bake at 375° for 12 to 15 minutes or until lightly browned. Let cool completely on wire racks.

Combine powdered sugar, 1 tablespoon plus 1 teaspoon milk, and vanilla, stirring well. Drizzle glaze in the shape of a cross over top of each bun. Yield: 1½ dozen.

Karen Tufte

The Global Gourmet
Concordia Language Villages
Moorhead, Minnesota

Sweet Potato Buns

These large, luscious sweet potato buns make perfect holiday fare. If you prefer a crispier crust rather than soft-sided buns, bake them on greased baking sheets at 375° for 20 minutes.

1 cup milk
⅔ cup butter or margarine
½ cup sugar
1 cup cooked, mashed sweet
   potato
1 teaspoon salt
1 package active dry yeast

½ cup warm water (105° to 115°)
2 large eggs, lightly beaten
6 to 7 cups all-purpose flour
½ teaspoon ground cardamom
1 (8-ounce) can crushed
   pineapple, drained
½ cup currants

Combine milk and butter in a saucepan; heat until butter melts, stirring occasionally. Stir in sugar, sweet potato, and salt. Let cool to room temperature.

Combine yeast and warm water in a 2-cup liquid measuring cup; let stand 5 minutes.

Combine sweet potato mixture, yeast mixture, and eggs in a large mixing bowl; beat at medium speed of an electric mixer until well blended. Add 2 cups flour and cardamom, beating until blended. Gradually add enough remaining flour to make a soft dough. Stir in pineapple and currants. (Dough will be sticky.)

Turn dough out onto a well-floured surface, and knead until smooth and elastic (about 8 to 10 minutes). Place in a well-greased bowl, turning to grease top.

Cover and let rise in a warm place (85°), free from drafts, 1 hour or until doubled in bulk.

Punch dough down. Cover and let rest 10 minutes. Divide dough in half. With lightly floured hands, divide each half into 9 equal portions. Shape each portion into a smooth ball, tucking edge under so that it resembles a mushroom cap; place in 3 greased 8-inch round cakepans. Cover and let rise in a warm place, free from drafts, 45 minutes or until doubled in bulk. Bake at 375° for 20 minutes or until golden. Yield: 1½ dozen.

Back Home Again
The Junior League of Indianapolis, Indiana

Orange Coffee Rolls

1 package active dry yeast
¼ cup water (105° to 115°)
1 cup sugar, divided
2 large eggs
½ cup sour cream
¼ cup plus 2 tablespoons butter
   or margarine, melted
1 teaspoon salt

2¾ to 3 cups all-purpose flour
2 tablespoons butter or
   margarine, melted and divided
1 cup flaked coconut, toasted
   and divided
2 tablespoons grated orange
   rind
Glaze

Combine yeast and warm water in a large mixing bowl; let stand 5 minutes. Add ¼ cup sugar and next 4 ingredients; beat at medium speed of an electric mixer until blended. Gradually stir in enough flour to make a soft dough.

Turn dough out onto a well-floured surface, and knead until smooth and elastic (about 5 minutes). Place in a well-greased bowl, turning to grease top. Cover and let rise in a warm place (85°), free from drafts, 1½ hours or until doubled in bulk.

Punch dough down, and divide in half. Roll one portion of dough into a 12-inch circle; brush with 1 tablespoon melted butter. Combine remaining ¾ cup sugar, ¾ cup coconut, and orange rind; sprinkle half of coconut mixture over dough. Cut into 12 wedges; roll up each wedge, beginning at wide end. Place in a greased 13- x 9- x 2-inch pan, point side down. Repeat with remaining dough, butter, and coconut mixture.

Cover and let rise in a warm place, free from drafts, 45 minutes or until doubled in bulk. Bake at 350° for 25 to 30 minutes or until golden. (Cover with aluminum foil after 15 minutes to prevent excessive browning, if necessary.) Spoon warm Glaze over warm rolls; sprinkle with remaining ¼ cup coconut. Yield: 2 dozen.

Glaze

¾ cup sugar
½ cup sour cream

¼ cup butter or margarine
2 teaspoons orange juice

Combine all ingredients in a small saucepan; bring to a boil. Boil 3 minutes, stirring occasionally. Let cool slightly. Yield: about 1⅓ cups.

Tastes and Traditions: The Sam Houston Heritage Cookbook
The Study Club of Huntsville
Huntsville, Texas

Cakes

Sour Cream-Spice Layer Cake, page 108

Mary Ball Washington's Gingerbread, 1784

George Washington's mother is credited with creating this dark, moist cake. It's flavored with molasses, cream sherry, ginger, and other spices.

½ cup butter or margarine, softened
½ cup firmly packed dark brown sugar
½ cup honey
½ cup molasses
¼ cup cream sherry
3 large eggs
3 cups all-purpose flour
2 tablespoons ground ginger
1½ teaspoons ground cinnamon
1½ teaspoons ground mace
1½ teaspoons ground nutmeg
1 teaspoon cream of tartar
½ cup warm milk (105° to 115°)
2 tablespoons grated orange rind
¼ cup orange juice
1 cup raisins
1 teaspoon baking soda
2 tablespoons warm water (105° to 115°)

Beat butter at medium speed of an electric mixer until creamy; gradually add sugar, beating well. Add honey, molasses, and sherry, beating well. Add eggs, one at a time, beating after each addition.

Combine flour and next 5 ingredients; add to butter mixture alternately with milk, beginning and ending with flour mixture. Mix at low speed after each addition until blended. Stir in orange rind, orange juice, and raisins. Dissolve baking soda in warm water; add to batter, stirring well. Pour batter into a greased 13- x 9- x 2-inch pan.

Bake at 350° for 40 to 50 minutes or until a wooden pick inserted in center comes out clean. Cool in pan on a wire rack. Yield: 15 servings.

Specialties of the House
Kenmore Association
Fredericksburg, Virginia

Lemon Texas Cake

Garnish each serving of cake with a fresh mint sprig and lemon rind bow knot to add pizzazz.

2 cups all-purpose flour
1 teaspoon baking soda
½ teaspoon salt
2 cups sugar
2 large eggs, lightly beaten
½ cup sour cream
1¼ cups plus 2 tablespoons
    butter or margarine, divided

¾ cup plus 2 tablespoons water
2 teaspoons grated lemon rind
2 tablespoons fresh lemon juice
1 tablespoon lemon extract
¼ cup plus 2 teaspoons milk
1 teaspoon lemon extract
3 cups sifted powdered sugar

Combine first 6 ingredients in a large mixing bowl; beat at medium speed of an electric mixer until blended.

Combine 1 cup butter and next 4 ingredients in a medium saucepan; bring to a boil. Add to flour mixture, stirring well. Pour into a greased and floured 15- x 10- x 1-inch jellyroll pan.

Bake at 350° for 20 minutes or until a wooden pick inserted in center comes out clean. Cool in pan on a wire rack 20 minutes.

Combine remaining ¼ cup plus 2 tablespoons butter, milk, and 1 teaspoon lemon extract in saucepan; bring to a boil. Remove from heat. Gradually add powdered sugar, stirring until mixture is spreading consistency. Spread frosting on top of cake. Let cool completely in pan on wire rack. Yield: 24 servings.

Specialties of Indianapolis, Volume 2
Home Economists' Guild of Indianapolis, Indiana

Peanut Butter Sheet Cake

1 cup water
½ cup vegetable oil
½ cup creamy peanut butter
½ cup butter or margarine
2 cups all-purpose flour
1 teaspoon baking soda

2 cups sugar
2 large eggs
½ cup milk
1 teaspoon vanilla extract
Frosting

Combine first 4 ingredients in a saucepan; cook over medium heat, stirring constantly, until smooth.

Combine flour, soda, and sugar in a large mixing bowl. Add eggs, milk, and vanilla; beat at low speed of an electric mixer until blended. Add peanut butter mixture; mix well. Pour batter into a greased and floured 13- x 9- x 2-inch pan.

Bake at 375° for 25 minutes or until a wooden pick inserted in center comes out clean. Cool completely in pan on a wire rack. Spread Frosting on top of cake. Yield: 15 servings.

Frosting

½ cup creamy peanut butter
½ cup butter or margarine
⅓ cup milk

4¾ cups sifted powdered sugar
1 teaspoon vanilla extract

Combine first 3 ingredients in a medium saucepan; cook over medium heat, stirring constantly, until smooth. Remove from heat. Add powdered sugar and vanilla, stirring until mixture is spreading consistency. Yield: 2½ cups.

Freddie Surkosky

Seasoned with Love
Woodbridge Lioness Club
Woodbridge, Virginia

Strawberry Heart Cake

This red and white heart-shaped cake is perfect for Valentine's Day or a wedding anniversary.

1¼ cups sugar, divided
3 tablespoons cornstarch
2 (10-ounce) packages frozen
    sliced strawberries, thawed
2 tablespoons fresh lemon juice
½ cup butter or margarine,
    softened
2 large eggs

1½ cups all-purpose flour
½ teaspoon baking powder
¼ teaspoon baking soda
½ teaspoon salt
½ cup buttermilk
1 teaspoon vanilla extract
Powdered sugar

Combine ¼ cup sugar and cornstarch in a medium saucepan. Add strawberries; cook over medium heat, stirring constantly, 15 minutes or until thickened. Remove from heat; stir in lemon juice. Let cool.

Beat butter at medium speed of an electric mixer until creamy; gradually add remaining 1 cup sugar, beating well. Add eggs, one at a time, beating after each addition.

Combine flour, baking powder, soda, and salt; add to butter mixture alternately with buttermilk, beginning and ending with flour mixture. Mix at low speed after each addition until blended. Stir in vanilla. Pour batter into a greased and floured 10-inch heart-shaped cakepan.

Bake at 325° for 35 minutes or until a wooden pick inserted in center comes out clean. Cool in pan on a wire rack 10 minutes; remove from pan, and let cool completely on wire rack.

Using a serrated knife, cut vertically to, but not through, bottom of cake, 1 inch from edge. Hollow out the heart-shaped center of cake, reserving for another use. Sprinkle cake with powdered sugar. Spoon strawberry mixture into center of cake. Cover and chill at least 3 hours. Yield: one 10-inch cake.

Liz D'Andrea

Candlelight and Wisteria
Lee-Scott Academy
Auburn, Alabama

Dark Chocolate Cake with White Chocolate Buttercream Frosting

1 cup unsalted butter or
  margarine, softened
1¾ cups sugar
4 large eggs
2 cups all-purpose flour
1½ teaspoons baking
  soda
¼ teaspoon salt

¼ teaspoon freshly grated
  nutmeg
1⅓ cups buttermilk
4 (1-ounce) squares unsweetened
  chocolate, melted
1 teaspoon vanilla extract
White Chocolate Buttercream
  Frosting

Grease two 9-inch round cakepans; line with wax paper. Grease wax paper. Set aside.

Beat butter at medium speed of an electric mixer until creamy; gradually add sugar, beating well. Add eggs, one at a time, beating after each addition. Combine flour and next 3 ingredients; add to butter mixture alternately with buttermilk, beginning and ending with flour mixture. Mix at low speed after each addition until blended. Stir in chocolate and vanilla. Pour batter into prepared pans.

Bake at 325° for 35 to 45 minutes or until a wooden pick inserted in center comes out clean. Cool in pans 10 minutes; remove from pans, and let cool completely on wire racks. Spread frosting between layers and on top and sides of cake. Yield: one 2-layer cake.

White Chocolate Buttercream Frosting

4 ounces white chocolate, finely
  chopped
¼ cup plus 2 tablespoons
  whipping cream

¼ cup white crème de cacao
1 cup unsalted butter or
  margarine, softened
4 cups sifted powdered sugar

Place chocolate in a bowl. Bring cream to a boil in a saucepan over medium-high heat. Pour over chocolate; stir until smooth. Stir in crème de cacao. Let cool completely, stirring occasionally. Beat butter at medium speed of an electric mixer until creamy. Gradually add sugar; beat until blended. Gradually add chocolate mixture; beat until spreading consistency. Yield: 3½ cups.   Nancy Hyland

Savor the Brandywine Valley, A Collection of Recipes
The Junior League of Wilmington, Delaware

Hawaiian Cake

Graham cracker crumbs combined with flaked coconut and pecans take the place of flour in this cake.

1 cup butter or margarine, softened
2 cups sugar
5 large eggs
1 teaspoon baking powder
¾ teaspoon baking soda
1 cup milk

1 (3½-ounce) can flaked coconut
1 cup pecans, chopped
1 (13½-ounce) package graham cracker crumbs
Pineapple Frosting

Grease three 9-inch round cakepans; line with wax paper. Grease and flour wax paper. Set aside.

Beat butter at medium speed of an electric mixer until creamy; gradually add sugar, beating well. Add eggs, one at a time, beating after each addition. Add baking powder and soda to butter mixture; beat well. Gradually add milk, beating until blended. Stir in coconut and pecans. Gradually add cracker crumbs, beating until blended. Pour batter into prepared pans.

Bake at 350° for 25 to 30 minutes or until a wooden pick inserted in center comes out clean. Cool in pans on wire racks 5 minutes; remove from pans, and let cool completely on wire racks. Spread Pineapple Frosting between layers and on top of cake. Yield: one 3-layer cake.

Pineapple Frosting

1 (20-ounce) can crushed pineapple, drained
¾ cup butter or margarine, melted

1 (16-ounce) package powdered sugar, sifted

Press pineapple between paper towels to remove excess moisture. Set aside.

Beat butter and sugar at medium speed of an electric mixer until well blended. Add pineapple, and beat until spreading consistency. Yield: 2¾ cups.

Among the Lilies
Women in Missions, First Baptist Church of Atlanta
Atlanta, Georgia

Sour Cream-Spice Layer Cake

½ cup butter or margarine, softened
1¼ cups firmly packed brown sugar
3 large eggs
1¾ cups all-purpose flour
2 teaspoons baking powder
½ teaspoon baking soda
¼ teaspoon salt
1 teaspoon ground cinnamon
½ teaspoon ground allspice
½ teaspoon ground nutmeg
¾ cup sour cream
½ cup finely chopped pecans or walnuts
2 (1-ounce) squares unsweetened chocolate
2 teaspoons butter or margarine
Frosting
Garnish: pecan or walnut halves

Beat ½ cup butter at medium speed of an electric mixer until creamy; gradually add brown sugar, beating well. Add eggs, one at a time, beating after each addition.

Combine flour and next 6 ingredients; add to butter mixture alternately with sour cream, beginning and ending with flour mixture. Mix at low speed after each addition until blended. Stir in ½ cup pecans. Pour batter into 2 greased and floured 8-inch round cakepans.

Bake at 350° for 30 to 35 minutes or until a wooden pick inserted in center comes out clean. Cool in pans on wire racks 10 minutes; remove from pans, and let cool completely on wire racks.

Combine chocolate squares and 2 teaspoons butter in a small saucepan. Cook over low heat until chocolate and butter melt, stirring often. Let cool. Spread Frosting between layers and on top and sides of cake. Spoon melted chocolate mixture on top of cake. Garnish, if desired. Yield: one 2-layer cake.

Frosting

½ cup butter or margarine, softened
3 tablespoons sour cream
Dash of salt
4 cups sifted powdered sugar
1 teaspoon vanilla extract

Beat butter, sour cream, and salt at low speed of an electric mixer until creamy. Gradually add powdered sugar, beating until spreading consistency. Stir in vanilla. Yield: 2⅓ cups.   Robin Fones

Hopeful Hearts Cookbook
Macoupin County Adopt-a-Pet Animal Shelter
Benld, Illinois

Chocolate Mirror

The shiny chocolate glaze inspired the title of this recipe. Use any leftover glaze to coat the cake a second time, or cover and store it in the refrigerator and enjoy it as a dessert sauce.

½ cup butter or margarine,
  softened
3 large eggs
1 cup buttermilk
1 cup strong brewed coffee
2 teaspoons vanilla extract

1¾ cups all-purpose flour
1 teaspoon baking powder
2 teaspoons baking soda
2 cups sugar
1 cup cocoa
Glaze

Grease a 12-cup Bundt pan; dust with cocoa, and set aside.

Beat butter at medium speed of an electric mixer until creamy. Add eggs, buttermilk, coffee, and vanilla, and beat until blended.

Sift together flour and next 4 ingredients. Add flour mixture to butter mixture; beat at low speed until blended. Beat at medium speed 2 minutes. Pour batter into prepared pan.

Bake at 350° for 45 to 50 minutes or until a wooden pick inserted in center comes out clean. Cool in pan on a wire rack 15 minutes; remove from pan, and let cool completely on wire rack. Place wax paper under wire rack. Pour warm Glaze over cake, letting excess drip down sides of cake onto wax paper. Chill at least 30 minutes before serving. Yield: one 10-inch cake.

Glaze

1 cup sugar
1 cup cocoa
1 cup whipping cream
2 tablespoons butter or
  margarine

1 tablespoon honey
1½ tablespoons vanilla extract

Combine first 5 ingredients in a heavy saucepan. Cook over low heat until mixture is smooth, stirring often (do not boil). Remove from heat, and stir in vanilla. Yield: about 2¼ cups.

For Goodness Taste
The Junior League of Rochester, New York

Pumpkin-Chocolate Chip Cake

2 cups sugar
1¼ cups vegetable oil
4 large eggs
1 (16-ounce) can pumpkin
3 cups all-purpose flour
2 teaspoons baking powder
2 teaspoons baking soda

1 teaspoon salt
2 teaspoons ground cinnamon
¾ cup semisweet chocolate morsels
¾ cup chopped pecans or walnuts, divided

Beat sugar and oil at medium speed of an electric mixer 5 to 7 minutes. Add eggs, one at a time, beating just until yellow disappears. Add pumpkin; beat at low speed just until blended.

Combine flour and next 4 ingredients; add to pumpkin mixture, and beat at low speed 2 to 3 minutes. Stir in chocolate morsels and ½ cup pecans. Pour batter into a greased and floured 10-inch tube pan. Sprinkle with remaining ¼ cup pecans.

Bake at 350° for 1 hour and 10 minutes or until a wooden pick inserted in center comes out clean. Cool in pan on a wire rack 10 to 15 minutes; remove from pan, and let cool completely on wire rack. Yield: one 10-inch cake.   Dorothy O'Neil

Come Savor Swansea
First Christian Congregational Church
Swansea, Massachusetts

Chocolate-Macaroon Pound Cake

1½ cups butter or margarine, softened
3 cups sugar
5 large eggs
2½ cups all-purpose flour
2 teaspoons baking powder

½ teaspoon salt
1 cup cocoa
1½ cups buttermilk
2 cups flaked coconut
2 teaspoons vanilla extract
2 teaspoons powdered sugar

Beat butter at medium speed of an electric mixer about 2 minutes or until soft and creamy. Gradually add 3 cups sugar, beating at medium speed 5 to 7 minutes. Add eggs, one at a time, beating just until yellow disappears.

Combine flour and next 3 ingredients; add to butter mixture alternately with buttermilk, beginning and ending with flour mixture. Mix at low speed just until blended after each addition. Stir in coconut and vanilla. Pour batter into a greased and floured 10-inch tube pan.

Bake at 350° for 50 minutes. Cover loosely with aluminum foil to prevent excessive browning. Bake an additional 45 to 50 minutes or until a wooden pick inserted in center of cake comes out clean. Cool in pan on a wire rack 10 to 15 minutes; remove from pan, and let cool completely on wire rack. Sprinkle with powdered sugar. Yield: one 10-inch cake.

Janet Mackey

The Feast
St. Mary's Catholic Community
Caldwell, Idaho

Pineapple Pound Cake

The crushed pineapple in this pound cake makes it moist and flavorful.

1 cup butter or margarine, softened	1 teaspoon baking powder
½ cup shortening	¼ cup milk
2¾ cups sugar	1 (15¼-ounce) can crushed pineapple, undrained
6 large eggs	1 teaspoon vanilla extract
3 cups all-purpose flour	

Beat butter and shortening at medium speed of an electric mixer about 2 minutes or until soft and creamy. Gradually add sugar, beating at medium speed 5 to 7 minutes. Add eggs, one at a time, beating just until yellow disappears.

Combine flour and baking powder; add to butter mixture alternately with milk, beginning and ending with flour mixture. Mix at low speed just until blended after each addition. Stir in pineapple and vanilla. Pour batter into a greased and floured 10-inch tube pan.

Bake at 350° for 1 hour and 30 minutes or until a wooden pick inserted in center comes out clean. Cool in pan on a wire rack 10 to 15 minutes; remove from pan, and let cool completely on wire rack. Yield: one 10-inch cake.

Cathy Lee

Golden Oldies Cook Book
Catholic Diocese of Belleville Ministry to Sick and Aged
Belleville, Illinois

Cidered-Up Pound Cake

Sweet apple cider gives this spiced pound cake its personality. Apple cider was a popular beverage in the early days of America.

1 cup butter or margarine,
  softened
½ cup shortening
3¼ cups sugar
6 large eggs
3¼ cups all-purpose flour
½ teaspoon baking powder

½ teaspoon salt
¾ teaspoon ground cinnamon
½ teaspoon ground allspice
½ teaspoon ground nutmeg
1 cup apple cider
1 teaspoon vanilla extract
Caramel Glaze

Beat butter and shortening at medium speed of an electric mixer about 2 minutes or until soft and creamy. Gradually add sugar, beating at medium speed 5 to 7 minutes. Add eggs, one at a time, beating just until yellow disappears.

Combine flour and next 5 ingredients; add to butter mixture alternately with apple cider, beginning and ending with flour mixture. Mix at low speed just until blended after each addition. Stir in vanilla. Pour batter into a greased and floured 10-inch tube pan.

Bake at 325° for 1 hour and 30 minutes or until a wooden pick inserted in center comes out clean. Cool in pan on a wire rack 10 to 15 minutes; remove from pan, and let cool completely on wire rack. Drizzle warm Caramel Glaze over cake. Yield: one 10-inch cake.

Caramel Glaze

½ cup sugar
¼ cup butter or margarine
¼ cup buttermilk

1½ tablespoons light corn syrup
¼ teaspoon baking soda
¼ teaspoon vanilla extract

Combine all ingredients in a small saucepan. Bring to a boil; reduce heat to medium, and cook 10 minutes, stirring often. Yield: 1 cup.

The Virginia Hostess
The Junior Woman's Club of Manassas, Virginia

Cranberry-Apple-Filled Walnut Cake Roll

2 large cooking apples, peeled, cored, and chopped
1 cup fresh cranberries
¼ cup sugar
¼ cup water
2 tablespoons brandy
1 teaspoon lemon juice
½ teaspoon ground cinnamon
¼ teaspoon ground nutmeg
⅔ cup all-purpose flour
1 teaspoon baking powder
¼ teaspoon salt

3 large eggs
¾ cup sugar
⅓ cup water
1 teaspoon vanilla extract
⅓ cup ground walnuts
2 to 3 tablespoons powdered sugar
1 cup whipping cream
½ teaspoon ground cinnamon
1 teaspoon vanilla extract
Garnishes: coarsely chopped walnuts, apple slices

Grease a 15- x 10- x 1-inch jellyroll pan. Line bottom of pan with wax paper; grease wax paper. Set aside.

Combine first 8 ingredients in a medium saucepan. Cook over medium heat, stirring constantly, about 10 minutes or until cranberry skins pop and liquid is absorbed. Let cool completely.

Combine flour, baking powder, and salt; set aside. Beat eggs in a large mixing bowl at high speed of an electric mixer 2 minutes. Gradually add ¾ cup sugar, beating 5 minutes or until thick and pale. Stir in ⅓ cup water and 1 teaspoon vanilla. Gradually fold flour mixture and ground walnuts into egg mixture with a wire whisk. Spread batter evenly in prepared pan. Bake at 375° for 12 minutes or until cake springs back when lightly touched in the center.

Sift powdered sugar in a 15- x 10-inch rectangle on a cloth towel. When cake is done, immediately loosen from sides of pan, and turn out onto towel. Peel off wax paper. Starting at narrow end, roll up cake and towel together; place, seam side down, on a wire rack to cool.

Unroll cake; spread with cranberry mixture. Reroll cake without towel; place, seam side down, on a serving plate.

Beat whipping cream, ½ teaspoon ground cinnamon, and 1 teaspoon vanilla at high speed until stiff peaks form. Pipe over cake. Garnish, if desired. Yield: 1 filled cake roll (5 to 6 servings).   Tama Hiles

Culinary Classics, From Our Kitchens
Mountain State Apple Harvest Festival
Martinsburg, West Virginia

Ice Cream Toffee Roll

¾ cup all-purpose flour
1 teaspoon baking powder
¼ teaspoon salt
2 tablespoons instant coffee
  granules
4 large eggs, separated
¾ cup sugar, divided
1 teaspoon vanilla extract

2 to 3 tablespoons powdered
  sugar
1 quart vanilla ice cream,
  softened
5 (1.4-ounce) English toffee-
  flavored candy bars,
  crushed (1 cup)
1 cup whipping cream, whipped

Grease a 15- x 10- x 1-inch jellyroll pan. Line bottom of pan with wax paper; grease and flour wax paper. Set aside.

Sift together first 4 ingredients; set aside. Beat egg yolks in a large mixing bowl at high speed of an electric mixer until thick and pale. Gradually add ¼ cup sugar, beating well. Stir in vanilla. Set aside.

Beat egg whites at high speed until foamy. Gradually add remaining ½ cup sugar, 1 tablespoon at a time, beating until stiff peaks form and sugar dissolves (2 to 4 minutes). Gently fold into egg yolk mixture. Gradually fold in flour mixture. Spread batter evenly in prepared pan. Bake at 350° for 15 minutes or until cake springs back when lightly touched in the center.

Sift powdered sugar in a 15- x 10-inch rectangle on a cloth towel. When cake is done, immediately loosen from sides of pan, and turn out onto sugared towel. Peel off wax paper. Starting at narrow end, roll up cake and towel together; place, seam side down, on a wire rack to cool completely.

Unroll cake; spread evenly with vanilla ice cream. Sprinkle ⅔ cup crushed candy bars over ice cream. Reroll cake without towel. Cover and freeze until firm. To serve, slice cake. Top each slice evenly with whipped cream and remaining ⅓ cup crushed candy bars. Yield: 1 filled cake roll (5 to 6 servings).   Carolyn Hardesty

Cooking with Christopher in Mind
Family and Friends of Christopher Lee Hamilton
East Peoria, Illinois

Pecan-Strawberry Shortcakes

Let the sliced fresh strawberries and sugar mixture stand at room temperature at least 20 minutes to extract the fruit juice and form a syrup.

6 cups sliced fresh strawberries
¼ cup sugar
1 tablespoon grated orange rind, divided
2 cups all-purpose flour
2 teaspoons baking powder
½ cup ground pecans

¼ cup sugar
½ cup butter or margarine
⅔ cup milk
1 large egg, lightly beaten
1 cup whipping cream
2 tablespoons sugar
½ teaspoon vanilla extract

Combine strawberries, ¼ cup sugar, and 1 teaspoon orange rind in a large bowl; stir gently. Let stand at room temperature at least 20 minutes.

Combine flour and next 3 ingredients in a medium bowl; cut in butter with pastry blender until mixture is crumbly. Combine remaining 2 teaspoons orange rind, milk, and egg; stir well. Add egg mixture to flour mixture, stirring just until dry ingredients are moistened.

Drop batter evenly into 9 mounds on an ungreased baking sheet; flatten mounds slightly with back of a spoon to ¾-inch thickness. Bake at 450° for 8 to 9 minutes or until lightly browned. Let cool completely on a wire rack.

Beat whipping cream until foamy; gradually add 2 tablespoons sugar and vanilla, beating until soft peaks form.

Split shortcakes in half horizontally. Place bottom halves, cut side up, on individual dessert plates. Spoon half of strawberry mixture and half of whipped cream evenly over shortcake bottoms. Top each with remaining shortcake halves, cut side down. Spoon remaining strawberry mixture and whipped cream evenly over each serving. Yield: 9 servings.

Margaret Lawrence

The Maine Collection
Portland Museum of Art
Portland, Maine

Almond Cheesecake with Fresh Nectarines

You'll need about 11 vanilla wafers, finely crushed, to yield ½ cup of vanilla wafer crumbs for this crust.

½ cup vanilla wafer crumbs
¼ cup ground blanched almonds, toasted
3 tablespoons unsalted butter or margarine, melted
½ teaspoon ground ginger
3 (8-ounce) packages cream cheese, softened
1 cup sugar

4 large eggs
2 teaspoons almond extract, divided
1 teaspoon vanilla extract
1 (8-ounce) carton sour cream
¼ cup sugar
1 large nectarine, peeled and thinly sliced
1 teaspoon lemon juice

Combine first 4 ingredients in a small bowl, and stir well. Firmly press crumb mixture on bottom of a 9-inch springform pan. Freeze until firm.

Beat cream cheese at medium speed of an electric mixer until creamy; gradually add 1 cup sugar, beating well. Add eggs, one at a time, beating after each addition. Stir in 1 teaspoon almond extract and vanilla. Pour batter into prepared pan.

Bake at 400° for 12 minutes. Reduce oven temperature to 225°, and bake 45 additional minutes or until center is almost set. Turn oven off. Leave cheesecake in oven 1 hour.

Combine sour cream, ¼ cup sugar, and remaining 1 teaspoon almond extract; spread evenly over cheesecake. Return cheesecake to oven; bake at 350° for 8 minutes. Let cool to room temperature in pan on a wire rack; cover and chill at least 8 hours. Carefully remove sides of springform pan. Toss nectarine slices with lemon juice; arrange on top of cheesecake in spoke fashion. Yield: 12 servings.

Sugar Snips & Asparagus Tips
Woman's Auxiliary of Infant Welfare Society of Chicago
Chicago, Illinois

Caramel-Pecan Cheesecake

Caramel topping and sour cream make a quick and easy finish for this rich cheesecake.

1 cup graham cracker crumbs
¾ cup ground pecans
¼ cup sugar
¼ cup butter or margarine, melted
12 ounces cream cheese, softened

¾ cup caramel topping, divided
3 large eggs
2 tablespoons milk
½ cup sour cream
Garnish: pecan halves

Combine first 4 ingredients in a small bowl; stir well. Firmly press crumb mixture on bottom and 1 inch up sides of an 8-inch spring-form pan. Set aside.

Beat cream cheese at medium speed of an electric mixer until creamy; gradually add ½ cup caramel topping, beating well. Add eggs, one at a time, beating after each addition. Stir in milk. Pour batter into prepared pan.

Bake at 350° for 40 to 45 minutes or until center is almost set. Let cool in pan on a wire rack 15 minutes.

Combine remaining ¼ cup caramel topping and sour cream; spread evenly over cheesecake. Let cool to room temperature in pan on wire rack; cover and chill at least 8 hours. Carefully remove sides of spring-form pan. Garnish, if desired. Yield: 10 servings.   Kim Dunagan

Appalachian Appetites
The Service League of Boone, North Carolina

Orange Blossom Cheesecake

To make slicing this cheesecake easier, cut the oranges for decorating the top into the thinnest possible slices.

3 cups gingersnap crumbs
¼ cup plus 2 tablespoons butter or margarine, melted
2 teaspoons grated orange rind
1½ cups fresh orange juice
⅓ cup unpeeled and thinly sliced fresh ginger
4 (8-ounce) packages cream cheese, softened
⅔ cup sugar

6 ounces white chocolate, melted
4 large eggs
2 tablespoons grated orange rind
1 tablespoon vanilla extract
4 cups water
2 cups sugar
2 oranges, unpeeled and cut into very thin slices

Combine first 3 ingredients in a bowl; stir well. Firmly press crumb mixture on bottom and up sides of a 9-inch springform pan. Chill.

Combine orange juice and ginger in a saucepan; bring to a boil. Reduce heat to medium-low; cook 20 minutes or until reduced to 3 tablespoons. Pour mixture through a wire-mesh strainer into a small bowl, discarding ginger. Set orange juice mixture aside.

Beat cream cheese at medium speed of an electric mixer until creamy. Add ⅔ cup sugar, beating well. Add strained orange juice mixture, and beat well. With mixer running, add chocolate in a steady stream, beating until blended. Add eggs, one at a time, beating after each addition. Stir in 2 tablespoons orange rind and vanilla. Pour batter into prepared pan.

Bake at 350° for 50 to 55 minutes or until center is almost set. Let cool to room temperature in pan on a wire rack; cover and chill at least 8 hours.

Cover a wire rack with wax paper; set aside. Combine water and 2 cups sugar in a large skillet; cook over medium heat until sugar dissolves, stirring often. Reduce heat; simmer 5 minutes. Add orange slices, one at a time, and simmer 1 hour. Turn orange slices, and simmer an additional hour or until tender and translucent. Arrange orange slices in a single layer on prepared rack. Let dry 1 hour.

Carefully remove sides of springform pan. Overlap orange slices in a decorative pattern on top of cheesecake. Yield: 12 servings.

Some Like It Hot
The Junior League of McAllen, Texas

Piña Colada Cheesecake

2 tablespoons butter or margarine
½ cup flaked coconut
½ cup finely chopped blanched almonds
¼ cup sugar
1⅔ cups fine, dry breadcrumbs
¼ cup sugar
½ cup butter or margarine, melted
4 (8-ounce) packages cream cheese, softened
¾ cup sugar
4 large eggs
1 (15¼-ounce) can crushed pineapple, well drained
1 (15-ounce) can cream of coconut
1 (8-ounce) carton sour cream
2 tablespoons cornstarch
1 teaspoon lemon juice
1 teaspoon vanilla extract
1 teaspoon rum extract

Melt 2 tablespoons butter in a medium skillet over medium-high heat. Add coconut, almonds, and ¼ cup sugar; cook, stirring constantly, until golden. Set aside.

Combine breadcrumbs, ¼ cup sugar, and ½ cup butter; stir well. Firmly press crumb mixture on bottom and 1 inch up sides of a 10-inch springform pan. Bake at 350° for 12 minutes. Let cool in pan on a wire rack.

Beat cream cheese at medium speed of an electric mixer until creamy; gradually add ¾ cup sugar, beating well. Add eggs, one at a time, beating after each addition. Stir in pineapple and next 6 ingredients. Pour batter into prepared pan.

Bake at 350° for 1 hour and 20 minutes or until center is almost set. Turn oven off. Sprinkle reserved coconut mixture evenly over cheesecake. Partially open oven door, and let cheesecake cool in oven 1 hour. Let cool to room temperature in pan on a wire rack; cover and chill at least 8 hours. Carefully remove sides of springform pan. Yield: 12 servings.

Debbie Heaney

Cookin' with Fire
Milford Permanent Firefighters Association
Milford, Massachusetts

Apricot-Chocolate Torte

This chunky chocolate torte is extremely rich, so you may want to serve small wedges.

3 (1-ounce) squares
   unsweetened chocolate
2 cups walnuts
1½ cups all-purpose flour
¾ cup firmly packed brown
   sugar
½ teaspoon salt
½ cup butter, cut into pieces
2 tablespoons cold water

2 teaspoons vanilla extract
1½ cups sugar
3 tablespoons all-purpose flour
¾ cup water
1 tablespoon fresh lemon juice
2 (6-ounce) packages dried
   apricot halves, chopped
Garnish: shaved semisweet or
   milk chocolate

Position knife blade in food processor bowl; add unsweetened chocolate. Process until coarsely chopped. Add walnuts, 1½ cups flour, brown sugar, and salt; process until chocolate and nuts are finely chopped. Add butter; process until well blended, stopping once to scrape down sides. Add 2 tablespoons cold water and vanilla. Pulse 2 or 3 times until dough is crumbly; set aside.

Combine 1½ cups sugar and 3 tablespoons flour in a saucepan; stir in ¾ cup water and lemon juice. Add apricots; bring to a boil over medium heat. Reduce heat, and simmer, uncovered, 25 minutes or until thickened, stirring often. Let cool.

Press two-thirds of dough on bottom and 1 inch up sides of a 9-inch springform pan. Top with apricot mixture, spreading evenly. Crumble remaining dough evenly over apricot mixture.

Bake at 350° for 40 minutes. Let cool completely in pan on a wire rack. Carefully remove sides of springform pan. Garnish, if desired. Yield: one 9-inch torte.

Carol Sue Coden

Still Fiddling in the Kitchen
National Council of Jewish Women
Southfield, Michigan

Cookies &
Candies

Poinsettia Cookies, page 125

Chocolate-Hazelnut Clusters

½ cup unsalted butter or
   margarine, softened
½ cup firmly packed dark
   brown sugar
½ cup sugar
1 large egg
1 teaspoon vanilla extract
1 teaspoon water

1½ cups regular oats, uncooked
¾ cup all-purpose flour
½ teaspoon baking powder
12 (1-ounce) squares bittersweet
   chocolate, coarsely chopped
½ cup hazelnuts, coarsely
   chopped

Beat butter at medium speed of an electric mixer until creamy; gradually add sugars, beating well. Add egg, vanilla, and water, and beat well.

Combine oats, flour, and baking powder; add to butter mixture, beating well (dough will be crumbly). Stir in chocolate and hazelnuts. Cover and chill 1 hour.

Drop cookie dough by heaping tablespoonfuls onto greased cookie sheets. Bake at 350° for 8 to 10 minutes. Cool 2 minutes on cookie sheets; remove to wire racks, and let cool completely. Yield: 2½ dozen.

From Portland's Palate
The Junior League of Portland, Oregon

Old-Time Cinnamon Jumbles

Bring back fond memories of sneaking a treat from Grandma's cookie jar with these old-fashioned cookies. They have just the right hint of cinnamon and nutmeg flavor.

¼ cup shortening
¼ cup butter or margarine,
   softened
1 cup sugar
1 large egg
¾ cup buttermilk
1 teaspoon vanilla extract

¼ teaspoon ground nutmeg
2 cups all-purpose flour
½ teaspoon baking soda
½ teaspoon salt
¼ cup sugar
½ teaspoon ground cinnamon

Beat shortening and butter at medium speed of an electric mixer until creamy; gradually add 1 cup sugar, beating well. Add egg, beating well. Add buttermilk, vanilla, and nutmeg, mixing until blended.

Combine flour, baking soda, and salt; add to shortening mixture, beating well. Cover and chill at least 2 hours.

Drop dough by heaping teaspoonfuls onto lightly greased cookie sheets. Combine ¼ cup sugar and cinnamon; sprinkle evenly over cookies. Bake at 375° for 8 to 10 minutes. Cool on wire racks. Yield: 4½ dozen.   Tolland Junior Woman's Club Story

Recipes and Remembrances of Tolland
The Tolland Historical Society
Tolland, Connecticut

Texas-Sized Almond Cookies

1 **cup butter or margarine, softened**	1 **teaspoon baking soda**
1 **cup sugar**	1 **teaspoon salt**
1 **cup sifted powdered sugar**	1 **teaspoon cream of tartar**
1 **cup vegetable oil**	2 **cups coarsely chopped almonds**
2 **large eggs**	1 **(6-ounce) package almond brickle chips**
1 **teaspoon almond extract**	**Sugar**
3½ **cups all-purpose flour**	
1 **cup whole wheat flour**	

Beat butter at medium speed of an electric mixer until creamy; gradually add 1 cup sugar and powdered sugar, beating well. Add oil, eggs, and almond extract; beat well.

Combine flours, baking soda, salt, and cream of tartar; add to butter mixture, beating well. Stir in almonds and almond brickle chips.

Shape cookie dough into 3-inch balls; roll in additional sugar. Place 5 inches apart on ungreased cookie sheets. Flatten cookies in a criss-cross pattern with a fork dipped in sugar. Bake at 350° for 10 to 12 minutes. Cool 1 minute on cookie sheets; remove to wire racks, and let cool completely. Yield: 3½ dozen.   Marian K. Bartlett

Phi Bete's Best
Theta Alpha Gamma Chapter
Bedford, Indiana

Melomacarona (Honey-Dipped Cakes)

½ cup butter or margarine,
  softened
¼ cup vegetable oil
¼ cup sugar
1 teaspoon grated orange rind
¼ cup orange juice
1 large egg
2¼ cups all-purpose flour
1½ teaspoons baking powder

¼ teaspoon salt
½ teaspoon ground cinnamon
½ cup chopped walnuts or
  blanched almonds
¾ cup honey
¼ cup sugar
¼ cup water
1 cup ground walnuts or
  blanched almonds

Beat butter at medium speed of an electric mixer until creamy; add oil and ¼ cup sugar, beating well. Add orange rind, orange juice, and egg, beating well.

Combine flour, baking powder, salt, and cinnamon; add to butter mixture, beating well. Stir in ½ cup chopped walnuts. Divide dough in half; cover and chill 30 minutes.

Work with one portion of dough at a time, keeping remaining dough chilled. Shape dough into 2½- x 1-inch ovals. Place on greased cookie sheets. Bake at 375° for 15 minutes or until lightly browned. Cool on wire racks. Place wax paper under wire racks.

Combine honey, ¼ cup sugar, and water; bring to a boil, stirring constantly. Using a fork, dip cookies in hot honey mixture. Place cookies on wire racks; sprinkle with ground walnuts. Let dry slightly before serving. Store between layers of wax paper in an airtight container. Yield: 2¼ dozen.

Mary Moore

Recipes & Remembrances
Hospice at Grady Memorial Hospital
Delaware, Ohio

Poinsettia Cookies

These pretty cookies are named for the decorative flower design on top of each one, which is made from red candied cherry wedges and butterscotch morsels.

2 cups butter or margarine, softened
2 cups sifted powdered sugar
2 large eggs
1 teaspoon vanilla extract
3 cups all-purpose flour
1 teaspoon salt

1 cup flaked coconut
1 cup butterscotch morsels, divided
Sugar
1 (4-ounce) container red candied cherries, cut into wedges

Beat butter at medium speed of an electric mixer until creamy; gradually add powdered sugar, beating well. Add eggs and vanilla, beating well.

Combine flour and salt; add to butter mixture, beating well. Stir in flaked coconut and ¾ cup butterscotch morsels. Cover and chill at least 8 hours.

Shape dough into 1-inch balls; place on ungreased cookie sheets. Dip a flat-bottomed glass in sugar, and flatten each ball to a 2-inch circle. Place a butterscotch morsel in the center of each cookie. Arrange 5 cherry wedges in a circular pattern around each butterscotch morsel to resemble a poinsettia. Bake at 350° for 9 to 10 minutes. Cool 1 minute on cookie sheets; remove to wire racks, and let cool completely. Yield: 5 dozen.

Mary Pantazis

What's Cookin'
Montgomery County Humane Society
Rockville, Maryland

German Vanilla Cookies

Let the cookie dough stand 10 minutes before shaping it into balls and the dough will be less sticky and easier to handle. If you prefer, you can fill the indentations in each cookie with raspberry jelly instead of the Chocolate Glaze.

1 cup butter or margarine,
   softened
¾ cup sifted powdered sugar
1 egg yolk

1 teaspoon vanilla extract
2¼ cups all-purpose flour
Chocolate Glaze

Beat butter at medium speed of an electric mixer until creamy; gradually add powdered sugar, beating well. Add egg yolk and vanilla; beat well. Gradually add flour to butter mixture, beating well. Let stand 10 minutes.

Shape dough into 1-inch balls; place on ungreased cookie sheets. Press thumb into each ball of dough, leaving an indentation. Bake at 325° for 15 minutes. Cool completely on wire racks. Spoon Chocolate Glaze into indentation of each cookie. Yield: 4 dozen.

Chocolate Glaze

3 (1-ounce) squares semisweet
   chocolate
2 tablespoons butter or
   margarine

1 tablespoon light corn syrup

Combine all ingredients in a small saucepan. Cook over low heat, stirring constantly, until chocolate and butter melt. Yield: ¼ cup plus 3 tablespoons.

Rita C. Leonard

Simple Elegance
Our Lady of Perpetual Help Women's Guild
Germantown, Tennessee

Lemon-Apricot Cookies

1 cup butter or margarine, softened
⅓ cup sugar
⅓ cup firmly packed brown sugar
1 large egg
1 teaspoon vanilla extract

2½ cups all-purpose flour
1 teaspoon baking powder
4 ounces dried apricot halves
½ cup water
3 tablespoons honey
⅛ teaspoon ground cinnamon
Lemon Icing

Beat butter at medium speed of an electric mixer until creamy; gradually add sugars, beating well. Add egg and vanilla; beat well.

Combine flour and baking powder; gradually add to butter mixture, stirring well (dough will be stiff).

Divide dough into 8 equal portions; shape into balls. Wrap in wax paper, and chill 1 hour.

Combine apricot halves and water in a small saucepan. Bring to a boil; cover, reduce heat, and simmer 10 to 15 minutes or until tender, stirring often. Remove from heat. Position knife blade in food processor bowl. Add apricot mixture, honey, and cinnamon; process until smooth. Cover and chill.

Shape each portion of dough into an 8-inch log. Place logs 4 inches apart on greased cookie sheets. Place the handle of a wooden spoon lengthwise down the center of each log; gently press handle to form a ½-inch-wide indentation. Spoon about 1½ tablespoons apricot mixture into each indentation. Bake at 350° for 18 to 20 minutes or until lightly browned. Cool 10 minutes on cookie sheets; remove to wire racks, and let cool completely. Drizzle Lemon Icing evenly over logs. Cut each log diagonally into 7 cookies. Yield: about 5 dozen.

Lemon Icing

1 cup sifted powdered sugar
1 tablespoon lemon juice

½ to 1 tablespoon water

Combine all ingredients in a bowl; stir until smooth. Yield: ¼ cup.

Plain & Elegant: A Georgia Heritage
West Georgia Medical Center Auxiliary
LaGrange, Georgia

Sicilian Slice Cookies

If red candied cherries aren't available, you can use chopped maraschino cherries. Be sure to drain the cherries well, and gently press them between layers of paper towels to remove excess moisture.

1 cup shortening
1 cup sugar
6 large eggs, beaten
1 tablespoon vanilla
  extract
4 cups all-purpose flour

1 tablespoon plus 1 teaspoon
  baking powder
½ cup coarsely chopped pecans
¼ cup chopped red candied
  cherries
Powdered sugar

Beat shortening at medium speed of an electric mixer until fluffy; gradually add 1 cup sugar, beating well. Add beaten eggs and vanilla, and beat well.

Combine flour and baking powder; gradually add to egg mixture, beating well. Stir in pecans and cherries. Let stand 5 minutes.

Divide dough into 3 equal portions. Place each portion 4 inches apart on greased cookie sheets; shape into 10-inch logs. Bake at 350° for 15 minutes or until golden. Let cool 10 minutes on cookie sheets.

Cut logs into ½-inch slices. Place slices on cookie sheets, cut side down. Bake at 350° for 10 minutes or until crisp and lightly browned. Cool completely on wire racks. Sprinkle with powdered sugar. Yield: 6 dozen.

Father Gabriell

Taste & Share the Goodness of Door County
St. Rosalia's Ladies Sodality of St. Rosalia's Catholic Church
Sister Bay, Wisconsin

Key Lime Cookie Bars

2 cups all-purpose flour
½ cup sifted powdered sugar
1 cup butter or margarine
4 large eggs

2 cups sugar
⅓ cup Key lime juice
¼ teaspoon salt
2 tablespoons powdered sugar

Combine flour and ½ cup powdered sugar in a large bowl; cut in butter with pastry blender until mixture is crumbly. Press into a greased 13- x 9- x 2-inch pan. Bake at 350° for 20 to 25 minutes or until golden. Set aside.

Beat eggs until thick and pale. Gradually add 2 cups sugar, lime juice, and salt, beating well after each addition. Spread evenly over baked layer in pan. Bake at 350° for 20 to 25 minutes or until lightly browned. Sprinkle with 2 tablespoons powdered sugar. Cool completely in pan on a wire rack. Cut into bars. Yield: 2½ dozen.   Sandy Ernst

Cooking Up a Storm, Florida Style
Brookwood Guild
St. Petersburg, Florida

Salted Peanut Chews

1½ cups all-purpose flour
½ teaspoon baking powder
¼ teaspoon baking soda
½ teaspoon salt
⅔ cup firmly packed brown
    sugar
½ cup butter or margarine,
    softened
2 egg yolks

1 teaspoon vanilla extract
3 cups miniature marshmallows
1 (10-ounce) package peanut
    butter morsels
⅔ cup light corn syrup
¼ cup butter or margarine
2 teaspoons vanilla extract
2 cups crisp rice cereal
2 cups salted roasted peanuts

Combine first 8 ingredients in a large mixing bowl. Beat at low speed of an electric mixer until crumbly. Press into an ungreased 13- x 9- x 2-inch pan. Bake at 350° for 12 to 15 minutes or until lightly browned. Sprinkle with marshmallows; bake 1 to 2 additional minutes or until marshmallows begin to puff. Cool in pan on a wire rack.

Combine peanut butter morsels, corn syrup, ¼ cup butter, and 2 teaspoons vanilla in a large saucepan; cook over low heat, stirring constantly, until smooth. Remove from heat; stir in cereal and peanuts. Spread cereal mixture over marshmallows. Cover and chill 1 hour or until firm. Cut into bars. Yield: 3 dozen.   Lisa Hodges

Cookin' for the Kids
Wal-Mart Distribution Center #6011
Brookhaven, Mississippi

Southern Pecan Bars

This rich bar cookie can do double-duty as a dessert square—just make each serving a little larger, and add a dollop of whipped cream.

1 cup butter or margarine, softened
¾ cup firmly packed brown sugar
2¼ cups all-purpose flour
½ teaspoon vanilla extract
1 egg white, lightly beaten
4 large eggs

1 cup light corn syrup
⅓ cup firmly packed brown sugar
¼ cup butter or margarine, melted
3 tablespoons all-purpose flour
1 teaspoon vanilla extract
2 cups coarsely chopped pecans

Beat 1 cup butter at medium speed of an electric mixer until creamy; gradually add ¾ cup brown sugar, beating well. Add 2¼ cups flour, beating well. Stir in ½ teaspoon vanilla. Press into bottom of an ungreased 13- x 9- x 2-inch pan. Brush with egg white. Bake at 350° for 15 minutes. Cool 5 minutes in pan on a wire rack.

Beat eggs in a large mixing bowl at medium speed of an electric mixer until thick and pale. Combine corn syrup and next 4 ingredients; add to beaten eggs, stirring until smooth. Fold in pecans. Spoon pecan mixture over crust. Bake at 350° for 30 minutes. Gently run a knife around edge of pan to release sides. Cool completely in pan on wire rack. Cut into bars. Store in an airtight container in the refrigerator. Yield: 4 dozen.

Barbara Saito

St. Stephen's Feast
St. Stephen Protomartyr Catholic Church
St. Louis, Missouri

Heavenly Honey Brownies

⅓ cup butter or margarine,
   softened
¾ cup sugar
½ cup honey
2 teaspoons vanilla extract
2 large eggs

½ cup all-purpose flour
½ teaspoon salt
⅓ cup cocoa
1 cup chopped pecans
Honey-Chocolate Frosting

Beat butter at medium speed of an electric mixer until creamy; gradually add sugar, beating well. Add honey and vanilla, beating well. Add eggs, one at a time, beating well after each addition.

Combine flour, salt, and cocoa; add to butter mixture, beating well. Stir in pecans. Spoon batter into a greased 8-inch square pan. Bake at 350° for 30 to 35 minutes or until a wooden pick inserted in center comes out clean. Cool completely in pan on a wire rack. Spread Honey-Chocolate Frosting on top of brownies. Cut into squares. Yield: 3 dozen.

Honey-Chocolate Frosting

3 tablespoons butter or
   margarine, softened
1 cup sifted powdered sugar
3 tablespoons cocoa

1 tablespoon honey
1 tablespoon milk
¾ teaspoon vanilla extract

Beat butter at medium speed of an electric mixer until creamy. Gradually add sugar and remaining ingredients, beating until blended. Yield: ½ cup.

The Pasquotank Plate
Christ Episcopal Churchwomen
Elizabeth City, North Carolina

Ricotta Brownies

The ricotta cheese in these brownies makes them unbelievably moist. Ricotta cheese is often used in desserts because it has a slightly sweet flavor.

1 cup butter or margarine	1 cup all-purpose flour
4 (1-ounce) squares unsweetened chocolate	1 cup ricotta cheese
	1 large egg
2½ cups sugar, divided	2 teaspoons vanilla extract
3 large eggs	1 cup chopped walnuts

Combine butter and chocolate in top of a double boiler; bring water to a boil. Reduce heat to low; cook until butter and chocolate melt, stirring occasionally. Remove from heat, and let cool slightly.

Combine 2 cups sugar and 3 eggs in a medium bowl; beat well with a wire whisk. Add to chocolate mixture, stirring until blended.

Combine remaining ½ cup sugar, flour, ricotta cheese, 1 egg, and vanilla in a medium bowl, and stir well. Add ricotta cheese mixture to chocolate mixture, stirring until blended. Spread mixture in a greased 13- x 9- x 2-inch pan. Sprinkle evenly with walnuts. Bake at 350° for 40 to 45 minutes or until a wooden pick inserted in center comes out clean. Cool completely in pan on a wire rack. Cut brownies into squares. Yield: 2 dozen.

Family & Company
The Junior League of Binghamton, New York

Fudge

1 tablespoon butter or margarine	2 cups milk chocolate morsels
4½ cups sugar	2 cups semisweet chocolate morsels
1 (12-ounce) can evaporated milk	1 (13-ounce) jar marshmallow creme
2 tablespoons butter or margarine	1 teaspoon vanilla extract
¼ teaspoon salt	2 cups chopped pecans

Butter a large heavy saucepan with 1 tablespoon butter. Combine sugar and next 3 ingredients in pan; cook over medium heat, stirring constantly, until sugar dissolves and mixture comes to a boil. Cover and cook 2 to 3 minutes to wash down sugar crystals from sides of pan. Uncover and cook, without stirring, until mixture reaches soft ball stage or candy thermometer registers 236°.

Combine milk mixture, chocolate morsels, and marshmallow creme in a large mixing bowl; beat at medium speed of an electric mixer until smooth. Add vanilla; beat until mixture thickens and begins to lose its gloss (about 10 minutes). Stir in pecans. Quickly pour into a buttered 13- x 9- x 2-inch dish. Let cool completely. Cut into squares. Yield: 5 pounds.   Rosalyn Skelton Weston

Discover Oklahoma Cookin'
Oklahoma 4-H Foundation
Stillwater, Oklahoma

Chocolate-Almond Balls

To drizzle the melted chocolate over this candy quickly and easily, try spooning the chocolate into a small zip-top plastic bag, and seal the bag. Then simply snip a tiny hole in one corner of the bag, using scissors.

1 (9-ounce) package chocolate wafers, crushed
1 cup finely chopped blanched almonds, toasted
1 cup sifted powdered sugar
⅓ cup crème de cacao or other chocolate-flavored liqueur
¼ cup light corn syrup
1 pound vanilla-flavored candy coating
2 (1-ounce) squares semisweet chocolate

Combine first 5 ingredients in a large bowl; stir well. Shape into 1-inch balls; chill until firm.

Place candy coating in top of a double boiler; bring water to a boil. Reduce heat to low; cook until candy coating melts, stirring often. Dip balls in melted candy coating, and coat well. Place on wax paper, and let dry.

Melt semisweet chocolate in a small saucepan over low heat, stirring constantly. Remove from heat, and let cool. Drizzle chocolate over balls. Store in an airtight container. Yield: 4 dozen.   Alice Tignor

Food for Thought
Indian Creek School Parent Teacher Organization
Crownsville, Maryland

Super Chocolate Candy

12 ounces peanut butter
  morsels
1 (4-ounce) package sweet
  baking chocolate

1½ cups pecan halves
½ cup flaked coconut (optional)

Place peanut butter morsels and chocolate in top of a double boiler; bring water to a boil. Reduce heat to low; cook until morsels and chocolate melt, stirring occasionally. Stir in pecans and coconut, if desired. Drop by rounded teaspoonfuls onto wax paper, and let cool completely. Yield: 1¼ pounds.   Sandra Graham Cude

The Jubilee of Our Many Blessings Cookbook
United Methodist Women
Highland Park United Methodist Church
Dallas, Texas

Goober Brittle

Although there are many varieties of peanuts, the two most popular are the Spanish (small and round) and the Virginia (large and oval shaped). You can use either variety of peanut in this candy recipe.

3 cups sugar
1 cup light corn syrup
1 cup water
2½ cups raw Spanish peanuts

2 tablespoons butter or
  margarine
1 tablespoon baking soda
1 teaspoon salt

Combine sugar, corn syrup, and water in a large saucepan. Cook over medium heat, stirring constantly, until sugar dissolves. Cover and cook over medium heat 2 to 3 minutes to wash down sugar crystals from sides of pan. Add peanuts; cook until mixture reaches hard crack stage (300°), stirring occasionally. Remove from heat. Stir in butter, baking soda, and salt.

Working rapidly, pour mixture into 2 buttered 15- x 10- x 1-inch jellyroll pans; spread in a thin layer. Let cool completely. Break into pieces. Store in an airtight container. Yield: about 2½ pounds.

The Wild Wild West
The Junior League of Odessa, Texas

Desserts

Lemon-Ginger Mousse, page 140

Melon Balls in Fruit Sauce

For a change of pace from the more familiar melons such as cantaloupe, honeydew, and watermelon, experiment with more unusual varieties like casaba, Crenshaw, Persian, and Santa Claus.

¾ cup fresh orange juice
½ cup currant jelly
¼ cup sugar
¼ cup fresh lime juice

1 teaspoon vanilla extract
4 cups assorted melon balls
Garnishes: orange slices, lime
    slices, fresh mint sprigs

Combine first 4 ingredients in a small saucepan. Bring to a boil, stirring occasionally; reduce heat, and simmer, uncovered, 3 minutes. Remove from heat; stir in vanilla. Let sauce cool completely.

Pour sauce over melon balls. Cover and chill thoroughly. Serve with a slotted spoon. Garnish, if desired. Yield: 4 servings.

The William & Mary Cookbook
Society of the Alumni, College of William and Mary
Williamsburg, Virginia

Sisson Holiday Cranberries

Looking for an easy holiday dessert? This baked cranberry and apple combo is certain to become a new family favorite.

3 cups chopped cooking
    apples
2 cups fresh cranberries
1¼ cups sugar
1½ cups quick-cooking oats,
    uncooked

½ cup firmly packed brown
    sugar
½ cup butter or margarine,
    melted
⅓ cup all-purpose flour
⅓ cup chopped pecans

Combine first 3 ingredients in an ungreased 2-quart casserole. Combine oats and remaining ingredients in a bowl; stir well. Sprinkle oat mixture over apple mixture. Bake at 350° for 1 hour or until lightly browned. Serve warm. Yield: 6 servings. Laura Boyer Sisson

New Additions and Old Favorites
Canterbury United Methodist Church
Birmingham, Alabama

Breakfast Pears

Try serving these baked pear halves as a sweet finish to your next breakfast.

3 medium-size firm ripe pears
½ cup pitted, chopped dates
½ cup orange juice
¼ cup honey
2 teaspoons butter or
    margarine, melted
Ground nutmeg

Peel and core pears; cut in half lengthwise. Place pears, cut side up, in an ungreased 11- x 7- x 1½-inch baking dish. Place 1 rounded tablespoon dates in cavity of each pear. Combine orange juice, honey, and butter; pour over pears. Sprinkle with nutmeg. Cover and bake at 350° for 25 minutes, basting occasionally with orange juice mixture. Serve warm. Yield: 6 servings.   Mary Lou Green

Angels & Friends Favorite Recipes II
Angels of Easter Seal
Youngstown, Ohio

Spicy Coconut Pears

1 (29-ounce) can pear halves in
    syrup, undrained
2 tablespoons cornstarch
¼ teaspoon ground cinnamon
¼ teaspoon ground nutmeg
⅛ teaspoon ground cloves
½ cup sugar
¼ cup lemon juice
2 tablespoons butter or
    margarine
½ cup flaked coconut, lightly
    toasted

Drain pears, reserving 1 cup syrup. Combine ¼ cup reserved syrup, cornstarch, and spices; set aside. Combine remaining ¾ cup syrup, sugar, lemon juice, and butter in a saucepan; bring to a boil. Reduce heat; gradually stir in cornstarch mixture. Cook over low heat, stirring constantly, until thickened.

Arrange pears in an 8-inch square baking dish. Pour syrup mixture over pears; sprinkle with coconut. Bake at 350° for 15 minutes. Serve warm. Yield: 4 servings.   Dwaine and Nancy Coley

Treasured Gems
Hiddenite Center Family
Hiddenite, North Carolina

Almond Cookie Cups with Raspberries and Caramel Sauce

These delicate cookies require a little extra attention when shaping. If they become too crisp to shape, simply reheat them at 350° for 30 seconds to soften.

1 cup blanched almonds, ground	2 tablespoons milk
¾ cup sugar	½ cup whipping cream
¼ cup plus 2 tablespoons unsalted butter, softened	¼ cup sugar
1 tablespoon plus 1 teaspoon all-purpose flour	4 cups fresh raspberries
	Caramel Sauce

Cut 12 (6-inch) squares of parchment paper. Place 2 parchment squares on an ungreased cookie sheet. Set aside.

Combine first 5 ingredients in a medium mixing bowl; beat at medium speed of an electric mixer until well blended. (Dough will be sticky.)

Place 1 tablespoon dough in center of each parchment square on cookie sheet. Dip a spoon into cold water; use back of a spoon to flatten dough into 3-inch rounds. Bake at 350° for 8 to 10 minutes or until golden. (Cookies will spread during baking.) Remove from oven, and let cool 1 minute on cookie sheet.

When cookies are cool enough to hold their shape, transfer to bottom of inverted muffin tins; remove parchment paper. Let cookies cool completely; remove carefully. Repeat procedure with remaining parchment squares and dough.

Beat whipping cream until foamy; gradually add ¼ cup sugar, beating until soft peaks form. Spoon sweetened whipped cream into each cookie cup. Top evenly with raspberries, and drizzle with Caramel Sauce. Yield: 12 servings.

Caramel Sauce

1 cup firmly packed light brown sugar	⅓ cup sugar
1 cup whipping cream	¼ cup light corn syrup
	¼ cup maple syrup

Combine all ingredients in a large saucepan, stirring well. Cook sugar mixture, uncovered, over medium-high heat, without stirring, until candy thermometer registers 220°. Remove from heat; let sauce cool 20 minutes. Yield: 2½ cups.

Sensational Seasons: A Taste & Tour of Arkansas
The Junior League of Fort Smith, Arkansas

Flan de Chocolate

Flan is a Spanish baked custard dessert with a caramelized sugar glaze. This flan takes on a new personality with the flavor of chocolate.

1 **cup sugar**	2 **(14-ounce) cans sweetened**
1¾ **cups water, divided**	**condensed milk**
2 **tablespoons cocoa**	4 **large eggs**
1 **tablespoon sugar**	1 **teaspoon vanilla extract**

Combine 1 cup sugar and ¼ cup water in a heavy saucepan; cook over medium heat, stirring constantly with a wooden spoon, until sugar crystallizes into lumps (about 15 minutes). Continue to cook, stirring constantly, until sugar melts and turns golden brown (about 15 minutes). Quickly pour hot caramelized sugar into an ungreased 8-inch round cakepan, tilting to coat bottom evenly. Set aside (mixture will harden).

Combine remaining 1½ cups water, cocoa, and 1 tablespoon sugar in a small saucepan. Bring to a boil over medium heat, stirring often. Remove from heat, and let cool.

Combine milk, eggs, and vanilla in container of an electric blender; cover and process just until blended. Add cocoa mixture; process until blended, stopping once to scrape down sides. Pour egg mixture over caramelized sugar in cakepan. Place cakepan in a large shallow baking dish. Add hot water to dish to depth of 1 inch. Cover and bake at 350° for 1½ hours or until a knife inserted near center comes out clean. Remove pan from water, and let cool. Cover and chill 8 hours.

To serve, loosen edge of flan with a spatula, and invert onto a serving plate. Yield: 6 servings.

Tropical Seasons, A Taste of Life in South Florida
Beaux Arts of the Lowe Art Museum of the University of Miami
Coral Gables, Florida

Lemon-Ginger Mousse

If you don't have fresh ginger on hand, you can substitute 1 teaspoon of ground ginger.

½ cup butter or margarine	1 tablespoon grated fresh ginger
1 cup sugar	4 large eggs
1 tablespoon grated lemon rind	1 cup whipping cream, whipped
⅓ cup fresh lemon juice	16 gingersnap cookies, divided

Melt butter in a medium saucepan over low heat; add sugar and next 3 ingredients. Cook over medium heat, stirring constantly, 5 minutes or until sugar dissolves.

Beat eggs at medium speed of an electric mixer 1 minute. Pour hot lemon mixture in a very thin stream over beaten eggs while beating constantly at low speed. Return egg mixture to saucepan; cook over medium heat, stirring constantly, 6 to 8 minutes or until thick.

Pour lemon mixture through a wire-mesh strainer into a bowl. Freeze 20 to 25 minutes or until chilled, stirring occasionally. Fold whipped cream into lemon mixture; cover and chill thoroughly.

Coarsely crush 10 gingersnap cookies. Place 1 rounded tablespoon cookie crumbs in each of 6 dessert glasses. Spoon ⅓ cup mousse mixture on top of cookie crumbs in dessert glasses; repeat layers. Top each serving with 1 remaining whole cookie. Serve immediately. Yield: 6 servings.

Judy Eller

Bethel's Bounty
Bethel Presbyterian Women
Davidson, North Carolina

Chocolate Chip and Raisin Bread Pudding with Crème Anglaise

1 (1-pound) loaf cinnamon-
   raisin bread
4 large eggs, lightly beaten
1½ cups milk
½ cup whipping cream
½ cup firmly packed brown
   sugar
⅓ cup Irish cream liqueur

¼ cup dark rum
4 ounces semisweet chocolate,
   chopped
½ cup raisins
1 tablespoon grated orange rind
1 tablespoon vanilla extract
Crème Anglaise

Remove crust from bread; reserve for other uses. Cut bread into cubes, and place in a large bowl.

Combine eggs and next 5 ingredients in a medium bowl; stir in chocolate and next 3 ingredients. Pour egg mixture over bread; stir well. Cover and chill 30 minutes.

Pour into a greased 9-inch springform pan. Bake, uncovered, at 350° for 50 minutes or until a knife inserted in center comes out clean. Cool in pan 5 minutes. Carefully remove sides of springform pan; cut into wedges. Serve warm with Crème Anglaise. Yield: 8 servings.

Crème Anglaise

1 vanilla bean
1⅓ cups whipping cream
⅔ cup milk

4 egg yolks
½ cup sugar
½ cup Irish cream liqueur

Cut a 2-inch piece of vanilla bean; reserve remaining bean for other uses. Split vanilla bean lengthwise. Combine vanilla bean, whipping cream, and milk in a heavy saucepan. Cook over medium heat, stirring constantly, until mixture reaches 185°.

Combine yolks and sugar in a bowl; beat with a wire whisk until blended. Gradually stir about one-fourth of hot mixture into yolks; add to remaining hot mixture, stirring constantly. Cook over low heat, stirring constantly, 6 minutes or until thickened. Discard vanilla bean; stir in liqueur. Cover and chill. Yield: 2⅔ cups.   Kim Bennett

Conflict-Free Cooking
National Court Reporters Foundation
Vienna, Virginia

Holiday Meringues

These crisp white meringues are filled with a scoop of lime sherbet and topped with a simple cranberry syrup to create a light and colorful holiday dessert.

3 egg whites
¼ teaspoon cream of tartar
1 teaspoon vanilla extract

1 cup sugar
1 quart lime sherbet
Cranberry Sauce

Combine first 3 ingredients in a large mixing bowl; beat at high speed of an electric mixer until foamy. Gradually add sugar, 1 tablespoon at a time, beating until stiff peaks form and sugar dissolves (2 to 4 minutes).

Drop mixture evenly into 10 mounds on a large baking sheet lined with unglazed brown paper or parchment paper. (Do not use recycled paper.) Make an indentation in center of each mound with back of a spoon. Bake at 225° for 1 hour; turn oven off, and let cool in oven at least 2 hours or up to 8 hours. Carefully remove meringues from paper.

Just before serving, scoop lime sherbet into center of each meringue. Drizzle with Cranberry Sauce. Serve immediately. Yield: 10 servings.

Cranberry Sauce

2 cups cranberry juice cocktail
½ cup sugar
2 tablespoons cornstarch

1 tablespoon lemon juice
⅛ teaspoon salt

Combine all ingredients in a medium saucepan. Bring to a boil over medium heat, stirring constantly; boil 1 minute. Cover and chill. Yield: 2⅓ cups.   Barbara Davock

Simple Elegance
Our Lady of Perpetual Help Women's Guild
Germantown, Tennessee

Rogue Pears

¼ cup firmly packed light brown sugar
¼ cup Triple Sec or other orange-flavored liqueur
1 teaspoon grated orange rind
3 tablespoons orange juice
4 large firm ripe pears, peeled, cored, and thinly sliced
1 tablespoon butter or margarine, melted
1 quart vanilla ice cream
Sugared Orange Peels

Combine first 4 ingredients in a small bowl; stir well, and set aside.

Cook pear slices in butter in a large skillet over low heat 20 minutes or until golden, stirring occasionally. Stir in sugar mixture. Bring to a boil over medium heat, stirring constantly; cook 2 to 3 minutes or until sauce thickens and clings to pear slices. Set aside, and keep warm.

Scoop ice cream into 6 individual dessert bowls. Spoon pear slices and sauce evenly over ice cream. Top each serving with a Sugared Orange Peel. Serve immediately. Yield: 6 servings.

Sugared Orange Peels

1 orange
¼ cup sugar

Cut a 9- x ¼ inch strip of orange rind, using a vegetable peeler or sharp knife. Twist orange rind strip around a pencil; wrap pencil in heavy-duty plastic wrap. Freeze until firm.

Remove orange rind from freezer; remove plastic wrap and pencil. Cut orange rind into 6 (1½-inch) pieces. Combine orange rind and sugar; toss gently. Yield: 6 orange rind peels.

Rogue River Rendezvous
The Junior Service League of Jackson County
Medford, Oregon

Amaretto Chantilly

3½ cups miniature
   marshmallows
⅔ cup amaretto
½ cup chopped maraschino
   cherries

1 tablespoon lemon juice
¼ teaspoon almond extract
2 cups whipping cream
2 tablespoons finely chopped
   pistachios or toasted almonds

Combine marshmallows and amaretto in top of a double boiler; bring water to a boil. Reduce heat to low; cook until marshmallows melt, stirring occasionally. Remove from heat. Stir in cherries, lemon juice, and almond extract. Let cool slightly.

Beat whipping cream until soft peaks form. Fold into marshmallow mixture. Spoon into individual dessert dishes, and sprinkle with nuts. Cover and freeze until firm. Yield: 8 servings.   Sharon Neal

Candlelight and Wisteria
Lee-Scott Academy
Auburn, Alabama

Peach-Macaroon Delight

This frozen ring mold dessert can be made ahead of time. For easier slicing, try using a serrated or an electric knife.

1 (13.75-ounce) package
   macaroon cookies
½ cup light rum
½ cup frozen coconut, thawed

¼ cup slivered almonds
1 quart peach ice cream, slightly
   softened
Fresh peach slices (optional)

Gently press cookies in bottom and up sides of a 9-inch ring mold. Gently fold rum, coconut, and almonds into ice cream. Spoon mixture over cookies in mold. Cover and freeze until firm.

Invert onto a serving platter. Serve immediately with peach slices, if desired. Yield: 8 servings.

Virginia Celebrates
The Council of the Virginia Museum of Fine Arts
Richmond, Virginia

Butterscotch Crunch Ice Cream Pie

If you want to maximize the butterscotch flavor of this ice cream dessert, simply top it with butterscotch sauce instead of caramel sauce.

1 cup all-purpose flour
¼ cup quick-cooking oats, uncooked
¼ cup firmly packed brown sugar
½ cup butter or margarine

½ cup chopped pecans or walnuts
1 (12-ounce) jar caramel sauce
½ gallon mocha fudge ice cream, softened

Combine flour, oats, and brown sugar in a medium bowl; cut in butter with pastry blender until mixture is crumbly. Stir in pecans. Firmly press oat mixture into bottom of an ungreased 13- x 9- x 2-inch pan. Bake at 400° for 15 minutes; stir to crumble. Let cool completely in pan on a wire rack.

Firmly press half of oat mixture into bottom of a buttered 9-inch springform pan; drizzle with half of caramel sauce. Spoon ice cream into prepared pan, spreading evenly; drizzle with remaining caramel sauce. Sprinkle with remaining oat mixture. Cover and freeze until firm. Let stand 5 minutes before serving. Yield: 16 servings.

Celebrate!
The Junior League of Sacramento, California

Mexican Cream Torte

2 cups crisp coconut cookie
crumbs, divided
3 pints chocolate ice cream,
softened and divided

¾ cup chocolate syrup, divided
1 pint orange sherbet, softened
1 cup crushed peanut brittle

Sprinkle ⅔ cup cookie crumbs in bottom of a lightly greased 8-inch springform pan. Spread half of chocolate ice cream over crumbs; pour ¼ cup chocolate syrup over ice cream layer. Cover and freeze until firm.

Sprinkle ⅔ cup crumbs over frozen syrup; spread sherbet over crumbs. Pour ¼ cup chocolate syrup over sherbet; cover and freeze until firm.

Sprinkle remaining ⅔ cup crumbs over syrup; spread remaining chocolate ice cream over crumbs. Pour remaining ¼ cup syrup over ice cream; sprinkle with peanut brittle. Cover and freeze at least 8 hours. Carefully remove sides of springform pan. Let stand 10 minutes before serving. Yield: 8 servings.   Della M. Works

First United Methodist Church Centennial Cookbook, 1993
United Methodist Women of First United Methodist Church
Casper, Wyoming

Mississippi Mocha Mud

The flavors of coffee and chocolate are deliciously paired in this frozen treat.

2 cups finely chopped pecans
⅔ cup firmly packed brown
sugar
¼ cup butter or margarine,
melted
½ teaspoon ground cinnamon
½ teaspoon instant coffee
granules

4 (1-ounce) squares
unsweetened chocolate
⅔ cup strong coffee
1 cup sugar
1 quart coffee ice cream,
softened

Combine first 5 ingredients; stir well. Firmly press pecan mixture into bottom of an ungreased 10- x 6- x 2-inch baking dish. Bake at 350° for 12 to 15 minutes or until lightly browned. Let cool in dish on a wire rack.

Combine chocolate and strong coffee in a saucepan. Cook over low heat, stirring constantly, until chocolate melts and mixture is smooth. Stir in 1 cup sugar; cook, stirring constantly, until sugar dissolves. Let cool completely. Cover and chill.

Spread ice cream evenly in prepared dish; cover and freeze until firm. Pour chocolate mixture over ice cream; cover and freeze at least 8 hours. Let stand 5 minutes before serving. Yield: 8 servings.

Heart & Soul
The Junior League of Memphis, Tennessee

Mexican Mocha Ice Cream

1 **cup half-and-half**
3 **(1-ounce) squares semisweet chocolate, coarsely chopped**
2 **teaspoons instant coffee granules**
4 **egg yolks**

⅔ **cup sugar**
1 **tablespoon butter or margarine**
1 **cup whipping cream, whipped**
2 **tablespoons Kahlúa or other coffee-flavored liqueur**

Combine half-and-half, chocolate, and coffee granules in a small saucepan; cook over low heat until chocolate melts, stirring occasionally. Set aside.

Beat egg yolks and sugar at high speed of an electric mixer until thick and pale. Gradually stir in chocolate mixture; cook over low heat, stirring constantly, 10 minutes or until thickened. Remove from heat; stir in butter. Let cool 15 minutes; stir in whipped cream and liqueur.

Pour mixture into freezer container of a 2-quart hand-turned or electric freezer. Freeze according to manufacturer's instructions.

Pack freezer with additional ice and rock salt, and let stand 1 hour before serving. Yield: about 4 cups.   Nancy Ward

Tri-State Center for the Arts Celebrity Cookbook
Tri-State Center for the Arts
Pine Plains, New York

Lemon Ice Cream

Thin lemon slices stud this old-fashioned and refreshing ice cream.

6 **medium lemons**
3 **cups sugar**

8 **cups half-and-half**

Cut 2 lemons into very thin slices. Combine lemon slices, juice from remaining 4 lemons, and sugar in a medium bowl; stir well. Let stand at room temperature at least 3 hours, stirring occasionally.

Combine lemon mixture and half-and-half. Pour mixture into freezer container of a 1-gallon hand-turned or electric freezer. Freeze according to manufacturer's instructions.

Pack freezer with additional ice and rock salt, and let stand 1 hour before serving. Yield: 1 gallon.

Seasoned Skillets & Silver Spoons
Columbus Museum Guild
Columbus, Georgia

Tropical Fruit Ice

4 **nectarines or fresh peaches, peeled and chopped**
2 **ripe bananas, sliced**
1 **(8-ounce) can crushed pineapple, undrained**

¾ **cup plus 2 tablespoons fresh orange juice**
½ **cup water**
¼ **cup fresh lemon juice**

Combine nectarine and banana in container of an electric blender; cover and process until smooth, stopping once to scrape down sides. Pour into a 13- x 9- x 2-inch dish. Stir in pineapple and remaining ingredients. Cover and freeze until firm. Let stand at room temperature 30 minutes before serving. Yield: 7½ cups.   Shay Caulkins

Recipes & Remembrances
Hospice at Grady Memorial Hospital
Delaware, Ohio

Eggs & Cheese

Garden Vegetable Soufflé, page 155

Swiss Cheese Scramble

6 slices white bread
1¾ cups milk
8 large eggs, lightly beaten
¾ teaspoon salt
⅛ teaspoon pepper
2 tablespoons butter or
  margarine
¼ teaspoon seasoned salt

1 (8-ounce) package sliced Swiss
  cheese
½ cup fine, dry breadcrumbs
2 tablespoons butter or
  margarine, melted
8 slices bacon, cooked and
  crumbled

Remove and discard crust from bread; cube bread. Combine bread cubes and milk in a small bowl; let stand 5 minutes. Drain, reserving bread and milk.

Combine milk, eggs, salt, and pepper in a large bowl; beat with a wire whisk until blended.

Melt 2 tablespoons butter in a large skillet over low heat. Add egg mixture, and cook over medium-low heat, without stirring, until mixture begins to set on bottom. Draw a spatula across bottom of pan to form large curds. Continue cooking until eggs are firm but still moist (do not stir constantly). Gently stir reserved bread into egg mixture.

Pour into a lightly greased 8-inch square baking dish; sprinkle with seasoned salt. Arrange cheese slices on top of egg mixture. Combine dry breadcrumbs and 2 tablespoons melted butter; sprinkle evenly over cheese. Top with crumbled bacon.

Bake, uncovered, at 400° for 10 to 12 minutes or until cheese melts. Serve immediately. Yield: 6 servings.

Heard in the Kitchen
The Heard Museum Guild
Phoenix, Arizona

Italian Frittata

This Italian version of a French omelet has the filling cooked in the omelet rather than folded inside. A frittata has a firmer texture than an omelet because it's cooked very slowly over low heat and finished under the broiler.

1 pound mild Italian link sausage
2 medium-size green peppers, cut into strips
1½ cups chopped purple onion
3 cloves garlic, sliced
2 tablespoons olive oil
2 tablespoons butter or margarine, melted
2 medium-size red potatoes, cooked, peeled, and diced
2 tomatoes, peeled and diced
2 tablespoons minced fresh parsley
1½ teaspoons dried basil
1½ teaspoons dried oregano
¼ teaspoon salt
¼ teaspoon pepper
8 large eggs, beaten
3 tablespoons water
½ cup grated Parmesan cheese

Place sausage in a large skillet; add water to skillet to depth of ½ inch. Bring to a boil; cover, reduce heat, and simmer 10 minutes or until sausage is done. Drain. Cut sausage into ½-inch slices; set aside.

Cook green pepper, onion, and garlic in oil and butter in a 12-inch ovenproof skillet over medium-high heat, stirring constantly, until tender. Add sausage, potato, and next 6 ingredients; cook 2 minutes, stirring constantly.

Combine eggs and 3 tablespoons water; pour over mixture in skillet. Cover, reduce heat to low, and cook 8 to 10 minutes or until eggs are set. Sprinkle with cheese.

Place skillet under broiler; broil 5½ inches from heat (with electric oven door partially opened) 3 to 5 minutes or until golden. Cut into wedges. Serve immediately. Yield: 8 servings.

The Bess Collection
The Junior Service League of Independence, Missouri

Cheese Blintz Casserole

Serve this cheese delicacy for breakfast or brunch topped with fresh berries, fruit preserves, sour cream, or lemon yogurt.

1 cup all-purpose flour
1 tablespoon baking powder
Dash of salt
1 cup butter or margarine, melted
½ cup sugar
¼ cup milk
2 large eggs, beaten

1 teaspoon vanilla extract
2 (8-ounce) packages cream cheese, softened
1¾ cups small-curd cottage cheese
¼ cup sugar
2 tablespoons fresh lemon juice
Dash of salt

Combine first 3 ingredients in a medium bowl. Add butter and next 4 ingredients, stirring well. Pour half of batter into a greased 13- x 9- x 2-inch pan (mixture will be thin in pan). Set pan and remaining batter aside.

Beat cream cheese at medium speed of an electric mixer until creamy. Add cottage cheese, ¼ cup sugar, lemon juice, and dash of salt; beat until blended. Spread cream cheese mixture over batter in pan, and pour remaining batter over cream cheese mixture. Bake, uncovered, at 300° for 55 minutes or until lightly browned. Serve immediately. Yield: 12 servings.

Karel Forrester

Georgia Land
Medical Association of Georgia Alliance
Atlanta, Georgia

Smoky Egg Casserole

This egg casserole gets its unique flavor from smoked cheese. We suggest smoked Gouda, but you can substitute another favorite variety.

1 cup frozen English peas
2 tablespoons butter or
   margarine
2 tablespoons all-purpose flour
1¼ cups milk
1 (6-ounce) package smoked
   Gouda cheese, shredded
12 large eggs, beaten
1 (6-ounce) jar sliced
   mushrooms, drained

1 tablespoon minced fresh
   chives
2 tablespoons butter or
   margarine
½ cup plain croutons
6 slices bacon, cooked and
   crumbled

Cook peas according to package directions; drain and set aside.

Melt 2 tablespoons butter in a heavy saucepan over low heat; add flour, stirring until smooth. Cook 1 minute, stirring constantly. Gradually add milk; cook over medium heat, stirring constantly, until mixture is thickened and bubbly. Add cheese, stirring until smooth. Set aside, and keep warm.

Combine peas, eggs, mushrooms, and chives in a large bowl. Melt 2 tablespoons butter in a large skillet over low heat. Add egg mixture, and cook over medium-low heat, without stirring, until mixture begins to set on bottom. Draw a spatula across bottom of pan to form large curds. Continue cooking until eggs are firm but still moist (do not stir constantly). Stir in cheese sauce.

Pour egg mixture into a greased 8-inch square baking dish. Bake, uncovered, at 350° for 20 minutes or until set and lightly browned. Sprinkle with croutons and bacon, and bake 10 additional minutes. Let stand 5 minutes before serving. Yield: 6 servings.

Moveable Feasts
Mystic Seaport Museum Stores
Mystic, Connecticut

Puffy Chile Relleno Casserole

3 (4½-ounce) cans whole green chiles, drained
4 (6-inch) corn tortillas, cut into 1-inch strips
4 cups (16 ounces) shredded Monterey Jack cheese
1 large tomato, sliced
8 large eggs
½ cup milk
½ teaspoon salt
½ teaspoon garlic powder
½ teaspoon ground cumin
½ teaspoon pepper
¼ teaspoon onion salt
Paprika

Make a lengthwise slit down each chile, and carefully remove seeds. Place half of chiles in bottom of a greased 8-inch square baking dish. Place half of tortilla strips over chiles, and sprinkle with half of cheese. Arrange tomato slices over cheese. Repeat layers with remaining chiles, tortilla strips, and cheese.

Combine eggs and next 6 ingredients in a bowl, beating with a wire whisk until blended. Pour over chile mixture; sprinkle with paprika. Bake at 350° for 40 to 45 minutes or until set and lightly browned. Let stand 5 minutes before serving. Yield: 6 servings.   Sheryl Dennis

Our Cherished Recipes, Second Edition
First Presbyterian Church
Skagway, Alaska

Fiesta Corn Flan

2 tablespoons minced onion
3 tablespoons finely chopped green pepper
1 tablespoon unsalted butter or margarine, melted
1½ cups fresh cut corn, divided
1½ tablespoons all-purpose flour
½ cup milk
1 cup whipping cream
3 large eggs
½ to 1 teaspoon salt
Freshly ground pepper to taste
¼ teaspoon ground nutmeg
⅛ teaspoon ground allspice
2 cups (8 ounces) shredded Monterey Jack cheese with jalapeño pepper

Cook onion and green pepper in melted butter in a medium skillet over medium-high heat, stirring constantly, until vegetables are tender. Add 1 cup corn, and cook, stirring constantly, 6 to 8 minutes or until corn is tender. Set vegetables aside.

Position knife blade in food processor bowl; add remaining ½ cup corn, flour, and next 7 ingredients. Process until smooth. Combine cooked vegetables, pureed mixture, and cheese. Pour into an ungreased 11- x 7- x 1½-inch baking dish. Set dish in a larger pan; add hot water to pan to depth of 1 inch. Bake, uncovered, at 350° for 1 hour or until set. Let stand 15 minutes before serving. Yield: 6 servings.

For Goodness Taste
The Junior League of Rochester, New York

Garden Vegetable Soufflé

Fresh cut corn is the garden vegetable that's showcased in this soufflé.

¼ **cup minced onion**	1 **cup fresh cut corn**
3 **tablespoons butter or**	¾ **teaspoon salt**
margarine, melted	½ **teaspoon ground nutmeg**
3 **tablespoons all-purpose flour**	6 **egg whites**
1 **cup milk**	¼ **teaspoon cream of tartar**
4 **egg yolks**	⅛ **teaspoon salt**

Cut a piece of aluminum foil long enough to fit around a 2-quart soufflé dish, allowing a 1-inch overlap; fold foil lengthwise into thirds. Lightly oil one side of foil and bottom of dish. Wrap foil around outside of dish, oiled side against dish, allowing it to extend 3 inches above rim to form a collar; secure with string.

Cook onion in butter in a saucepan over medium-high heat, stirring constantly, until tender. Add flour, stirring until blended. Cook 1 minute, stirring constantly. Gradually add milk; cook over medium heat, stirring constantly, until mixture is thickened and bubbly.

Beat egg yolks until thick and pale. Gradually stir about one-fourth of hot mixture into yolks; add to remaining hot mixture, stirring constantly. Stir in corn, ¾ teaspoon salt, and nutmeg.

Beat egg whites, cream of tartar, and ⅛ teaspoon salt at high speed of an electric mixer until stiff peaks form. Gently stir 1 cup beaten egg white into corn mixture. Fold remaining egg white into corn mixture. Pour into prepared soufflé dish. Bake at 375° for 40 to 45 minutes or until puffed and golden. Serve immediately. Yield: 8 servings.

The Wild Wild West
The Junior League of Odessa, Texas

Crabmeat Cheesecake

Pair this rich, crabmeat-filled cheesecake with a tossed green salad to create a satisfying meal, or turn it into a terrific appetizer by chilling and serving it with assorted crackers.

1 cup round buttery cracker crumbs (20 to 25 crackers)
3 tablespoons butter or margarine, melted
2 (8-ounce) packages cream cheese, softened
3 large eggs
¾ cup sour cream, divided

2 teaspoons grated onion
1 teaspoon lemon juice
½ teaspoon hot sauce
⅛ teaspoon freshly ground pepper
1 cup fresh crabmeat, drained and flaked

Combine cracker crumbs and butter. Firmly press crumb mixture on bottom of an ungreased 9-inch springform pan. Bake at 350° for 10 minutes; let cool on a wire rack.

Beat cream cheese, eggs, and ¼ cup sour cream at medium speed of an electric mixer until creamy. Add onion, lemon juice, hot sauce, and pepper, beating well. Stir in crabmeat. Pour into prepared pan.

Bake, uncovered, at 325° for 50 minutes or until center is almost set. Gently run a knife around edge of pan to release sides. Let cool in pan on wire rack. Carefully remove sides of springform pan. Spread remaining ½ cup sour cream over top. Serve immediately. Yield: 6 servings.

Phyllis E. Murphy

Dock 'n Dine in Dorchester
Long Wharf Lighthouse Committee
Cambridge, Maryland

Bacon-Asparagus Quiche

For convenience, you can substitute 1 (10-ounce) package frozen cut asparagus for fresh in this recipe. Simply thaw and drain the frozen asparagus before using it. No blanching is necessary.

½ pound fresh asparagus spears
1 unbaked 9-inch pastry shell
4 slices bacon, cooked and crumbled
1 cup (4 ounces) shredded Swiss cheese
2 large eggs, lightly beaten

2 egg whites, lightly beaten
1 cup milk
¼ teaspoon dried tarragon
¼ teaspoon ground nutmeg
⅛ teaspoon freshly ground pepper

Snap off tough ends of asparagus. Remove scales from stalks with a knife or vegetable peeler, if desired. Cut asparagus diagonally into 1-inch pieces. Blanch asparagus in boiling water 3 to 5 minutes or until crisp-tender. Drain and set aside.

Prick bottom and sides of pastry with a fork. Bake at 450° for 8 to 10 minutes; let cool on a wire rack. Sprinkle bacon in bottom of pastry shell; top with asparagus, and sprinkle with cheese.

Combine eggs and remaining ingredients, stirring well. Pour egg mixture over cheese. Bake, uncovered, at 350° for 35 minutes or until a knife inserted in center comes out clean. Let stand 10 minutes before serving. Yield: one 9-inch quiche.   Barbara Osborne

Harbor Hills Book Club's Lunch Bag
Harbor Hills Book Club
Davidsonville, Maryland

Mexican Quiche

⅔ cup cornmeal
⅓ cup whole wheat flour
1 teaspoon onion powder
¼ teaspoon baking soda
½ teaspoon salt
¼ cup plus 2 tablespoons butter
  or margarine, divided
¼ cup cold water
½ cup finely chopped onion
1 cup fresh cut or frozen whole
  kernel corn, thawed
¼ cup finely chopped tomato

3 large eggs, beaten
1 cup milk
½ cup (2 ounces) shredded
  sharp Cheddar cheese
1 large clove garlic, minced
½ teaspoon salt
1 teaspoon chili powder
1 teaspoon dried oregano
¼ teaspoon freshly ground
  pepper
1½ jalapeño peppers, seeded
  and chopped

Combine first 5 ingredients; cut in ¼ cup butter with pastry blender until mixture is crumbly. Sprinkle cold water (1 tablespoon at a time) evenly over surface; stir with a fork until dry ingredients are moistened. Shape into a ball. Chill.

Roll pastry to ⅛-inch thickness on a lightly floured surface. Line a 9-inch quiche dish with pastry; trim excess pastry along edges. Prick bottom and sides of pastry with a fork.

Bake at 400° for 3 minutes; remove from oven, and gently prick bottom and sides of pastry with a fork. Bake 5 additional minutes. Let cool on a wire rack.

Melt remaining 2 tablespoons butter over medium-high heat in a large skillet. Add onion, and cook 2 minutes, stirring constantly. Add corn, and cook, stirring constantly, until onion is golden. Remove from heat; stir in tomato.

Combine eggs and next 7 ingredients in a large bowl. Add corn mixture to egg mixture; stir well. Stir in jalapeño pepper.

Pour mixture into prepared pastry shell. Bake at 400° for 30 to 35 minutes or until a knife inserted in center comes out clean. Let stand 10 minutes before serving. Yield: one 9-inch quiche.

The Impossible Diet Cookbook
The Recovery Alliance
Milford, Connecticut

Onion Tart with Spinach and Pine Nuts

Pine nuts, also called pignoli, have a wonderfully delicate flavor. Because of their high fat content, store them in an airtight container in the refrigerator up to three months or in the freezer up to nine months.

1 **unbaked 9-inch pastry shell**
½ **pound fresh spinach**
2 **medium onions, thinly sliced**
3 **tablespoons unsalted butter or margarine, melted**
1½ **cups half-and-half**
4 **large eggs, lightly beaten**

½ **teaspoon salt**
½ **teaspoon pepper**
¼ **teaspoon ground nutmeg**
2 **tablespoons pine nuts, toasted**
2 **tablespoons grated Parmesan cheese**

Line pastry shell with aluminum foil; fill with dried beans or pie weights. Bake at 400° for 10 minutes. Carefully remove beans and foil; bake 8 additional minutes or until golden. Set aside.

Remove stems from spinach; wash leaves thoroughly, and pat dry. Chop spinach, and set aside.

Cook onion in butter in a large skillet over medium-high heat, stirring constantly, 10 to 12 minutes or until tender. Stir in spinach; remove from heat. Spoon onion mixture into prepared pastry shell. Combine half-and-half and next 4 ingredients; pour over onion mixture. Sprinkle with pine nuts and cheese.

Bake at 350° for 35 to 40 minutes or until a knife inserted in center comes out clean. Let stand 10 minutes before serving. Yield: one 9-inch tart.

Jamie Hawks Pack

The Heritage Collection
Western Kentucky University Home Economics
Alumni Association
Bowling Green, Kentucky

Herb Omelet Torte

For easy slicing, use an electric knife to cut this stately torte.

1 (17¼-ounce) package frozen puff pastry sheets, thawed
1 pound fresh spinach
1 clove garlic, minced
1 tablespoon butter or margarine, melted
1 tablespoon olive oil
½ teaspoon salt
½ teaspoon freshly grated nutmeg
¼ teaspoon pepper
2 medium-size sweet red peppers, cut into strips
1 tablespoon butter or margarine, melted
6 large eggs
2 tablespoons chopped fresh parsley

1½ tablespoons chopped green onions or fresh chives
1 tablespoon chopped fresh dill
1 tablespoon chopped fresh tarragon
¼ teaspoon salt
¼ teaspoon pepper
2 tablespoons butter or margarine, divided
3 cups (12 ounces) shredded Swiss cheese
½ pound thinly sliced cooked ham, turkey, or chicken
⅓ cup sliced ripe olives
1 large egg, lightly beaten

Unfold pastry sheets, and cut an 8-inch circle out of each sheet. Press one of the circles in bottom of an ungreased 8-inch springform pan; chill remaining circles. Press enough remaining pastry scraps on sides of springform pan to form crust, leaving ¼ inch extending above pan. Seal seams by moistening with water and pressing together. Chill. Make decorative shapes from any remaining pastry scraps, if desired, and chill.

Remove stems from spinach; wash leaves thoroughly, and pat dry. Cook spinach and garlic in 1 tablespoon butter and oil in a large Dutch oven over medium-high heat, stirring constantly, until spinach wilts and liquid evaporates. Remove from heat; stir in ½ teaspoon salt, nutmeg, and ¼ teaspoon pepper. Chill.

Cook red pepper strips in 1 tablespoon butter in a large skillet over medium-high heat, stirring constantly, until tender. Set aside.

Combine 6 eggs and next 6 ingredients in a large bowl; beat with a wire whisk until well blended. Heat an 8-inch omelet pan or heavy skillet over medium heat. Add 1 tablespoon butter, and rotate pan to coat. Add half of egg mixture. As egg mixture starts to cook, gently lift edges of omelet with a spatula, and tilt pan so uncooked portion flows underneath. Allow uncooked portion on top to set; transfer omelet to a plate. Repeat procedure with remaining 1 tablespoon butter and egg mixture.

Remove pastry from refrigerator. Place 1 omelet in prepared pan. Arrange half each of spinach mixture, cheese, and ham over omelet. Arrange red pepper strips and olives over ham. Repeat layers in reverse order with remaining ham, cheese, spinach mixture, and omelet. Top with remaining pastry circle; fold edges under and crimp. Arrange decorative pastry pieces on top of pastry circle. Brush top of pastry with beaten egg. Place pan on a baking sheet. Bake at 350° for 50 to 60 minutes. Let stand 15 minutes before serving. Carefully remove sides of springform pan. Yield: 8 servings.

Cranbrook Reflections: A Culinary Collection
Cranbrook House and Gardens Auxiliary
Bloomfield Hills, Michigan

Croissant French Toast

5 large eggs
⅔ cup whipping cream
⅓ cup Triple Sec or other
    orange-flavored liqueur
2 tablespoons sugar
2 teaspoons ground cinnamon

6 day-old croissants, cut in half
    lengthwise
¼ cup plus 2 tablespoons butter
    or margarine, melted and
    divided
Powdered sugar

Combine eggs and whipping cream in a large bowl; beat with a wire whisk until blended. Add Triple Sec, 2 tablespoons sugar, and cinnamon; beat well. Pour egg mixture into a shallow bowl.

Dip 2 croissant halves into egg mixture. Cook in 1 tablespoon butter over medium heat until golden, turning once. Set aside, and keep warm. Repeat procedure twice with remaining croissants, egg mixture, and butter. Sift powdered sugar over croissants. Serve immediately. Yield: 6 servings.

Diane Bosworth-Kitchin

Come Savor Swansea
First Christian Congregational Church
Swansea, Massachusetts

Grilled Apple and Cheese Sandwiches

Tired of plain old grilled cheese sandwiches? Try this fabulous flavor teaser—a combination of shredded sharp Cheddar cheese, tart apple, and pimiento-stuffed olives.

1 cup (4 ounces) shredded sharp Cheddar cheese
1 cup finely chopped cooking apple
⅓ cup minced pimiento-stuffed olives

¼ cup mayonnaise
8 slices white or whole wheat bread
Melted butter or margarine

Combine Cheddar cheese, apple, olives, and mayonnaise in a medium bowl, and stir well.

Spread cheese mixture evenly on 1 side of 4 slices of bread to within ¼ inch of edges. Top with remaining bread slices; brush top slices of bread with melted butter, and invert onto a hot griddle. Immediately brush other sides of sandwiches with melted butter; cook over medium heat until golden. Turn sandwiches, and brown other sides. Yield: 4 servings.

Joan K. Bartley

Culinary Classics, From Our Kitchens
Mountain State Apple Harvest Festival
Martinsburg, West Virginia

Fish & Shellfish

Louisiana Baked Shrimp, page 178

Ahi with Sesame-Cilantro Marinade

To broil this tuna instead of grilling it, place it on a greased rack in a broiler pan. Broil 5½ inches from heat (with electric oven door partially opened) 6 minutes on each side or until fish flakes easily when tested with a fork.

3 pounds Ahi tuna steaks	2 cloves garlic, crushed
1 cup thinly sliced green onions	½ cup soy sauce
1 cup chopped fresh cilantro	¼ cup dark sesame oil
2 tablespoons sesame seeds, toasted	¼ cup honey
	1 teaspoon hot sauce

Place steaks in a large shallow dish. Combine green onions and next 3 ingredients in a small bowl. Combine soy sauce and next 3 ingredients; stir well. Add onion mixture to soy sauce mixture; stir well. Pour over steaks. Cover and marinate in refrigerator 8 hours, turning steaks occasionally.

Remove steaks from marinade, discarding marinade. Grill steaks, covered, over medium-hot coals (350° to 400°) about 4 minutes on each side or until fish flakes easily when tested with a fork. Yield: 6 servings.

Desert Treasures
The Junior League of Phoenix, Arizona

Broiled Bluefish with Salsa

4 plum tomatoes, peeled, seeded, and chopped	2½ tablespoons fresh lemon juice
1 medium-size sweet red pepper, chopped	1 tablespoon vegetable oil
1 small purple onion, chopped	½ teaspoon ground cumin
1 small jalapeño pepper, seeded and finely chopped	½ teaspoon chili powder
1 tablespoon chopped fresh cilantro	4 bluefish fillets (about 1½ pounds)
	½ teaspoon salt
	¼ teaspoon pepper

Combine first 9 ingredients in a medium bowl, and stir well. Set salsa aside.

Sprinkle fillets with salt and pepper. Place fillets on a lightly greased rack; place rack in broiler pan. Top fillets evenly with salsa. Broil 5½ inches from heat (with electric oven door partially opened) 6 to 8 minutes or until fish flakes easily when tested with a fork. Serve immediately. Yield: 4 servings.   James E. Griffin

Rhode Island Cooks
American Cancer Society, Rhode Island Division
Pawtucket, Rhode Island

Catfish Bake

6 slices bacon
1⅓ cups chopped onion
6 farm-raised catfish fillets
   (about 2 pounds)
1 (8-ounce) package cream
   cheese, softened
2 tablespoons Dijon mustard
½ teaspoon salt

¼ teaspoon prepared
   horseradish
Dash of pepper
½ cup dry sherry
Paprika
Garnishes: fresh parsley sprigs,
   lemon slices

Cook bacon in a large skillet until crisp; remove bacon, reserving drippings in skillet. Crumble bacon, and set aside.

Cook onion in drippings in skillet over medium-high heat, stirring constantly, until tender. Set aside.

Place fillets in a lightly greased 13- x 9- x 2-inch baking dish. Combine cream cheese and next 4 ingredients in a medium mixing bowl; beat at low speed of an electric mixer until blended. Add sherry, and beat at low speed until smooth. Stir in onion. Pour cream cheese mixture evenly over fillets; sprinkle with reserved bacon and paprika.

Bake, uncovered, at 350° for 30 to 35 minutes or until fish flakes easily when tested with a fork. Serve immediately. Garnish, if desired. Yield: 6 servings.   Mary Lee Childs

The Summerhouse Sampler
Wynnton Elementary School PTA
Columbus, Georgia

Crispy Seasoned Flounder

The Tartar Sauce served with these crispy flounder fillets gets a flavor twist from the addition of basil. The spicy seasoning mix used to coat the flounder will work well for most any type of fish.

1 large egg	2 pounds flounder fillets
¼ cup milk	¼ cup vegetable oil
1 cup all-purpose flour	Tartar Sauce
Seasoning Mix	

Combine egg and milk in a large bowl; beat with a wire whisk until blended. Set aside.

Combine flour and 1½ teaspoons Seasoning Mix. Rub remaining Seasoning Mix on both sides of fillets.

Dip fillets into egg mixture, and dredge in flour mixture. Cook fillets in hot oil in a large skillet over medium-high heat 3 minutes on each side or until fish flakes easily when tested with a fork. Serve with Tartar Sauce. Yield: 4 servings.

Seasoning Mix

1 tablespoon salt	½ teaspoon dried thyme
1 teaspoon onion powder	¼ teaspoon dry mustard
1 teaspoon paprika	¼ teaspoon black pepper
½ teaspoon garlic powder	⅛ teaspoon ground red pepper
½ teaspoon dried oregano	

Combine all ingredients in a small bowl, and stir well. Yield: 2½ tablespoons.

Tartar Sauce

½ cup mayonnaise	½ teaspoon dried basil
1½ teaspoons lemon juice	Dash of hot sauce

Combine all ingredients in a small bowl; stir well. Cover and chill. Yield: ½ cup.

Family & Company
The Junior League of Binghamton, New York

Grouper Cutlets over Black Beans with Tomato-Ginger Relish

Pounding the pieces of fish to flatten them to ¼-inch thickness ensures that they will cook quickly and evenly.

2 medium tomatoes, peeled, seeded, and chopped
1 shallot, diced
½ jalapeño pepper, seeded and diced
1 tablespoon minced fresh ginger
1 teaspoon chopped fresh cilantro
1 teaspoon olive oil
1 teaspoon raspberry vinegar
¼ teaspoon salt

⅛ teaspoon freshly ground pepper
1 (15-ounce) can black beans, rinsed and drained
1½ pounds grouper fillets, cut into 12 pieces
¼ teaspoon salt
¼ teaspoon freshly ground pepper
2 tablespoons all-purpose flour
2 tablespoons olive oil, divided
Chopped green onions

Combine first 9 ingredients in a small bowl; stir well. Set relish aside.

Place beans in a small saucepan. Cook over medium heat until thoroughly heated, stirring often. Set aside, and keep warm.

Place fish pieces between 2 sheets of heavy-duty plastic wrap; flatten to ¼-inch thickness, using a meat mallet or rolling pin. Sprinkle with ¼ teaspoon salt and ¼ teaspoon pepper; dredge in flour.

Cook half of fish pieces in 1 tablespoon oil in a large skillet over medium-high heat 1 to 2 minutes on each side or until fish flakes easily when tested with a fork. Remove from skillet; set aside, and keep warm. Repeat procedure with remaining fish pieces and remaining 1 tablespoon oil.

To serve, spoon warm beans evenly onto serving plates; place fish on top of beans. Top evenly with relish. Sprinkle with chopped green onions. Serve immediately. Yield: 4 servings.   Scott Roark

Heart Choice Recipes from Charleston's Greatest Chefs
Medical University of South Carolina Heart Center
Charleston, South Carolina

Pecan Grouper

½ cup all-purpose flour	½ cup butter, divided
½ teaspoon salt	½ cup coarsely chopped pecans
¼ teaspoon pepper	¼ cup chopped fresh parsley
2 pounds grouper fillets	Lemon wedges

Combine first 3 ingredients; dredge fillets in flour mixture.

Melt 3 tablespoons butter in a large skillet over medium-high heat. Add fillets, and cook 5 minutes on each side or until fish flakes easily when tested with a fork. Remove fillets to a serving platter; set aside, and keep warm.

Melt remaining ¼ cup plus 1 tablespoon butter in skillet over medium heat. Add pecans, and cook, stirring constantly, 2 minutes or until butter begins to brown. Pour over fillets; sprinkle with parsley. Serve immediately with lemon wedges. Yield: 4 servings.

Still Gathering: A Centennial Celebration
Auxiliary to the American Osteopathic Association
Chicago, Illinois

Orange Roughy Parmesan

2 pounds orange roughy fillets	3 tablespoons chopped green onions
2 tablespoons lemon juice	
½ cup grated Parmesan cheese	¼ teaspoon salt
¼ cup butter or margarine, softened	⅛ teaspoon freshly ground pepper
3 tablespoons mayonnaise	Dash of hot sauce

Place fillets on a greased rack; place rack in broiler pan. Brush fillets with lemon juice, and let stand at room temperature 10 minutes.

Combine Parmesan cheese and next 6 ingredients; set aside.

Broil fillets 8 inches from heat (with electric oven door partially opened) 8 minutes. Spread Parmesan cheese mixture evenly over fillets. Broil 5 additional minutes or until fish flakes easily when tested with a fork. Yield: 4 servings.

Carolyn Lamar

Kailua Cooks
Le Jardin Academy
Kailua, Hawaii

Orange Roughy with Cucumber Relish

1 (11-ounce) can mandarin
    oranges, drained and coarsely
    chopped
1 small cucumber, peeled,
    seeded, and finely chopped

⅓ cup white vinegar
1 green onion, minced
1 tablespoon minced fresh dill
1¼ pounds orange roughy fillets

Combine first 5 ingredients in a small bowl; stir well. Cover relish, and let stand at room temperature 1 hour, stirring occasionally.

Place fillets on a lightly greased rack; place rack in broiler pan. Brush 1 tablespoon liquid from relish over fillets. Broil 3 inches from heat (with electric oven door partially opened) 3½ minutes on each side or until fish flakes easily when tested with a fork. Transfer fillets to a serving platter. Spoon reserved relish evenly over fillets. Yield: 4 servings.   Jean Featherstone

Meals by Mildred and Other Fine Methodist Cooks
First United Methodist Church
Hickory, North Carolina

Cray's Cajun Salmon

To broil salmon instead of grilling it, place on a lightly greased rack in a broiler pan. Broil 5½ inches from heat (with electric oven door partially opened) 5 minutes on each side or until fish flakes easily when tested with a fork.

¼ cup plus 2 tablespoons butter
    or margarine, melted
1 teaspoon salt
1 teaspoon dried basil
1 teaspoon dried thyme

1 teaspoon paprika
1 teaspoon black pepper
½ teaspoon ground red pepper
4 (6-ounce) salmon steaks,
    1 inch thick

Combine first 7 ingredients in a small bowl; stir well. Brush butter mixture evenly over both sides of salmon steaks. Grill, covered, over hot coals (400° to 500°) 7 minutes on each side or until fish flakes easily when tested with a fork. Yield: 4 servings.   Andy T. Cray

A Taste of Reno
The Food Bank of Northern Nevada
Sparks, Nevada

Taku Grilled Salmon

Fresh salmon is grilled and basted with a brown sugar-butter mixture in this quick entrée. It takes its name from the Taku Glacier on the Alaska-British Columbia border where fresh salmon are plentiful.

⅓ cup butter or margarine
⅔ cup firmly packed brown
   sugar
2 tablespoons lemon juice
1 tablespoon dry white wine
8 (10-ounce) salmon fillets

Melt butter in a medium saucepan over medium heat. Add brown sugar, stirring just until blended. Add lemon juice and wine; cook 2 minutes, stirring constantly. Set aside.

Place half of salmon fillets in a greased grilling basket. Grill, covered, over medium-hot coals (350° to 400°) 5 minutes on each side or until fish flakes easily when tested with a fork, basting often with brown sugar mixture during the last 5 minutes of cooking. Repeat procedure with remaining half of salmon fillets and brown sugar mixture. Yield: 8 servings.   Anne Hightower

New Additions and Old Favorites
Canterbury United Methodist Church
Birmingham, Alabama

Greek Snapper

Vegetable cooking spray
1 tablespoon olive oil
1 cup chopped onion
1 clove garlic, minced
3 medium tomatoes, peeled,
   seeded, and chopped
¼ cup dry white wine
1 teaspoon dried oregano
¼ teaspoon salt
⅛ teaspoon pepper
6 (4-ounce) red snapper fillets
2 ounces feta cheese, crumbled
2 tablespoons chopped fresh
   parsley
1 tablespoon chopped ripe
   olives

Coat a large skillet with cooking spray; add olive oil. Place over medium heat until hot. Add onion and garlic; cook until tender, stirring constantly. Stir in tomato and next 4 ingredients. Bring to a boil; reduce heat, and simmer, uncovered, 20 minutes.

Place fillets in a 13- x 9- x 2-inch baking dish coated with cooking spray. Spoon tomato mixture over fillets. Bake, uncovered, at 350° for

20 minutes or until fish flakes easily when tested with a fork. Sprinkle with cheese, parsley, and olives. Serve immediately. Yield: 6 servings.

Simply Heavenly
Woman's Synodical Union of the Associate Reformed
Presbyterian Church
Greenville, South Carolina

Big Daddy's Trout Almondine

You'll have to crush about three packs of crackers to get enough crumbs to dredge the fillets. To crush the crackers, place them in a heavy-duty, zip-top plastic bag. Seal the bag securely, and crush with a rolling pin.

6 trout fillets (about 2½ pounds), skinned
1 cup milk
1 large egg, beaten
1 teaspoon almond extract
3 cups finely crushed saltine crackers
½ cup vegetable oil, divided
½ cup slivered or sliced almonds, toasted

Place fillets in a large shallow dish. Combine milk, egg, and almond extract; pour over fillets. Turn fillets to coat. Cover and chill 2 hours, turning once.

Remove fillets from milk mixture, discarding milk mixture. Dredge fillets in cracker crumbs.

Cook fillets, 2 at a time, in ¼ cup plus 2 tablespoons oil in a large skillet over medium-high heat 3 to 4 minutes on each side or until fish flakes easily when tested with a fork. Drain fillets, and place on a serving platter; set aside, and keep warm. Cook remaining fillets in batches, adding 1 tablespoon oil to oil in skillet with each batch. Sprinkle with almonds. Yield: 6 servings.   Robertson's Cafeteria

Gracious Goodness, Charleston!
Bishop England High School Endowment Fund
Charleston, South Carolina

Tuna Glazed with Ginger and Lime

Try this recipe with mahimahi steaks instead of tuna steaks. Mahimahi is a type of dolphin with a firm, flavorful flesh that stands up to grilling.

6 (8-ounce) tuna steaks
3 cloves garlic, crushed
1 tablespoon grated fresh ginger
1 teaspoon sugar
½ teaspoon dried crushed red pepper

3 tablespoons fresh lime juice
2 tablespoons low-sodium soy sauce
1 tablespoon dark sesame oil

Place steaks in a large shallow dish. Combine garlic and remaining ingredients in a small bowl; stir well. Pour marinade mixture over steaks. Cover and marinate in refrigerator 1 hour, turning once.

Remove steaks from marinade, reserving marinade. Bring marinade to a boil in a small saucepan. Grill steaks, covered, over medium-hot coals (350° to 400°) about 20 minutes or until fish flakes easily when tested with a fork, turning once and basting often with marinade. Yield: 6 servings.

Cooking with Class, A Second Helping
Charlotte Latin School
Charlotte, North Carolina

Beth's Crab and Spinach Casserole

1 (10-ounce) package frozen chopped spinach
1 cup (4 ounces) shredded sharp Cheddar cheese
2 tablespoons minced onion
¼ cup plus 2 tablespoons butter or margarine, melted
2 tablespoons all-purpose flour

1 cup milk
1 pound fresh crabmeat, drained and flaked
1 tablespoon lemon juice
½ teaspoon salt
⅛ teaspoon curry powder
¾ cup soft breadcrumbs

Cook spinach according to package directions. Drain spinach well, pressing between layers of paper towels. Arrange spinach in a greased 11- x 7- x 1½-inch baking dish; sprinkle with cheese. Set aside.

Cook onion in butter in a heavy saucepan over medium-high heat, stirring constantly, until tender. Reduce heat to low; add flour, stirring until blended. Cook 1 minute, stirring constantly. Gradually add milk; cook over medium heat, stirring constantly, until mixture is thickened and bubbly. Stir in crabmeat and next 3 ingredients. Spoon crabmeat mixture evenly over cheese. Sprinkle with breadcrumbs. Bake, uncovered, at 350° for 30 minutes. Yield: 6 servings.   Shirley Miller

Carolina Harvest: 20 Years of Culinary Heritage
American Cancer Society, South Carolina Division
Columbia, South Carolina

Oven Crabmeat Tetrazzini

1 (8-ounce) package medium
  egg noodles
¾ pound fresh mushrooms,
  sliced
1 small onion, chopped
1 clove garlic, minced
½ cup butter or margarine,
  melted
2 tablespoons all-purpose flour

2½ cups half-and-half
1 pound fresh crabmeat,
  drained and flaked
¾ cup dry sherry
2 teaspoons coarsely ground
  pepper
¾ cup freshly grated Parmesan
  cheese

Cook noodles according to package directions; drain and set aside.

Cook mushrooms, onion, and garlic in butter in a large skillet over medium-high heat, stirring constantly, until tender. Remove mushroom mixture from skillet with a slotted spoon, reserving butter in skillet; set mushroom mixture aside.

Reduce heat to low; add flour to butter in skillet, stirring until smooth. Cook 1 minute, stirring constantly. Gradually add half-and-half; cook over medium heat, stirring constantly, until mixture is thickened and bubbly. Stir in noodles, mushroom mixture, crabmeat, sherry, and pepper.

Pour mixture into an ungreased 2½-quart baking dish. Sprinkle with Parmesan cheese. Bake, uncovered, at 350° for 20 to 25 minutes or until thoroughly heated. Yield: 6 servings.

Food for Thought
Indian Creek School Parent Teacher Organization
Crownsville, Maryland

Colonial Oysters and Ham

Smithfield ham is considered by many to be the best country-cured ham on the market. Cured and processed in the area of Smithfield, Virginia, the ham can be purchased from gourmet butcher shops or by mail order.

6 commercial frozen puff pastry patty shells
½ cup hot water
1 teaspoon chicken-flavored bouillon granules
1 pint oysters, undrained
3 tablespoons butter or margarine
3 tablespoons all-purpose flour
1 cup whipping cream
⅛ teaspoon onion salt
⅛ teaspoon dry mustard

½ teaspoon lemon juice
¼ teaspoon Worcestershire sauce
2 tablespoons butter or margarine, melted
⅔ cup chopped cooked country ham
1 to 2 teaspoons chopped fresh parsley
⅛ teaspoon freshly ground pepper

Bake patty shells according to package directions; set aside.

Combine water and bouillon granules, stirring to dissolve; set aside.

Drain oysters, reserving liquid. Add enough water to oyster liquid to equal ½ cup. Set oysters and liquid aside.

Melt 3 tablespoons butter in a heavy saucepan over low heat; add flour, stirring until smooth. Cook 1 minute, stirring constantly. Gradually add reserved bouillon mixture, oyster liquid, and whipping cream; cook over medium heat, stirring constantly, until sauce is thickened and bubbly. Stir in onion salt and next 3 ingredients. Remove from heat; set aside, and keep warm.

Cook oysters in 2 tablespoons melted butter in a large skillet over medium-high heat 3 to 5 minutes or until edges of oysters begin to curl, stirring occasionally. Drain.

Add sauce and ham to oysters. Cook, uncovered, over low heat until thoroughly heated, stirring occasionally. Spoon evenly into patty shells; sprinkle with parsley and pepper. Serve immediately. Yield: 6 servings.

The William & Mary Cookbook
Society of the Alumni, College of William and Mary
Williamsburg, Virginia

Baked Sea Scallops and Feta Cheese

3 tablespoons olive oil, divided
1½ pounds fresh sea scallops
¼ teaspoon salt
⅛ teaspoon freshly ground
  black pepper
2 green peppers, cut into thin
  strips
1 sweet red pepper, cut into thin
  strips
1 small onion, sliced
2 teaspoons minced garlic
1½ cups coarsely chopped plum
  tomatoes

½ cup dry white wine
16 Greek olives, pitted
2 teaspoons chopped fresh
  oregano
½ teaspoon fennel seeds
⅛ teaspoon dried crushed red
  pepper
¼ teaspoon salt
⅛ teaspoon black pepper
6 ounces crumbled feta cheese

Grease 4 gratin dishes with 1 tablespoon olive oil. Arrange scallops evenly in prepared dishes; sprinkle evenly with ¼ teaspoon salt and ⅛ teaspoon pepper.

Cook peppers, onion, and garlic in remaining 2 tablespoons oil in a large skillet over medium-high heat, stirring constantly, until tender. Add tomato and next 7 ingredients; stir well. Bring to a boil; reduce heat, and simmer, uncovered, 5 minutes.

Spoon tomato mixture evenly over scallops; sprinkle with feta cheese. Bake, uncovered, at 450° for 15 minutes or until scallops are opaque and cheese is lightly browned. Serve immediately. Yield: 4 servings.

Nancy Anderson

Trinity and Friends Finest
Women of Holy Trinity
Churchville, Maryland

Scallops and Mushrooms in Creamy Tomato Sauce

Sea scallops average 1½ inches in diameter. Bay scallops (about ½ inch in diameter) can be substituted, but don't cut them in half, as this recipe directs, and be sure to decrease the cooking time a little.

1 (8-ounce) package linguine
1 medium onion, thinly sliced
2 tablespoons butter or
  margarine, melted
1 pound fresh sea scallops, cut
  in half crosswise
1¾ cups sliced fresh
  mushrooms

2 tablespoons all-purpose flour
1 cup half-and-half
¼ cup tomato paste
2 drops of hot sauce
Salt and pepper to taste
Garnish: fresh dill sprigs

Cook linguine according to package directions; drain well. Set aside, and keep warm.

Cook onion in melted butter in a large skillet over medium-high heat, stirring constantly, until tender. Add scallops, and cook over medium heat 5 minutes or until scallops are opaque. Add mushrooms; sprinkle with flour. Stir in half-and-half, and cook, stirring constantly, until mixture is thickened and bubbly. Add tomato paste, hot sauce, and salt and pepper to taste; cook, stirring constantly, just until thoroughly heated. Serve scallop mixture immediately over linguine. Garnish, if desired. Yield: 4 servings.

Catherine Sabanos

St. Mary's of the Hills Favorite Recipes
St. Isaac Jogues Senior Guild, St. Mary's of the Hills
Catholic Church
Rochester Hills, Michigan

Clam-Stuffed Shrimp

1 pound unpeeled jumbo fresh shrimp

¾ cup crushed round buttery crackers

3 tablespoons butter, melted

1 (6½-ounce) can minced clams, drained

2 tablespoons chopped fresh parsley

⅛ teaspoon garlic powder

⅛ teaspoon salt

Dash of pepper

⅓ cup dry sherry

Peel and devein shrimp, leaving tails intact; cut a slit almost through back of shrimp. Open shrimp, and flatten. Set aside.

Combine cracker crumbs and butter. Stir in clams and next 4 ingredients. Top each shrimp evenly with mixture. Place in an ungreased 11- x 7- x 1½-inch baking dish. Bake at 350° for 20 minutes, basting occasionally with sherry. Yield: 4 servings.   Pam Fenimore

Ronald McDonald House of Burlington, Vermont
Anniversary Edition Cookbook
Ronald McDonald House of Burlington, Vermont

Shrimp Carolyn

2 pounds unpeeled medium-size fresh shrimp

8 ounces fettuccine, uncooked

6 green onions, chopped

1 tablespoon butter or margarine, melted

1 (4-ounce) can sliced mushrooms, drained

¼ teaspoon salt

¼ teaspoon ground red pepper

1 cup plus 2 tablespoons sour cream

Peel shrimp, and devein, if desired. Set aside.

Cook pasta according to package directions; drain well. Set aside, and keep warm.

Cook green onions in butter in a skillet over medium heat, stirring constantly, until tender. Add shrimp, mushrooms, salt, and pepper; cook, stirring constantly, 5 minutes or until shrimp turn pink. Reduce heat; stir in sour cream. Cook until thoroughly heated (do not boil). Serve immediately over pasta. Yield: 4 servings.

Good Food, Good Company
Junior Service League of Thomasville, Georgia

Louisiana Baked Shrimp

Serve these tasty New Orleans-style baked shrimp with plenty of crusty bread to sop up the rich, buttery sauce.

¾ pound unpeeled medium-size fresh shrimp
3 tablespoons unsalted butter or margarine
2 tablespoons dry red wine
1 teaspoon chili powder
1 teaspoon freshly ground black pepper
1 teaspoon minced garlic
2 teaspoons Worcestershire sauce
¼ teaspoon salt
⅛ teaspoon ground red pepper
French or Italian bread

Peel shrimp, and devein, if desired. Place shrimp in a single layer in an ungreased 10- x 6- x 2-inch baking dish.

Combine butter and next 7 ingredients in a saucepan. Cook over medium heat, stirring constantly, until butter melts. Pour over shrimp. Bake, uncovered, at 400° for 6 to 8 minutes or until shrimp turn pink. Serve with bread. Yield: 2 servings.   Anne Blackman

A Cook's Tour of the Bayou Country
Churchwomen of the Southwest Deanery of the Episcopal
Diocese of Louisiana
Franklin, Louisiana

Kiawah Island Shrimp with Cheese Rice

This beach specialty, which gets its name from a sea island off the coast of Georgia, South Carolina, and Florida, is loaded enough to be a one-dish meal.

2½ pounds unpeeled medium-size fresh shrimp
1 cup chopped onion
1 cup chopped green pepper
⅔ cup chopped celery
½ cup chopped bacon
2 cloves garlic, minced
½ cup olive oil
1 (28-ounce) can Italian-style tomatoes, undrained
2 (6-ounce) cans tomato paste

1 cup water
2 teaspoons Worcestershire sauce
1½ teaspoons sugar
½ teaspoon hot sauce
½ teaspoon salt
¼ teaspoon pepper
½ pound Polish sausage, thinly sliced
Cheese Rice

Peel shrimp, and devein, if desired. Set aside.

Cook onion and next 4 ingredients in olive oil in a large skillet over medium-high heat, stirring constantly, until vegetables are tender. Drain well. Add tomatoes and next 7 ingredients. Bring to a boil; reduce heat, and simmer, uncovered, 30 minutes.

Brown sausage in a large skillet over medium-high heat; drain.

Add shrimp and sausage to tomato mixture; bring to a boil. Reduce heat, and simmer, uncovered, 5 minutes or until shrimp turn pink. Serve immediately over Cheese Rice. Yield: 6 servings.

Cheese Rice

4½ cups water
2 cups long-grain rice, uncooked
1 cup chopped onion

2 teaspoons salt
1 cup (4 ounces) shredded sharp Cheddar cheese

Bring water to a boil; stir in rice, onion, and salt. Cover, reduce heat, and simmer 25 to 30 minutes or until water is absorbed and rice is tender. Stir in cheese. Yield: 6½ cups.   William Collins

Georgia Land
Medical Association of Georgia Alliance
Atlanta, Georgia

Madagascar Shrimp

This shrimp entrée gets its distinctive flavors from Madagascar, an island in the Indian Ocean. You'll find curry, bay leaves, thyme, and red pepper complemented by tomatoes, raisins, and almonds.

7½ cups water
2½ pounds unpeeled large fresh shrimp
1 cup chopped onion
1 cup chopped green pepper
1 cup diced celery
½ cup loosely packed celery leaves, chopped
¼ cup olive oil
3 (16-ounce) cans crushed tomatoes

½ cup chili sauce
½ cup raisins
¼ cup chopped fresh parsley
2 bay leaves
1 teaspoon curry powder
½ teaspoon salt
½ teaspoon dried thyme
½ teaspoon ground red pepper
½ teaspoon black pepper
½ cup slivered almonds, toasted
Hot cooked rice

Bring water to a boil; add shrimp, and cook 3 to 5 minutes or until shrimp turn pink. Drain well; rinse with cold water. Peel shrimp, and devein, if desired. Set aside.

Cook onion, green pepper, celery, and celery leaves in olive oil in a large skillet over medium-high heat, stirring constantly, until tender. Add tomatoes and next 9 ingredients; stir well. Bring to a boil; reduce heat, and simmer, uncovered, 1 hour or until thickened, stirring occasionally. Stir in shrimp and almonds. Serve immediately over rice. Yield: 6 servings.

Sandy Alan Hofstetter

All Hallows' Episcopal Parish Cookbook, 300th Anniversary Edition
All Hallows' Episcopal Church
Davidsonville, Maryland

Tequila Shrimp

1 pound unpeeled large fresh
  shrimp
¼ cup olive oil
¼ cup tequila
¼ cup fresh lime juice
2 cloves garlic, crushed
1 tablespoon dried crushed red
  pepper

2 tablespoons red wine vinegar
½ teaspoon salt
1 medium-size sweet red
  pepper, cut into thin strips
1 medium-size green pepper,
  cut into thin strips
1 medium-size purple onion,
  cut into eighths

Peel shrimp, and devein, if desired. Place shrimp in an ungreased
13- x 9- x 2-inch baking dish. Set aside.

Combine olive oil and next 6 ingredients in a jar. Cover tightly, and
shake vigorously. Pour over shrimp in dish. Place sweet red pepper,
green pepper, and onion on top of shrimp. Cover and marinate in
refrigerator 1 hour.

Remove shrimp and vegetables from marinade, reserving marinade.
Set shrimp and vegetables aside. Bring marinade to a boil in a small
saucepan; set aside.

Thread shrimp evenly onto 3 (10-inch) metal skewers. Grill shrimp,
covered, over medium coals (300° to 350°) 2 minutes on each side,
basting occasionally with boiled marinade. Set aside, and keep warm.

Cook vegetables in any remaining marinade in a large skillet over
medium-high heat, stirring constantly, until tender. Serve shrimp with
vegetables. Yield: 4 servings.

Culinary Masterpieces
Birmingham Museum of Art
Birmingham, Alabama

Sassy Seafood Sauté

For a clever presentation of this seafood sauté, select a wide-rimmed serving dish and sprinkle some of the chopped fresh parsley around the rim rather than on the food alone.

1 (8-ounce) package linguine
1 pound unpeeled medium-size fresh shrimp
3 tablespoons chopped green onions
1 tablespoon sugar
2 tablespoons ketchup
1 tablespoon cocktail sauce
1 tablespoon dry sherry
1 tablespoon soy sauce
¼ teaspoon salt
¼ teaspoon dry mustard
5 cloves garlic, minced
½ teaspoon dried crushed red pepper
¼ cup olive oil
1 pound fresh bay scallops
¼ cup chopped fresh parsley

Cook pasta according to package directions; drain well. Set aside, and keep warm.

Peel shrimp, and devein, if desired. Set aside.

Combine green onions and next 7 ingredients in a small bowl; stir well, and set aside.

Cook garlic and crushed red pepper in oil in a large skillet over medium heat, stirring constantly, 4 minutes or until garlic is tender. Add shrimp and scallops; cook, stirring constantly, until shrimp turn pink and scallops are opaque. Stir in green onion mixture, and cook until thoroughly heated. Spoon seafood mixture over pasta. Sprinkle with chopped parsley; serve immediately. Yield: 4 servings.

From Portland's Palate
The Junior League of Portland, Oregon

Meats

Roasted Pork Loin with Mushrooms and Garlic, page 198

Regency Beef Tenderloin with Royal Butter

The perfect entrée for a special occasion or Sunday dinner, this tenderloin and flavored butter can also be served as an appetizer on small dinner rolls.

1 cup soy sauce	1 teaspoon garlic powder
⅔ cup vegetable oil	1 green onion, chopped
3 tablespoons brown sugar	1 (5- to 6-pound) beef
2 tablespoons Dijon mustard	tenderloin, trimmed
1 tablespoon white vinegar	Royal Butter

Combine first 7 ingredients in a medium bowl; stir well.

Place tenderloin in a large heavy-duty, zip-top plastic bag. Pour marinade mixture over tenderloin. Seal bag securely. Marinate in refrigerator 8 hours, turning occasionally.

Remove tenderloin from marinade, reserving marinade. Bring marinade to a boil in a small saucepan; set aside.

Place tenderloin on a rack in a shallow roasting pan. Bake at 400° for 45 to 55 minutes or until thermometer inserted in thickest part registers 145° (medium-rare) or 160° (medium), basting occasionally with marinade. Let stand 10 minutes before slicing. Serve with Royal Butter. Yield: 12 servings.

Royal Butter

½ cup butter or margarine, softened	¼ cup mayonnaise
1 (8-ounce) package cream cheese, softened	¼ cup prepared horseradish, drained

Combine all ingredients in a medium mixing bowl; beat at medium speed of an electric mixer until blended. Serve at room temperature. Yield: 2 cups.

Gracious Goodness, Charleston!
Bishop England High School Endowment Fund
Charleston, South Carolina

Catalan Pot Roast

The thin sauce served with this cinnamon-spiced roast is subtly flavored with orange juice. If you prefer a thicker sauce, increase the amount of cornstarch.

¼ cup olive oil, divided
1 large clove garlic, crushed
1 tablespoon minced fresh
  parsley
1 teaspoon ground cinnamon
¾ teaspoon salt
¼ teaspoon dried marjoram
¼ teaspoon ground cloves
¼ teaspoon pepper
1 (4- to 5-pound) bottom round
  roast

¾ cup chopped onion
¾ cup minced green pepper
1 (16-ounce) can crushed
  tomatoes
1 cup dry red wine
½ cup fresh orange juice
1 tablespoon cornstarch
¼ cup cold water

Combine 2 tablespoons oil, garlic, and next 6 ingredients in a small bowl; rub herb mixture over entire surface of roast. Cover and chill 5 to 6 hours. Remove roast from refrigerator; let stand 30 minutes.

Brown roast in remaining 2 tablespoons oil in a large Dutch oven. Remove roast, reserving drippings in pan. Cook onion and green pepper in drippings in pan over medium-high heat, stirring constantly, until tender. Return roast to pan; add tomatoes, wine, and orange juice. Bring to a boil; cover, reduce heat, and simmer 3 to 4 hours or until meat is tender, turning occasionally.

Remove roast, reserving liquid in pan; let roast stand 20 minutes. Combine cornstarch and water, stirring until smooth. Stir into liquid in pan; cook over medium heat, stirring constantly, until slightly thickened. Serve roast with warm sauce. Yield: 10 servings.

Tampa Treasures
The Junior League of Tampa, Florida

London Broil with Hunter's Sauce

1 (2-pound) flank steak
2 tablespoons peanut oil
½ teaspoon salt
½ teaspoon pepper
3 tablespoons butter
2 cups sliced fresh mushrooms
1 tablespoon chopped shallots
1 tablespoon butter, melted
¼ teaspoon salt

⅛ teaspoon pepper
⅓ cup dry red wine
½ cup peeled and chopped
   tomato
½ cup beef broth
½ teaspoon chopped fresh
   tarragon
1 teaspoon cornstarch
2 tablespoons cold water

Brush both sides of steak with oil; sprinkle with ½ teaspoon salt and ½ teaspoon pepper. Place steak on rack; place rack in broiler pan. Broil 5½ inches from heat (with electric oven door partially opened) 3 to 5 minutes on each side or to desired degree of doneness. Remove steak to a hot serving platter; dot with 3 tablespoons butter. Let stand 5 minutes; reserve juices.

Cook mushrooms and shallot in 1 tablespoon butter in a skillet over medium heat, stirring constantly, until tender. Add ¼ teaspoon salt and ⅛ teaspoon pepper. Add wine; simmer 2 minutes. Add reserved juices, tomato, broth, and tarragon. Cook 5 minutes, stirring occasionally. Combine cornstarch and water, stirring until smooth. Stir into sauce. Cook, stirring constantly, 3 minutes or until thickened.

To serve, slice steak diagonally across grain into thin slices. Serve steak with warm sauce. Yield: 6 servings.

Family & Company
The Junior League of Binghamton, New York

Cowpoke Steak

2 pounds boneless round steak,
   1 inch thick
½ cup all-purpose flour
1 teaspoon garlic salt
½ teaspoon pepper
¼ cup vegetable oil

1 (28-ounce) can whole
   tomatoes, undrained
1 medium-size green pepper,
   cut into rings
1 small onion, sliced and
   separated into rings

Trim excess fat from steak; cut into 8 pieces. Combine flour, garlic salt, and ½ teaspoon pepper in a small bowl; dredge steak in flour mixture. Brown steak in oil in a skillet over medium heat. Remove steak to an ungreased 13- x 9- x 2-inch baking dish.

Place tomatoes in container of an electric blender; cover and process until smooth, stopping once to scrape down sides. Pour over steak; top with green pepper and onion. Cover and bake at 325° for 2 hours and 30 minutes. Yield: 8 servings.

The Wild Wild West
The Junior League of Odessa, Texas

Carbonnade Flamande

Brown sugar and prunes lend a touch of sweetness to this Belgian beef stew. Serve this dish on its own or spoon it over hot cooked noodles or rice.

1¼ cups pitted prunes
1 (12-ounce) can beer
1 (1½- to 2-pound) sirloin steak, cut into ½-inch pieces
2 tablespoons vegetable oil, divided

2 medium onions, sliced
½ cup water
1 tablespoon brown sugar
Salt and pepper to taste

Combine prunes and beer in a medium bowl; set aside.

Brown steak in 1 tablespoon oil in a large skillet over medium heat. Remove steak, reserving drippings in skillet. Set steak aside.

Cook onion in drippings and remaining 1 tablespoon oil in skillet over medium-high heat, stirring constantly, until tender.

Combine prune mixture, steak, cooked onion, water, and brown sugar in a Dutch oven; bring to a boil. Cover, reduce heat, and simmer 1½ hours or until steak is tender. Add salt and pepper to taste. Yield: 6 servings.   Madeleine Stallings

Southern Savoir Faire
The Altamont School
Birmingham, Alabama

Santa Barbara Shish Kabobs

Need a sure winner for your next party? Try this kabob recipe starring three kinds of meat plus an abundance of chunky fruits and vegetables.

½ cup vegetable oil
½ cup dry red wine
¼ cup soy sauce
3 cloves garlic, crushed
2 tablespoons ketchup
1½ teaspoons curry powder
1 teaspoon ground ginger
¼ teaspoon pepper
¼ teaspoon hot sauce
1 pound sirloin steak, cut into
   1-inch cubes
1 pound boneless leg of lamb,
   cut into 1-inch cubes

1 pound pork tenderloin, cut
   into ½-inch cubes
2 medium cooking apples
10 fresh mushrooms
1 eggplant, unpeeled and cut
   into ½-inch cubes
1 medium-size green pepper,
   cut into 1-inch pieces
1 (15¼-ounce) can pineapple
   chunks, drained
½ pound sliced bacon

Combine first 9 ingredients in container of an electric blender or food processor. Cover and process until smooth, stopping once to scrape down sides. Set aside ¼ cup marinade mixture.

Place each meat in a large shallow dish. Pour remaining marinade evenly over meats. Cover and marinate in refrigerator 8 hours, stirring twice.

Peel and core apples. Cut each apple into 6 wedges.

Combine reserved ¼ cup marinade, apple, mushrooms, eggplant, green pepper, and pineapple in a large bowl; stir well. Cover and marinate at room temperature 2 to 3 hours, stirring occasionally. Drain, reserving marinade.

Drain meats, discarding meat marinades. Cut bacon slices in half crosswise; wrap a half slice of bacon around each cube of lamb.

Alternately thread beef, mushrooms, lamb, eggplant, pineapple, pork, green pepper, and apple on 10 (15-inch) metal skewers. Grill, covered, over medium-hot coals (350° to 400°) 5 to 10 minutes or to desired degree of doneness, turning and basting occasionally with reserved vegetable marinade. Yield: 10 servings.

California Sizzles
The Junior League of Pasadena, California

South-of-the-Border Mexican Lasagna

Tortillas replace lasagna noodles in this southwestern take on lasagna.

12 (6-inch) corn tortillas, divided
1½ pounds ground beef
1 (16-ounce) can whole tomatoes, undrained and chopped
1½ teaspoons ground cumin
1 teaspoon salt
1 tablespoon chili powder
1 teaspoon black pepper
¼ teaspoon garlic powder
¼ teaspoon ground red pepper
2 cups small-curd cottage cheese
1½ cups (6 ounces) shredded Cheddar cheese, divided
1 large egg, beaten
2 cups shredded iceberg lettuce
½ cup chopped tomato
¼ cup sliced ripe olives
3 green onions, chopped

Line bottom and sides of an ungreased 13- x 9- x 2-inch baking dish with 6 tortillas.

Brown ground beef in a large skillet over medium heat, stirring until it crumbles. Drain meat, discarding drippings; return meat to skillet. Add canned tomatoes and next 6 ingredients; cook, uncovered, over medium heat until thoroughly heated, stirring occasionally. Spoon over tortillas in dish. Top with remaining 6 tortillas.

Combine cottage cheese, 1 cup Cheddar cheese, and egg in a medium bowl; stir well. Spread cottage cheese mixture over tortillas. Cover and bake at 350° for 15 minutes; uncover and bake 15 additional minutes. Top with diagonal rows of remaining ½ cup Cheddar cheese, shredded lettuce, ½ cup chopped tomato, olives, and green onions. Serve immediately. Yield: 8 servings.   Staci D. Freeman

Discover Oklahoma Cookin'
Oklahoma 4-H Foundation
Stillwater, Oklahoma

Oslo Macaroni Bake

1½ cups elbow macaroni,
   uncooked
1 pound ground round
2 tablespoons butter, melted
1 cup sliced fresh mushrooms
1 medium onion, chopped
½ cup chopped sweet red
   pepper
1 teaspoon salt
⅛ teaspoon pepper
1 (16-ounce) can whole tomatoes,
   drained and chopped
¼ cup butter or margarine
¼ cup all-purpose flour
2½ cups milk
2 cups (8 ounces) shredded
   Jarlsberg cheese, divided
1 (8-ounce) can tomato sauce

Cook pasta according to package directions; drain and set aside.

Brown meat in 2 tablespoons butter in a skillet over medium heat, stirring until it crumbles. Add mushrooms and next 4 ingredients; cook until vegetables are tender, stirring often. Stir in tomatoes.

Melt ¼ cup butter in a saucepan over low heat; add flour, stirring until smooth. Cook 1 minute, stirring constantly. Gradually add milk; cook over medium heat, stirring constantly, until thickened and bubbly. Stir in pasta and 1 cup cheese. Place half of pasta mixture in a greased 2½-quart baking dish. Top with half of meat mixture. Repeat layers. Top with tomato sauce. Bake, uncovered, at 350° for 25 minutes. Top with remaining 1 cup cheese; bake 5 minutes. Let stand 5 minutes before serving. Yield: 6 servings.   Sister Elizabeth Weier

Franciscan Centennial Cookbook
Franciscan Sisters
Little Falls, Minnesota

Veal Chops with Orange-Tomato Sauce

4 (6-ounce) veal loin chops
¼ teaspoon salt
⅛ teaspoon pepper
¼ cup plus 1 tablespoon butter,
   melted and divided
¾ cup fresh orange juice
½ cup dry white wine
¼ cup minced shallots
2 tablespoons grated orange
   rind, divided
¼ cup whipping cream
1 cup peeled, seeded, and
   chopped tomato
¼ cup thinly sliced fresh basil

Sprinkle veal with salt and pepper. Cook veal in 1 tablespoon melted butter in a large skillet over medium heat 4 to 5 minutes on each side or until done. Remove veal to a serving platter. Set veal aside, and keep warm.

Combine orange juice, wine, shallot, and 1 tablespoon orange rind in a small saucepan; bring to a boil over medium-high heat. Boil 10 minutes or until mixture is reduced to 3 tablespoons. Stir in whipping cream, and boil an additional minute. Stir in remaining ¼ cup butter, remaining 1 tablespoon orange rind, tomato, and basil. Remove from heat. Spoon warm sauce over veal. Serve immediately. Yield: 4 servings.

From Generation to Generation
Sisterhood of Temple Emanu-El
Dallas, Texas

Veal Medaillons with Lime-Cream Sauce

2 tablespoons all-purpose flour
½ teaspoon salt
¼ teaspoon pepper
1¼ pounds veal cutlets
1 tablespoon butter or margarine, melted
1 tablespoon olive oil
1½ cups dry white wine
1 teaspoon grated lime rind
1 tablespoon fresh lime juice
¼ cup whipping cream
12 green peppercorns
Garnish: fresh lime wedges

Combine first 3 ingredients in a small bowl; sprinkle flour mixture evenly over veal, lightly coating both sides.

Cook veal in butter and oil in a large skillet over medium heat 4 to 5 minutes on each side or until done. Remove veal to a serving platter, reserving drippings in skillet. Set aside, and keep warm.

Add wine, lime rind, and lime juice to drippings in skillet; stir well. Bring to a boil; boil until mixture is reduced by half. Stir in whipping cream and peppercorns; bring just to a boil. Spoon warm sauce over veal. Garnish, if desired. Serve immediately. Yield: 4 servings.

Back Home Again
The Junior League of Indianapolis, Indiana

Veal Strips with Artichokes

The marinade from these artichoke hearts creates a flavorful base for the sauce. Sour cream and chicken broth tame its concentrated flavor.

¾ **pound veal cutlets**
2 **tablespoons all-purpose flour**
¼ **teaspoon salt**
⅛ **teaspoon pepper**
⅛ **teaspoon paprika**
3 **tablespoons butter or**
  margarine, melted
1 **(6-ounce) jar marinated**
  artichoke hearts, undrained

1 **medium onion, sliced**
½ **cup sour cream**
¼ **cup chicken broth**
2 **tablespoons grated Parmesan**
  cheese
1 **tablespoon lemon juice**
Hot cooked spinach noodles

Place veal between 2 sheets of heavy-duty plastic wrap, and flatten to ⅛-inch thickness, using a meat mallet or rolling pin. Cut veal into ¾-inch strips.

Combine flour and next 3 ingredients. Dredge veal in flour mixture. Cook veal in butter in a large skillet over medium-high heat 2 to 3 minutes on each side or until done. Remove veal, reserving drippings in skillet. Set veal aside, and keep warm.

Drain artichoke hearts, reserving liquid; set artichoke hearts aside. Add liquid and onion to drippings in skillet; cook over medium-high heat, stirring constantly, 5 minutes or until onion is tender. Stir in sour cream and next 3 ingredients; cook over medium heat, stirring constantly, until thoroughly heated (do not boil). Add veal and artichoke hearts; cook just until thoroughly heated. Serve over noodles. Yield: 4 servings.

Desert Treasures
The Junior League of Phoenix, Arizona

Veal and Apple Pie

2 pounds boneless veal, cut into 1-inch pieces
2 tablespoons butter or margarine, melted
2 medium onions, sliced
½ pound fresh mushrooms, halved
1½ cups sparkling apple cider, divided
1 tablespoon ground coriander
1 tablespoon Dijon mustard
⅛ teaspoon pepper
½ pound carrots, scraped and cut into 1-inch pieces
2 large cooking apples, peeled, cored, and sliced
¼ cup all-purpose flour
½ (17¼-ounce) package frozen puff pastry sheets, thawed
1 large egg, lightly beaten
1 tablespoon half-and-half or milk

Brown veal in butter in a large Dutch oven over medium heat; drain. Return veal to pan. Add onion, mushrooms, 1 cup cider, coriander, mustard, and pepper; bring to a boil. Cover, reduce heat, and simmer 15 minutes. Add carrot and apple, and simmer 20 additional minutes. Combine flour and remaining ½ cup cider, stirring until smooth. Stir into veal mixture.

Spoon veal mixture into an ungreased 2½-quart oval casserole. Place puff pastry over veal mixture; trim, seal, and flute edges. Combine egg and half-and-half; brush over pastry. Bake at 400° for 20 minutes or until golden. Yield: 8 servings.

Good to the Core
The Apple Corps of the Weller Center for Health Education
Easton, Pennsylvania

Citrus Lamb Roast with Orange Gravy

The citrus-flavored gravy provides a light and refreshing contrast to the full-bodied flavor of this lamb roast.

⅓ cup sliced green onions
¼ cup chopped fresh parsley
2 tablespoons butter or
   margarine, softened
1 teaspoon grated orange rind

¼ teaspoon pepper
⅛ teaspoon salt
1 (3-pound) rolled boneless
   leg of lamb
Orange Gravy

Combine first 6 ingredients in a small bowl; stir well.

Remove strings from lamb. Spread green onion mixture down center of lamb to within 1 inch of edges.

Reroll lamb, tying securely with heavy string at 2-inch intervals. Place lamb on a rack in a shallow roasting pan. Bake at 325° for 1 hour and 50 minutes or until meat thermometer inserted in thickest part registers 150° (medium-rare). Remove lamb to a serving platter, reserving drippings. Let stand 15 minutes before serving. Serve with warm Orange Gravy. Yield: 6 servings.

Orange Gravy

⅔ cup orange juice
¼ cup pan drippings
1 tablespoon cornstarch
½ teaspoon chicken-flavored
   bouillon granules

¼ teaspoon dried basil
Salt and pepper to taste

Combine first 5 ingredients in a small saucepan. Cook over medium heat, stirring constantly, until thoroughly heated. Stir in salt and pepper to taste. Yield: 1 cup.   Linda St. Lawrence

Coastal Cuisine, Texas Style
The Junior Service League of Brazosport, Texas

Mom's Really Good Lamb Shanks

Mom knows that although lamb shanks are very flavorful, they are also a tough cut of meat. The long cooking time in liquid helps to tenderize them while preserving their wonderful flavor.

2 cloves garlic, minced
¼ cup vegetable oil
3 to 4 pounds (2-inch-thick) cross-cut lamb shanks
½ teaspoon salt
¼ teaspoon pepper
¼ cup white vinegar
½ cup ketchup
¼ cup water
2 carrots, scraped and cut into 1-inch pieces
2 medium-size baking potatoes, peeled and cut into 1-inch pieces
1 large onion, cut into very thin strips

Cook garlic in oil in a Dutch oven over medium-high heat, stirring constantly, until lightly browned.

Sprinkle lamb with salt and pepper. Add lamb to Dutch oven, and cook until browned. Add vinegar; cover, reduce heat to medium, and cook 15 minutes.

Combine ketchup and water, stirring well. Add ketchup mixture, carrot, and remaining ingredients to pan. Cover and bake at 350° for 1 hour and 30 minutes or until meat and vegetables are tender, stirring occasionally. Yield: 3 servings.

Marj Smith

Women Cook for a Cause
Women's Resource Center of Schoolcraft College
Livonia, Michigan

Grilled Lamb and Green Tomatoes

Here's a great recipe to use the green tomatoes at the end of the growing season. Their firm texture makes them ideal for skewering and grilling.

½ cup chopped fresh mint
½ cup raspberry vinegar
⅓ cup olive oil
¼ cup molasses
½ teaspoon coarsely ground
  pepper

¼ teaspoon salt
18 large fresh mushrooms
18 small green tomatoes
1 (4-pound) boneless leg of
  lamb, cut into 1½-inch pieces

Combine first 6 ingredients in a large bowl; stir well. Reserve half of marinade mixture for basting.

Remove stems from mushrooms; reserve for other uses. Combine remaining half of marinade, mushrooms caps, tomatoes, and lamb in a shallow dish; stir gently to coat. Cover and marinate in refrigerator 3 to 4 hours, stirring occasionally.

Remove vegetables and lamb from marinade, discarding marinade; thread alternately on eight 12-inch skewers.

Grill, covered, over medium-hot coals (350° to 400°) 6 minutes on each side or until done, basting occasionally with reserved half of marinade. Yield: 4 servings.   Brenda K. Rinearson

Soroptimist Cooks
Soroptimist International of Dixon, California

W.R. Coe's Favorite Lamb Curry

Lots of ingredients add up to lots of flavor for this dish. Serve the spicy mixture over hot cooked rice.

2 pounds boneless lamb, cut into 1-inch pieces
½ cup plus 2 tablespoons butter or margarine, melted and divided
3 stalks celery, chopped
1 large onion, chopped
1 medium cooking apple, peeled, cored, and chopped
1 medium-size green pepper, chopped
1 carrot, scraped and chopped
1 clove garlic, crushed
2 medium tomatoes, peeled, seeded, and chopped
1 tablespoon chopped fresh parsley
2 whole cloves
1 bay leaf
¼ teaspoon dried basil
¼ teaspoon dried thyme
⅛ teaspoon dried marjoram
⅛ teaspoon dried mint flakes
2 tablespoons all-purpose flour
2 tablespoons curry powder
½ teaspoon salt
½ teaspoon black pepper
¼ teaspoon ground nutmeg
¼ teaspoon ground red pepper
2 cups chicken broth
1 cup dry white wine
1 cup raisins
1 cup coarsely chopped fresh pineapple
Chopped fresh parsley

Brown lamb in 3 tablespoons butter in a large Dutch oven over medium heat. Drain and set aside.

Cook celery and next 5 ingredients in remaining melted butter in Dutch oven over medium-high heat, stirring constantly, until tender. Add tomato and next 7 ingredients; cook 2 additional minutes.

Combine flour and next 5 ingredients; sprinkle over vegetable mixture. Cook 2 minutes, stirring constantly.

Add lamb, chicken broth, and wine to pan. Bring to a boil; reduce heat, and simmer, uncovered, 30 minutes, stirring occasionally. Add raisins and pineapple; cook 5 minutes or until thoroughly heated. Remove and discard bay leaf. Sprinkle with additional chopped parsley just before serving. Yield: 4 servings.

Coe Hall Cooks!
Coe Hall
Oyster Bay, New York

Roasted Pork Loin with Mushrooms and Garlic

1 (3- to 4-pound) rolled
　　boneless pork loin roast
2 tablespoons lemon juice
1¼ teaspoons salt
½ teaspoon freshly ground
　　pepper
5 cloves garlic, thinly sliced
¼ teaspoon salt
3 fresh mushrooms, cut into
　　¼-inch strips

1 teaspoon cornstarch
1 tablespoon cold water
1 (8-ounce) carton sour cream
⅛ teaspoon salt
⅛ teaspoon freshly ground
　　pepper
Garnishes: sliced fresh
　　mushrooms, fresh rosemary
　　sprigs

Remove strings from roast; trim fat. Cut ½-inch diagonal slits at 1-inch intervals on top of roast. Brush with lemon juice; sprinkle with 1¼ teaspoons salt and ½ teaspoon pepper.

Sprinkle garlic slices with ¼ teaspoon salt; insert a garlic slice and mushroom strip into each slit. Reroll roast, tying securely with heavy string at 2-inch intervals. Place roast on a rack in a shallow roasting pan. Bake, uncovered, at 325° for 1 hour and 10 minutes or until meat thermometer inserted in thickest part registers 160° (medium).

Remove roast to a serving platter, reserving drippings in pan. Set roast aside, and keep warm. Cover and freeze pan drippings 10 minutes; remove and discard solidified fat from top of drippings.

Combine cornstarch and water in a small saucepan, stirring until smooth. Add pan drippings, sour cream, ⅛ teaspoon salt, and ⅛ teaspoon pepper. Cook over low heat, stirring constantly, until thickened (do not boil). Serve roast with warm gravy. Garnish, if desired. Yield: 10 servings.

Dining with Southern Elegance
Terrebonne Association for Family and Community Education
Houma, Louisiana

Roast Pork Tenderloin, Chinese Style

The tangy-sweet sauce that forms while the pork bakes is perfect for serving over hot cooked rice.

2 (1-pound) pork tenderloins
1 small clove garlic, minced
¼ cup soy sauce
¼ cup honey
2 tablespoons dry sherry
1 tablespoon lemon juice
1 teaspoon salt

1 teaspoon chicken-flavored
  bouillon granules
½ teaspoon ground cinnamon
¼ teaspoon ground ginger
2 tablespoons cornstarch
1 to 1½ cups water

Place tenderloins in a large heavy-duty, zip-top plastic bag. Combine garlic and next 8 ingredients; stir well. Pour marinade over tenderloins. Seal bag securely; marinate in refrigerator 2 hours, turning occasionally.

Remove tenderloins from marinade, reserving marinade. Pat tenderloins dry; dredge in cornstarch. Place in a greased roasting pan. Pour marinade over tenderloins. Bake, uncovered, at 325° for 55 minutes or until meat thermometer inserted in thickest part registers 160° (medium), basting frequently with marinade. Add 1 to 1½ cups water to pan drippings as necessary to keep drippings from burning and to form the sauce. Serve tenderloins with warm sauce. Yield: 6 servings.

Eileen Galloway

Dundee Presbyterian Church Cook Book
Dundee Presbyterian Church
Omaha, Nebraska

Mandarin Pork and Vegetables

1¼ cups cold water
⅓ cup soy sauce
⅓ cup light corn syrup
2 tablespoons cornstarch
¼ teaspoon dried crushed
   red pepper
¼ cup vegetable oil, divided
1 pound lean boneless pork, cut
   into ½-inch strips

2 cloves garlic, minced
2 cups fresh broccoli flowerets
2 medium onions, cut into
   wedges
1 carrot, scraped and sliced
   diagonally
½ pound fresh mushrooms,
   sliced
Hot cooked rice

Combine first 5 ingredients in a small bowl; stir well.

Pour 2 tablespoons oil around top of a preheated wok, coating sides; heat at medium-high heat (375°) for 2 minutes. Add pork and garlic; stir-fry 5 minutes or until pork is done. Remove pork and garlic from wok; set aside.

Heat remaining 2 tablespoons oil in wok; add broccoli, onion, and carrot, and stir-fry 2 minutes. Add mushrooms; stir-fry 1 minute or until vegetables are crisp-tender. Stir in pork mixture. Add soy sauce mixture, and stir-fry until sauce is slightly thickened. Serve over rice. Yield: 4 servings.

Barbara Pease

Cookin' with C.L.A.S.S.
Citizens League for Adult Special Services
Lawrence, Massachusetts

Oven-Barbecued Pork Chops

Here's an easy dish. Just top these chops with the sauce, and relax as they bake.

8 (1-inch-thick) bone-in pork
   loin chops, trimmed
1 tablespoon vegetable oil
½ teaspoon salt
¼ teaspoon pepper

1 medium onion, thinly sliced
1 small lemon, thinly sliced
1 (8-ounce) can tomato sauce
½ cup firmly packed brown
   sugar

Brown pork chops in oil in a large skillet over medium-high heat. Sprinkle with salt and pepper.

Remove pork chops to an ungreased 15- x 10- x 2-inch baking dish; top with onion and lemon slices. Combine tomato sauce and brown sugar, stirring well. Pour over pork chops. Cover and bake at 325° for 1 hour, basting occasionally with tomato sauce mixture. Uncover and bake 15 additional minutes. Yield: 8 servings.   Violet Sakai

A Collection of Favorite Recipes
Po'okela Church
Makawao, Hawaii

Cox's Memphis in May Ribs

This recipe makes quite a bit of Barbecue Sauce. Set some aside before basting to serve with the ribs; then store any leftover sauce in an airtight container in the refrigerator up to a month.

4 to 6 pounds spareribs or back ribs
¼ cup paprika
2 teaspoons salt
2 teaspoons onion powder
2 teaspoons garlic powder

2 teaspoons ground white pepper
2 teaspoons black pepper
1 teaspoon ground red pepper
Barbecue Sauce

Place ribs in a large shallow dish. Combine paprika and next 6 ingredients in a small bowl; stir well. Rub paprika mixture over entire surface of ribs. Cover and chill 3 hours.

Heat one side of charcoal or gas grill. Place ribs on cool side of grill. Grill, covered, over medium coals (300° to 350°) for 2 to 2½ hours, turning every 30 minutes. Brush ribs with Barbecue Sauce during last 30 minutes of grilling time. Yield: 4 servings.

Barbecue Sauce

2 cups water
2 cups white vinegar
2 cups ketchup
½ cup chopped onion

3 tablespoons salt
3 tablespoons sugar
3 tablespoons chili powder
3 tablespoons pepper

Combine all ingredients in a large saucepan. Bring to a boil; reduce heat, and simmer, uncovered, 1½ hours, stirring often. Yield: 3 cups.

Heart & Soul
The Junior League of Memphis, Tennessee

Golden Glazed Ham

1 (7-pound) fully cooked ham
   half
2 cups firmly packed brown
   sugar, divided

3 (8-ounce) cans beer
2 tablespoons honey
2 tablespoons Dijon mustard
½ cup bourbon

Place ham, fat side up, in a deep roasting pan. Press 1 cup brown sugar onto all sides of ham. Pour beer into pan. Insert meat thermometer, making sure it does not touch fat or bone. Cover and bake at 325° for 30 minutes. Remove 2 cups drippings from pan.

Combine remaining 1 cup brown sugar, honey, mustard, and bourbon in a saucepan; cook over medium heat, stirring constantly, until sugar melts. Baste ham with sugar mixture. Return ham to oven; bake, uncovered, 1 hour or until meat thermometer registers 140°, basting with drippings and sugar mixture every 10 minutes. Let stand 10 minutes before slicing. Yield: 14 servings.   Adelaide Sauthoff

Golden Oldies Cook Book
Catholic Diocese of Belleville Ministry to Sick and Aged
Belleville, Illinois

Ham Steak with Sauce

Try this feisty mustard mixture as a basting sauce for chicken or turkey, too.

¼ cup prepared mustard
¼ cup ginger ale
2 tablespoons dark brown sugar
½ teaspoon prepared
   horseradish

1 (1-inch-thick) slice fully
   cooked ham, about 2 pounds

Combine first 4 ingredients in a small bowl, and stir well. Spread mustard mixture over ham. Grill, covered, over medium-hot coals (350° to 400°) 5 minutes on each side, basting occasionally with remaining mustard mixture. Yield: 4 servings.   Judy Sheppard

June Fete Fare
The Women's Board of Abington Memorial Hospital
Abington, Pennsylvania

Pasta, Rice & Grains

Cumin Rice Timbales, page 218

Angel of Hearts

The intriguing recipe title was inspired by the angel hair pasta and artichoke hearts in this heavenly recipe. Angel hair pasta is a very thin pasta that complements this recipe's delicate cream sauce.

1 (8-ounce) package angel hair
   pasta
1 cup sliced fresh shiitake
   mushrooms
4 cloves garlic, minced
¼ cup extra virgin olive oil
4 skinned and boned chicken
   breast halves, cut into 1-inch
   strips

1 cup all-purpose flour
1 (14-ounce) can artichoke
   hearts, drained and quartered
½ cup sweet vermouth
1 cup chicken broth
¼ cup lemon juice
1 cup whipping cream
1 cup grated Parmesan cheese
1 teaspoon dried tarragon

Cook pasta according to package directions; drain well. Set aside, and keep warm.

Cook mushrooms and garlic in oil in a large skillet over medium-high heat, stirring constantly, until tender. Remove mushrooms and garlic, reserving oil in skillet; set vegetables aside, and keep warm.

Dredge chicken in flour; brown chicken in oil in skillet over medium heat. Remove chicken, reserving drippings in skillet; set chicken aside, and keep warm.

Add artichoke hearts to drippings; cook over medium-high heat, stirring constantly, until golden. Remove artichoke hearts, reserving drippings in skillet; set artichokes aside, and keep warm.

Add vermouth to drippings in skillet; cook over high heat, deglazing pan by scraping particles that cling to bottom. Add chicken broth and lemon juice, and simmer 1 minute. Add mushrooms, garlic, chicken, and artichoke hearts. Add whipping cream and Parmesan; bring just to a boil. Reduce heat, and simmer 5 to 7 minutes, stirring constantly. Place pasta on a large serving platter, and top with chicken mixture. Sprinkle with tarragon, and serve immediately. Yield: 4 servings.

Jonathan S. Juhasz

Five Star Sensations
Auxiliary of University Hospitals of Cleveland
Shaker Heights, Ohio

Angel Hair Pasta with Lobster Sauce

For an elegant presentation of this pasta dish, serve it on a bed of spinach leaves. For even more drama, slice the leaves into very thin strips or ribbons to create a chiffonade, a French culinary term that means "made of rags."

9 ounces angel hair pasta,
   uncooked
4 (8-ounce) fresh or frozen
   lobster tails, thawed
8 fresh mushrooms, sliced
5 green onions, sliced
¾ cup thinly sliced sweet red
   and green pepper
½ cup chopped sun-dried
   tomatoes
2 tablespoons unsalted butter or
   margarine, melted

1 tablespoon olive oil
6 slices bacon, cooked and
   crumbled
2 cups whipping cream
1 tablespoon chopped fresh
   basil
1 tablespoon lemon juice
¼ teaspoon pepper
Fresh spinach leaves (optional)
Garnish: lemon slices

Cook pasta according to package directions; drain well. Set aside, and keep warm.

Place lobster tails in boiling water to cover. Return to a boil; reduce heat, and simmer 12 to 15 minutes or until lobster is done. Drain well; carefully remove lobster meat from shells. Cut meat into ¼-inch pieces; set aside.

Cook mushrooms and next 3 ingredients in butter and oil in a large skillet over medium-high heat, stirring constantly, until tender. Add lobster and bacon; stir well.

Add pasta, whipping cream, basil, lemon juice, and pepper; cook, stirring constantly, until thoroughly heated. Serve immediately over fresh spinach leaves, if desired. Garnish, if desired. Yield: 6 servings.

Holy Cow, Chicago's Cooking!
The Church of the Holy Comforter
Kenilworth, Illinois

Basil Alfredo Pasta

Pungent fresh basil and hearty plum tomatoes give a color and flavor burst to this fettuccine Alfredo.

2 cups whipping cream
1 cup chopped fresh basil
1 (8-ounce) package fettuccine
2⅔ cups freshly grated
   Parmesan cheese

½ cup seeded and diced plum
   tomatoes
½ cup thinly sliced fresh basil
Freshly ground pepper to taste

Bring whipping cream to a boil in a heavy saucepan; reduce heat, and simmer, uncovered, 30 minutes or until thickened, stirring frequently. Add chopped basil, and cook 3 additional minutes. Set aside, and keep warm.

Cook pasta according to package directions; drain. Combine pasta, whipping cream mixture, and cheese; toss. Transfer mixture to a serving platter. Top with tomato, sliced basil, and pepper to taste. Serve immediately. Yield: 4 servings. Betty Cribbs

From the Hearts and Homes of Bellingham Covenant Church
Covenant Women's Ministries of Bellingham Covenant Church
Bellingham, Washington

Chicken Fettuccine with Walnut Sauce

¾ cup walnuts, toasted
1½ teaspoons butter
1 clove garlic
½ teaspoon salt
⅛ teaspoon pepper
1 tablespoon olive oil
¼ cup half-and-half
2 tablespoons freshly grated
   Parmesan cheese

¼ cup chopped fresh parsley
1½ teaspoons fresh lemon juice
¼ teaspoon dried Italian
   seasoning
1 (8-ounce) package fettuccine
1 pound skinned and boned
   chicken breast halves, cooked
   and cubed
Freshly grated Parmesan cheese

Position knife blade in food processor bowl; add first 5 ingredients. Process until smooth, stopping once to scrape down sides. Pour olive oil through food chute with processor running, processing until combined. Transfer to a large bowl; gradually add half-and-half and next 4 ingredients, stirring with a wire whisk until blended. Set aside.

Cook pasta according to package directions; drain, reserving ½ cup water. Stir water into half-and-half mixture. Add pasta and chicken; toss. Sprinkle with cheese. Serve immediately. Yield: 6 servings.

Taste the Good Life
The Assistance League of Omaha, Nebraska

Chinese Garden Pasta

3 tablespoons soy sauce, divided
¼ cup plus 2 tablespoons dark
   sesame oil, divided
1½ teaspoons brown sugar
1 pound skinned and boned
   chicken breast halves, cut
   into strips
1 (8-ounce) package linguine
1 tablespoon ground ginger
2 cloves garlic, minced
1 pound fresh mushrooms,
   sliced
3 cups fresh broccoli flowerets
3 cups fresh cauliflower flowerets

2 medium carrots, scraped and
   thinly sliced
1 medium-size green pepper,
   cut into strips
1 medium-size sweet red
   pepper, cut into strips
1 medium-size sweet yellow
   pepper, cut into strips
1 (8-ounce) can sliced water
   chestnuts, drained
1 bunch green onions, cut into
   very thin 2-inch strips
1 tablespoon white wine vinegar
½ teaspoon cracked pepper

Combine 1 tablespoon soy sauce, 1 tablespoon oil, and sugar; stir well. Place chicken in a shallow dish; pour marinade mixture over chicken. Cover and marinate in refrigerator 2 hours, turning occasionally.

Cook pasta according to package directions; drain well. Set aside, and keep warm.

Pour 2 tablespoons oil around top of preheated wok, coating sides; heat at medium-high (375°) for 2 minutes. Add ginger and garlic, and stir-fry 1 minute. Add chicken, and stir-fry 5 minutes. Pour 2 tablespoons oil into wok. Add mushrooms and next 6 ingredients, and stir-fry 4 to 5 minutes. Add water chestnuts and green onions, and stir-fry 1 to 2 minutes. Set aside, and keep warm.

Add remaining 2 tablespoons soy sauce, remaining 1 tablespoon oil, vinegar, and cracked pepper to wok; cook until thoroughly heated. Add to pasta; toss. Serve chicken mixture over pasta. Yield: 6 servings.

Above & Beyond Parsley
The Junior League of Kansas City, Missouri

Linguine with Clam-Artichoke Sauce

1 (8-ounce) package linguine
¼ cup olive oil
¼ cup butter or margarine
1 teaspoon all-purpose flour
1 cup chicken broth
2 or 3 cloves garlic, crushed
1 tablespoon minced fresh
  parsley
2 teaspoons lemon juice

¼ teaspoon salt
⅛ teaspoon pepper
1 (14-ounce) can artichoke
  hearts, drained and quartered
1 (10-ounce) can whole baby
  clams, drained
2 to 3 tablespoons freshly
  grated Parmesan cheese
2 teaspoons capers, chopped

Cook pasta according to package directions; drain well. Set aside, and keep warm.

Heat oil and butter in a large skillet over medium heat. Add flour, and cook 3 minutes, stirring often. Stir in broth, and cook, uncovered, 1 minute. Add garlic and next 4 ingredients; reduce heat to low, and cook, uncovered, 5 minutes. Stir in artichoke hearts, clams, cheese, and capers; cook 10 minutes, stirring often. Serve immediately over pasta. Yield: 4 servings.   Christina Sherburne

Enough to Feed an Army
West Point Officers Wives' Club
West Point, New York

Spicy Shrimp Pasta à la Mark Hicks

1 pound unpeeled medium-size
  fresh shrimp
10 ounces linguine, uncooked
1 small onion, chopped
4 cloves garlic, crushed
½ cup extra virgin olive oil
2 tablespoons butter or
  margarine, melted
1 (2-ounce) can anchovies,
  drained and mashed

1 to 2 teaspoons dried crushed
  red pepper
1½ teaspoons hot sauce
1 (28-ounce) can whole Italian-
  style tomatoes, drained and
  coarsely chopped
2 tablespoons minced fresh
  parsley
Freshly grated Parmesan cheese

Peel shrimp, and devein, if desired; set aside.

Cook pasta according to package directions; drain well. Set pasta aside, and keep warm.

Cook onion and garlic in oil and butter in a skillet over medium heat, stirring constantly, until tender. Add anchovies, red pepper, and hot sauce; cook 2 minutes. Add shrimp; cook 3 minutes or until shrimp turn pink. Add tomatoes and parsley; cook until heated.

Combine pasta and 3 tablespoons tomato liquid from shrimp mixture; toss gently. Serve shrimp mixture over pasta; sprinkle with cheese. Serve immediately Yield: 4 servings.   Linda Spencer

Some Like It Hot
The Bement School
Deerfield, Massachusetts

Wilted Greens over Pasta

Penne (pronounced pen-nay) pasta is tube shaped and cut on the diagonal. It works well in this recipe, standing up to the chunky spinach and bacon sauce.

1 **pound fresh spinach**
1 **(10-ounce) package penne pasta**
5 **slices bacon**
½ **cup chopped onion**
1 **clove garlic, minced**
½ **teaspoon dried crushed red pepper**

2 **tablespoons white wine vinegar**
1 **teaspoon sugar (optional)**
2 **teaspoons Dijon mustard**
1 **cup freshly grated Romano or Parmesan cheese**
½ **cup coarsely chopped pecans, toasted**

Remove stems from spinach; wash leaves thoroughly, and pat dry. Slice spinach into thin strips. Set aside.

Cook pasta according to package directions; drain. Set aside.

Cook bacon in a Dutch oven over medium heat until crisp; remove bacon, reserving 2 tablespoons drippings in pan. Crumble bacon; set aside. Cook onion, garlic, and pepper in drippings in pan over medium heat, stirring constantly, until vegetables are tender. Add spinach; cook until spinach wilts.

Combine pasta, vinegar, sugar, if desired, and mustard in a large bowl. Add spinach mixture and cheese; toss well. Sprinkle with bacon and pecans. Serve immediately. Yield: 6 servings.

Cooking with Herb Scents
Western Reserve Herb Society
Bay Village, Ohio

Penne, Peppers, and Salmon in Garlic

Smoked salmon, fresh dill, and sweet peppers transform pasta into a classy luncheon entrée. Try serving half-portions as an appetizer.

½ cup whipping cream
4 cloves garlic, crushed
¼ cup fresh lemon juice
¾ cup olive oil
2 tablespoons minced fresh dill
2 tablespoons minced fresh parsley
¼ teaspoon salt
⅛ teaspoon pepper
1 (16-ounce) package penne pasta

6 ounces smoked salmon, cut into 2- x ⅓-inch strips
1 large sweet red pepper, cut into very thin strips
1 large green pepper, cut into very thin strips
1 small purple onion, thinly sliced
Garnish: fresh dill sprigs

Bring whipping cream and garlic to a boil in a heavy saucepan over medium heat; reduce heat, and simmer 15 minutes or until garlic is tender and mixture is reduced to ¼ cup.

Pour garlic mixture into container of an electric blender. Cover and process until smooth. Add lemon juice, and blend well. With blender running on high speed, gradually add oil in a slow, steady stream, processing until well blended and slightly thickened. Add minced dill, parsley, salt, and pepper; blend well.

Cook pasta according to package directions; drain well, and place in a large bowl. Reserve 24 strips of salmon. Add remaining salmon, peppers, and onion to pasta. Add sauce, and toss gently. Top with reserved salmon strips. Garnish, if desired. Serve immediately. Yield: 4 servings.

Jane Martin

Savor the Brandywine Valley, A Collection of Recipes
The Junior League of Wilmington, Delaware

Summer Rigatoni

2 cups whipping cream
1 teaspoon garlic powder
1 teaspoon ground sage
½ teaspoon pepper
2 tablespoons freshly grated
  Parmesan cheese
8 ounces rigatoni, uncooked
12 fresh asparagus spears
3 carrots, scraped and cut into
  very thin strips
¼ cup chopped onion
1½ teaspoons vegetable oil
½ pound smoked turkey breast,
  cut into very thin strips
¾ cup chicken broth
¼ cup chopped pecans
Freshly grated Parmesan cheese

Combine first 4 ingredients in a medium saucepan; bring to a boil. Reduce heat to medium-low, and cook, uncovered, 15 minutes or until thickened. Stir in 2 tablespoons Parmesan cheese. Set aside, and keep warm.

Cook pasta according to package directions; drain well. Set aside, and keep warm.

Snap off tough ends of asparagus. Remove scales with a knife or vegetable peeler, if desired. Cut into 1-inch pieces.

Cook asparagus, carrot, and chopped onion in oil in a large skillet over medium-high heat, stirring constantly, until tender. Stir in turkey and chicken broth. Bring to a boil; reduce heat, and simmer, uncovered, 1 minute. Stir in whipping cream mixture.

Combine pasta and sauce; toss gently. Sprinkle with pecans and additional Parmesan cheese. Yield: 4 servings.

Culinary Masterpieces
Birmingham Museum of Art
Birmingham, Alabama

Fried Spaghetti

Spaghetti becomes a unique dinner for two when it's teamed with ham, eggs, and cheese and fried into a pancake.

1 (7-ounce) package spaghetti
4 ounces chopped cooked ham
2 green onions, sliced
2 large eggs, lightly beaten
⅓ cup grated Parmesan cheese
2 teaspoons chopped fresh
  parsley

¾ teaspoon dried oregano
¼ teaspoon salt
⅛ teaspoon pepper
5 cloves garlic, minced
¼ cup olive oil
1 cup (4 ounces) shredded
  mozzarella cheese

Cook spaghetti according to package directions; drain. Combine spaghetti, ham, and next 7 ingredients in a large bowl, tossing gently.

Cook garlic in oil in a 10-inch skillet over medium heat, stirring constantly, until tender. Add garlic and oil to spaghetti mixture, tossing gently to combine.

Heat skillet over medium heat until hot; return spaghetti mixture to skillet, and cook 3 to 4 minutes on each side or until lightly browned. Sprinkle with mozzarella cheese; cover and cook until cheese melts. Serve immediately. Yield: 2 servings.

Ken Green

Education That's Cooking, Our Favorite Recipes
Rowan-Cabarrus Community College
Phi Beta Lambda & Phi Theta Kappa
Salisbury, North Carolina

Macaroni-Cheese Casserole

1½ cups elbow macaroni,
  uncooked
2 tablespoons butter or
  margarine
2 tablespoons all-purpose flour
1 cup milk
1 cup (4 ounces) shredded
  process American cheese

¼ teaspoon salt
⅛ teaspoon pepper
1½ cups diced cooked ham
2 tablespoons prepared
  horseradish
2 teaspoons prepared mustard

Cook macaroni according to package directions; drain and set aside. Melt butter in a heavy saucepan over low heat; add flour, stirring until smooth. Cook 1 minute, stirring constantly. Gradually add milk; cook over medium heat, stirring constantly, until mixture is thickened and bubbly. Add cheese, salt, and pepper, stirring until cheese melts. Stir in ham, horseradish, and mustard.

Combine macaroni and sauce, stirring well. Pour into a greased 1-quart baking dish. Bake, uncovered, at 350° for 20 minutes or until thoroughly heated. Yield: 4 servings.   Sister Beata Lorsung

Franciscan Centennial Cookbook
Franciscan Sisters
Little Falls, Minnesota

Beef- and Tomato-Stuffed Shells

8 jumbo macaroni shells,
   uncooked
¾ pound ground beef
2 cups sliced fresh mushrooms
½ cup chopped onion
½ cup chopped green pepper
1 clove garlic, minced
1 (16-ounce) can whole
   tomatoes, undrained and
   chopped

¼ cup dry red wine
1 tablespoon cornstarch
2 tablespoons tomato paste
½ teaspoon salt
½ teaspoon dried oregano
¼ teaspoon fennel seeds,
   crushed
¼ cup grated Parmesan cheese

Cook pasta according to package directions; drain and set aside.

Brown ground beef, mushrooms, onion, green pepper, and garlic in a large skillet over medium heat, stirring until meat crumbles. Drain and set aside.

Combine tomatoes and next 6 ingredients in a large saucepan. Cook, stirring constantly, until thickened and bubbly. Stir ½ cup tomato mixture into ground beef mixture.

Spoon about ¼ cup ground beef mixture into each shell. Arrange shells in a lightly greased 10- x 6- x 2-inch baking dish. Stir remaining ground beef mixture into remaining tomato mixture; pour over shells. Sprinkle with cheese. Bake, uncovered, at 350° for 25 minutes or until thoroughly heated. Yield: 4 servings.   Beth Clark

American Buffet
General Federation of Women's Clubs
Washington, DC

Noodles Ontario

Cook once, eat twice with this recipe. Just fix and freeze the second pan of noodles, up to two months ahead, without baking it. Thaw it in the refrigerator, and bake it as directed.

1 pound mild Italian sausage
2 (28-ounce) cans crushed tomatoes
1 bay leaf
2 teaspoons minced garlic
2 teaspoons sugar
1 teaspoon dried basil
½ teaspoon dried oregano
¼ teaspoon pepper
⅛ teaspoon salt
1 (12-ounce) package extra wide egg noodles

4 large eggs
½ cup Parmesan cheese, divided
⅛ teaspoon ground nutmeg
⅛ teaspoon pepper
2 (10-ounce) packages frozen chopped spinach, thawed and well drained
4 green onions, sliced
4 cups (16 ounces) shredded mozzarella cheese

Remove and discard casing from sausage. Brown sausage in a large saucepan over medium heat, stirring until it crumbles; drain. Return sausage to pan; add tomatoes and next 7 ingredients. Bring to a boil; reduce heat, and simmer, uncovered, 1 hour, stirring occasionally. Remove and discard bay leaf. Set sausage mixture aside.

Cook noodles according to package directions; drain well. Rinse noodles with cold water, and drain well. Set aside.

Combine eggs, ¼ cup Parmesan cheese, nutmeg, and ⅛ teaspoon pepper in a large bowl; beat with a wire whisk until well blended. Stir in noodles, spinach, and green onions.

Divide half of pasta mixture between 2 greased 9-inch square pans. Layer one-fourth of sausage mixture over pasta mixture in each pan. Sprinkle 1 cup mozzarella cheese over sausage mixture in each pan. Repeat layers using remaining pasta mixture, sausage mixture, and mozzarella cheese. Sprinkle with remaining ¼ cup Parmesan cheese. Bake, uncovered, at 350° for 30 minutes or until hot and bubbly. Let stand 15 minutes before serving. Yield: 8 servings.

For Goodness Taste
The Junior League of Rochester, New York

Charleston Red Rice

Red rice, a delicately seasoned tomato-based rice, has its roots in the Low Country of eastern South Carolina. Rice became one of the area's first sources of great economic wealth.

2 cups long-grain rice, uncooked
6 slices bacon
2 medium onions, finely chopped
1 (8-ounce) can tomato sauce
1 (6-ounce) can tomato paste
1 tablespoon sugar
2 teaspoons Worcestershire sauce
Dash of hot sauce

Cook rice according to package directions; set aside.

Cook bacon in a medium skillet until crisp; remove bacon, reserving ¼ cup drippings in skillet. Crumble bacon, and set aside.

Cook onions in drippings in skillet over medium-high heat, stirring constantly, until tender. Add tomato sauce and next 4 ingredients. Bring to a boil; reduce heat, and simmer, uncovered, 10 minutes. Stir in rice.

Place rice mixture in a buttered 2-quart casserole. Bake, uncovered, at 325° for 45 minutes or until liquid is absorbed and rice is tender. Sprinkle with bacon. Serve immediately. Yield: 8 servings.

Simply Heavenly
Woman's Synodical Union of the Associate Reformed
Presbyterian Church
Greenville, South Carolina

Lemon-Fried Rice

Lemon rind and hot sauce transform fried rice into a distinctive new side dish. Serve it with beef, pork, and chicken for a change of pace.

¼ cup butter, melted
½ cup sliced green onions
¼ cup minced fresh parsley
1 (10-ounce) package frozen
   English peas, thawed

4 cups cold cooked rice
2 tablespoons soy sauce
2 teaspoons grated lemon rind
⅛ teaspoon hot sauce

Pour butter around top of preheated wok, coating sides; heat at medium-high (375°) for 2 minutes. Add green onions and parsley; stir-fry 1 minute. Add peas and remaining ingredients; stir-fry until thoroughly heated. Serve immediately. Yield: 8 servings.   Chris Dimov

A Taste of South Central Pennsylvania
South Central Pennsylvania Food Bank
Harrisburg, Pennsylvania

Spicy Monterey Rice

2 cups water
1 cup long-grain rice, uncooked
1 tablespoon chicken-flavored
   bouillon granules
1 (16-ounce) carton sour cream
1½ cups (6 ounces) shredded
   Cheddar cheese, divided

1 cup (4 ounces) shredded
   Monterey Jack cheese
½ cup chopped sweet red
   pepper
1 (4½-ounce) can chopped
   green chiles, undrained
⅛ teaspoon pepper

Combine water, rice, and bouillon granules in a medium saucepan. Bring to a boil; cover, reduce heat, and simmer 20 minutes or until liquid is absorbed and rice is tender.

Combine sour cream, 1 cup Cheddar cheese, and next 4 ingredients. Stir in rice. Spoon into a buttered 1½-quart casserole. Bake at 350° for 25 minutes. Sprinkle with remaining ½ cup Cheddar cheese; bake 5 additional minutes. Yield: 6 servings.   Christy Drake

Recipes from the End of the Road
Homer Special Olympics
Homer, Alaska

Vidalia Onion and Rice Casserole

1 cup water
½ cup long-grain rice, uncooked
7 medium Vidalia onions or other sweet onions, sliced (about 4½ pounds)
¼ cup butter or margarine, melted
1 cup (4 ounces) shredded Swiss cheese
⅔ cup half-and-half
1 teaspoon salt

Bring water to a boil. Stir in rice; cover, reduce heat, and simmer 20 minutes or until water is absorbed and rice is tender.

Cook onion in butter in a Dutch oven over medium heat, stirring constantly, until tender. Remove from heat. Stir in rice, cheese, half-and-half, and salt. Spread in a greased 13- x 9- x 2-inch baking dish. Bake at 325° for 1 hour or until browned. Yield: 8 servings.

Among the Lilies
Women in Missions, First Baptist Church of Atlanta
Atlanta, Georgia

Rice Pilaf with Vegetables

1 cup peeled and diced eggplant
1 small sweet red pepper, diced
1 small zucchini, diced
5 ounces fresh mushrooms, thinly sliced
1 clove garlic, crushed
½ cup butter or margarine, melted
1 large tomato, peeled, seeded, and chopped
1 (14½-ounce) can ready-to-serve chicken broth
1 cup long-grain rice, uncooked
Salt and pepper to taste

Cook first 5 ingredients in butter in a large skillet over medium heat 10 minutes, stirring occasionally. Stir in tomato, chicken broth, rice, and salt and pepper to taste.

Spoon mixture into an ungreased 11- x 7- x 1½-inch baking dish. Cover and bake at 350° for 1 hour or until liquid is absorbed and rice is tender, stirring after 30 minutes. Yield: 6 servings.   Mary Rossi

Angels & Friends Favorite Recipes II
Angels of Easter Seal
Youngstown, Ohio

Bayou Risotto

A traditional risotto is made by gradually adding hot broth to a rice mixture while stirring. Though not technically a risotto, this simpler version has the same creamy texture plus the bayou flavors of okra, tomatoes, and hot sauce.

4 slices bacon, diced
1 cup converted rice, uncooked
¾ cup chopped onion
2 cloves garlic, crushed
1 (14½-ounce) can ready-to-serve chicken broth
1¼ cups water

½ cup chopped green pepper
¼ to ½ teaspoon pepper
Hot sauce to taste
1 cup frozen whole okra, thawed, drained, and cut in half crosswise
1 small tomato, diced

Cook bacon in a large saucepan until crisp. Add rice, onion, and garlic, and cook over medium heat, stirring constantly, until tender.

Add chicken broth and next 4 ingredients; bring to a boil. Cover, reduce heat, and simmer 25 minutes. Remove from heat; stir in okra and tomato. Cover and let stand 5 minutes or until liquid is absorbed. Serve immediately. Yield: 6 servings.   Shelia Parker

Cookin' for the Kids
Wal-Mart Distribution Center #6011
Brookhaven, Mississippi

Cumin Rice Timbales

Cumin seed is an ancient spice shaped like a caraway seed. Lightly toasting the cumin seeds brings out their aroma and nutty flavor.

½ cup minced onion
1 teaspoon cumin seeds
⅛ teaspoon dried crushed red pepper
2 tablespoons olive oil
1 cup converted rice, uncooked

2 cups chicken broth
¼ teaspoon salt
1 tablespoon minced fresh parsley
½ teaspoon cumin seeds, lightly toasted

Cook first 3 ingredients in oil in a large saucepan over medium-high heat, stirring constantly, until onion is tender. Add rice; cook 1 minute, stirring constantly. Stir in chicken broth and salt. Bring to a boil; cover, reduce heat, and simmer 20 minutes or until liquid is absorbed and rice is tender. Remove from heat, and stir in parsley. Cover and let stand 5 minutes.

Pack warm rice mixture into 6 oiled 6-ounce custard cups. Immediately invert onto a serving platter. Sprinkle with toasted cumin seeds. Yield: 6 servings.

Tampa Treasures
The Junior League of Tampa, Florida

Bulgur Pilaf

In place of rice, try this quick and easy pilaf made with bulgur. Bulgur, a Middle Eastern staple, is wheat kernels that have been steamed, dried, and crushed.

2 tablespoons minced onion	1 cup bulgur (cracked wheat), uncooked
2 tablespoons chopped green pepper	1 (3-ounce) can sliced mushrooms, drained
2 tablespoons butter or margarine, melted	½ teaspoon salt
2 cups chicken broth	Dash of pepper

Cook minced onion and green pepper in butter in a large skillet over medium-high heat, stirring constantly, 3 minutes or until tender. Add chicken broth and remaining ingredients; bring to a boil. Cover, reduce heat, and simmer 15 minutes or until liquid is absorbed and bulgur is tender. Yield: 4 servings.   F. Norris

Our Cherished Recipes, Second Edition
First Presbyterian Church
Skagway, Alaska

Bulgur Pilaf with Onions

Either chicken or beef broth will work deliciously in this bulgur.

1 large onion, chopped	2 medium tomatoes, peeled and
2 banana peppers, chopped	chopped
2 tablespoons butter, melted	4 cups beef or chicken broth
2 cups bulgur (cracked wheat),	¼ teaspoon salt
uncooked	¼ teaspoon pepper

Cook onion and banana pepper in butter in a skillet over medium-high heat, stirring constantly, until tender. Add bulgur; cook, stirring constantly, 2 minutes. Add tomato; reduce heat, and simmer 3 minutes, stirring constantly. Stir in broth, salt, and pepper. Bring to boil; cover, reduce heat, and simmer 30 to 35 minutes or until liquid is absorbed and bulgur is tender. Yield: 10 servings.   Berrin Gürsan

Anatolian Feast, Food of Türkiye
American Turkish Association
Houston, Texas

Wild Rice and Barley Pilaf

½ cup chopped pecans	½ teaspoon dried thyme
¼ cup plus 1 tablespoon	1 (6-ounce) package wild rice
unsalted butter or margarine,	¼ cup pearl barley, uncooked
melted	2 cups beef broth
1 medium onion, diced	½ cup minced fresh parsley

Cook pecans in butter in a large skillet over medium-high heat, stirring constantly, until toasted. Remove pecans with a slotted spoon, reserving butter in skillet. Set pecans aside.

Cook onion and thyme in butter in skillet over medium heat, stirring constantly, until tender. Add rice and barley; cook 1 minute, stirring constantly. Add broth; bring to a boil. Cover, reduce heat, and simmer 1 hour or until rice is tender. Drain, if necessary. Stir in pecans and parsley. Yield: 8 servings.   Lael Rhino

Taste & Share the Goodness of Door County
St. Rosalia's Ladies Sodality of St. Rosalia's Catholic Church
Sister Bay, Wisconsin

Pies & Pastries

Florida Frost, page 228

Blueberry-Peach Pie

Serve this double-crust delicacy with scoops of vanilla ice cream or dollops of whipped cream.

2 cups all-purpose flour
1 teaspoon salt
⅔ cup plus 2 tablespoons shortening
3 to 5 tablespoons cold water
¾ cup sugar

⅓ cup all-purpose flour
1½ teaspoons ground cinnamon
2½ to 3 cups fresh blueberries
2 cups peeled, sliced fresh peaches

Combine 2 cups flour and salt; cut in shortening with pastry blender until mixture is crumbly. Sprinkle cold water (1 tablespoon at a time) evenly over surface; stir with a fork until dry ingredients are moistened. Shape into a ball.

Roll half of pastry to ⅛-inch thickness on a lightly floured surface. Place in a 9-inch pieplate; set aside.

Combine sugar, ⅓ cup flour, and cinnamon in a large bowl. Add blueberries and peach slices, and toss gently. Spoon into pastry shell.

Roll remaining pastry to ⅛-inch thickness; transfer to top of pie. Trim off excess pastry along edges. Fold edges under, and crimp. Cut slits in top of pastry to allow steam to escape. Bake at 425° for 40 to 50 minutes or until lightly browned. (Cover edges of pastry with strips of aluminum foil to prevent excessive browning, if necessary.) Let stand 10 minutes before serving. Serve warm. Yield: one 9-inch pie.

Holy Cow, Chicago's Cooking!
The Church of the Holy Comforter
Kenilworth, Illinois

Traverse City Cherry-Berry Pie

Traverse City is the capital of Michigan's cherry-producing region, so you can bet this pie is a winner. If you prefer, you can make it with a decorative lattice crust instead of a double crust. It will bake in the same length of time.

Pastry for double-crust 9-inch pie
1 **(10-ounce) package frozen raspberries in light syrup, thawed**
¾ **cup sugar**
3 **tablespoons cornstarch**
½ **teaspoon salt**
2 **cups pitted fresh tart red cherries**
½ **teaspoon ground cinnamon**
1 **quart vanilla or cinnamon ice cream**

Roll half of pastry to ⅛-inch thickness on a lightly floured surface. Place in a 9-inch pieplate; set aside.

Drain raspberries, reserving syrup. Set raspberries aside. Add water to syrup to equal 1 cup. Combine syrup mixture, sugar, cornstarch, and salt in a saucepan; stir well. Stir in cherries. Cook over medium heat, stirring constantly, until mixture is thickened and bubbly. Remove from heat; add raspberries and cinnamon, stirring gently. Pour into pastry shell.

Roll remaining pastry to ⅛-inch thickness; transfer to top of pie. Trim off excess pastry along edges. Fold edges under, and crimp. Cut slits in top of pastry to allow steam to escape. Bake at 375° for 35 minutes or until golden. (Cover edges of pastry with strips of aluminum foil to prevent excessive browning, if necessary.) Cool on a wire rack. Serve with ice cream. Yield: one 9-inch pie.

Cranbrook Reflections: A Culinary Collection
Cranbrook House and Gardens Auxiliary
Bloomfield Hills, Michigan

Cranberry-Apple-Cheese Pie

1 unbaked 9-inch pastry shell
1 (8-ounce) package cream
  cheese, softened
⅓ cup firmly packed brown
  sugar
2½ tablespoons cornstarch
⅛ teaspoon salt

1 (16-ounce) can jellied
  whole-berry cranberry sauce
2 cups peeled and thinly sliced
  Rome or other tart cooking
  apple
Walnut Streusel Topping

Line pastry with aluminum foil or wax paper, and fill with pie weights or dried beans.

Bake at 425° for 15 minutes. Remove foil, and bake 5 additional minutes. Cool completely on a wire rack.

Beat cream cheese in a small mixing bowl at medium speed of an electric mixer until creamy. Spread evenly on bottom of pastry shell.

Combine brown sugar, cornstarch, and salt; add cranberry sauce and apple, stirring gently. Spoon evenly over cream cheese; sprinkle with Walnut Streusel Topping. Bake at 375° for 45 minutes. (Cover edges of pastry with strips of aluminum foil to prevent excessive browning after 15 minutes.) Cool on wire rack. Yield: one 9-inch pie.

Walnut Streusel Topping

½ cup chopped walnuts
⅓ cup all-purpose flour
3 tablespoons firmly packed
  brown sugar

¼ teaspoon ground cinnamon
¼ cup butter or margarine

Combine first 4 ingredients in a bowl. Cut in butter with pastry blender until mixture is crumbly. Yield: 1½ cups.   Patsy Ernest

Women's Ministry Daily Bread
Word of Life Fellowship
Steubenville, Ohio

Pumpkin-Apple Pie

This pie's like two favorite pies in one. Tucked under a creamy layer of a traditional pumpkin filling is a spicy apple mixture.

1 unbaked 9-inch pastry shell
3 medium-size cooking apples, peeled and coarsely chopped
1½ teaspoons ground cinnamon, divided
1 teaspoon ground allspice
½ teaspoon ground nutmeg, divided
¼ cup butter or margarine, melted

¼ cup apple juice
2 tablespoons sugar
1 tablespoon all-purpose flour
1 cup canned pumpkin
1 large egg
⅓ cup sugar
¼ teaspoon ground cloves
½ cup half-and-half

Bake pastry shell at 425° for 5 minutes; set aside.

Cook apple, 1 teaspoon cinnamon, allspice, and ¼ teaspoon nutmeg in butter in a large skillet over medium-high heat 5 minutes, stirring occasionally. Stir in apple juice, 2 tablespoons sugar, and flour; cook 1 minute. Spoon apple mixture into pastry shell; set aside.

Combine pumpkin, egg, ⅓ cup sugar, remaining ½ teaspoon cinnamon, remaining ¼ teaspoon nutmeg, and cloves in a bowl, stirring with a wire whisk until blended. Stir in half-and-half. Pour pumpkin mixture over apple mixture. Bake at 425° for 15 minutes. Reduce oven temperature to 350°, and bake 30 additional minutes. Cool on a wire rack. Yield: one 9-inch pie.   Rose Marie Fowler

Exclusively Pumpkin Cookbook
Coventry Historical Society
Coventry, Connecticut

Walnut Crunch-Pumpkin Pie

This pumpkin pie with its crunchy walnut and brown sugar topping is best served at room temperature. If you have any leftover pie, store it in the refrigerator, and then let it return to room temperature before serving.

1 (16-ounce) can pumpkin
1 (12-ounce) can evaporated
  milk
2 large eggs, lightly beaten
¾ cup firmly packed brown
  sugar
1½ teaspoons ground cinnamon
½ teaspoon salt
½ teaspoon ground ginger

½ teaspoon ground nutmeg
1 unbaked 9-inch pastry shell
1 cup chopped walnuts
¾ cup firmly packed brown
  sugar
¼ cup butter or margarine,
  melted
Whipped cream

Combine first 8 ingredients in a large bowl; stir well. Pour pumpkin mixture into pastry shell. Bake at 400° for 45 to 50 minutes or until a knife inserted 1 inch from center comes out clean. Cool completely on a wire rack.

Combine walnuts, ¾ cup brown sugar, and butter; stir well. Sprinkle walnut mixture over cooled pie. Broil 8 inches from heat (with electric oven door partially opened) 3 minutes or until sugar dissolves. Let cool slightly before serving. Serve with whipped cream. Yield: one 9-inch pie.

Janet Mackey

The Feast
St. Mary's Catholic Community
Caldwell, Idaho

Chocolate-Macadamia Pie

If you aren't a macadamia nut fan, try substituting pecans in this luscious mocha-flavored pie.

4 large eggs, lightly beaten
¾ cup light corn syrup
½ cup firmly packed brown sugar
¼ cup butter or margarine, melted
2 teaspoons Kahlúa or other coffee-flavored liqueur
2 teaspoons vanilla extract
1 cup semisweet chocolate morsels
1 (7-ounce) jar macadamia nuts
1 unbaked 9-inch pastry shell
Coffee Cream
¼ cup shaved semisweet chocolate

Combine first 6 ingredients in a medium bowl; stir well. Stir in chocolate morsels and nuts.

Pour into pastry shell; bake at 425° for 10 minutes. Reduce oven temperature to 350°, and bake 30 additional minutes or until set. (Cover edges of pastry with strips of aluminum foil to prevent excessive browning, if necessary.) Cool completely on a wire rack; cover and chill thoroughly. Spoon Coffee Cream on top of pie; sprinkle with shaved chocolate. Cover and chill 30 minutes. Yield: one 9-inch pie.

Coffee Cream

1 cup whipping cream
2 tablespoons powdered sugar
2 tablespoons Kahlúa or other coffee-flavored liqueur

Combine all ingredients in a large mixing bowl; beat at high speed of an electric mixer until stiff peaks form. Yield: 2 cups.

Tastes and Traditions: The Sam Houston Heritage Cookbook
The Study Club of Huntsville
Huntsville, Texas

Old Virginia Peanut Pie

1 cup dark corn syrup
⅔ cup sugar
⅓ cup butter or margarine, melted
3 large eggs, lightly beaten
1 teaspoon vanilla extract
⅛ teaspoon salt
1 cup unsalted roasted peanuts
1 unbaked deep-dish 9-inch pastry shell
1 cup whipping cream, whipped

Combine first 6 ingredients in a large bowl; stir well. Stir in peanuts. Pour into pastry shell. Bake at 350° for 50 minutes or until a knife inserted in center comes out clean. (Cover edges of pastry with strips of aluminum foil to prevent excessive browning after 25 minutes, if necessary.) Cool completely on a wire rack. Serve with whipped cream. Yield: one 9-inch pie.

The William & Mary Cookbook
Society of the Alumni, College of William and Mary
Williamsburg, Virginia

Florida Frost

1½ cups gingersnap crumbs
¼ cup unsalted butter or margarine, melted
2 tablespoons sugar
½ gallon orange sherbet, softened
3 tablespoons fresh lemon juice
2 teaspoons grated orange rind
Garnishes: fresh orange segments, fresh mint sprigs

Combine first 3 ingredients. Firmly press crumb mixture evenly in bottom and up sides of a 9-inch pieplate. Bake at 375° for 6 to 8 minutes or until edges are browned. Cool completely on a wire rack.

Combine orange sherbet, lemon juice, and 1½ teaspoons orange rind in a large bowl; stir well. Spoon sherbet mixture into prepared crust, mounding and swirling with a small spatula. Sprinkle with remaining ½ teaspoon orange rind. Freeze until firm. Garnish, if desired. Yield: one 9-inch pie.

Perfect Endings: The Art of Desserts
Friends of the Arts of the Tampa Museum of Art
Tampa, Florida

Ice Cream Pie

You can use ¼ cup graham cracker crumbs instead of crushed vanilla wafers for this crust, if someone secretly finished off the vanilla wafers at your house.

1⅓ cups flaked coconut
¼ cup crushed vanilla wafers
1 tablespoon sugar, divided
2 teaspoons butter or margarine, melted
¾ cup flaked coconut
½ cup chopped pecans or walnuts
1 teaspoon butter or margarine, melted
1 quart vanilla ice cream, softened
Sauce

Combine 1⅓ cups coconut, vanilla wafer crumbs, 2 teaspoons sugar, and 2 teaspoons butter; stir well. Firmly press crumb mixture in bottom and up sides of a 9-inch pieplate. Bake at 325° for 12 to 15 minutes or until lightly browned. Cool completely on a wire rack.

Combine ¾ cup coconut, chopped pecans, remaining 1 teaspoon sugar, and 1 teaspoon butter; stir well. Spread on an ungreased baking sheet. Bake at 325° for 5 to 7 minutes or until lightly browned, stirring frequently.

Spoon softened ice cream into cooled crust. Sprinkle coconut-pecan mixture over ice cream; lightly press into ice cream. Freeze at least 2 hours or until firm. Let stand at room temperature 5 minutes before serving. Serve with warm Sauce. Yield: one 9-inch pie.

Sauce

½ cup butter or margarine
1 cup firmly packed brown sugar
⅓ cup whipping cream
2 teaspoons light corn syrup

Melt butter in a small saucepan over low heat. Add brown sugar, whipping cream, and corn syrup, stirring well. Bring sauce mixture to a boil; reduce heat, and simmer 1 minute, stirring constantly. Yield: 1⅓ cups.

Kathy Burchfield

A Taste of History
University of North Alabama Women's Club
Florence, Alabama

Walnut Tart

⅓ cup butter or margarine, softened
¼ cup sugar
1 egg yolk
1 cup all-purpose flour
2 cups coarsely chopped walnuts, toasted

⅔ cup firmly packed brown sugar
¼ cup butter or margarine
¼ cup dark corn syrup
1 cup whipping cream, divided

Beat ⅓ cup butter and ¼ cup sugar at medium speed of an electric mixer until light and fluffy. Add egg yolk; beat well. Gradually add flour, mixing at low speed until blended. (Mixture will be crumbly.) Shape into a ball. Press pastry in bottom and up sides of a 9-inch tart pan with removable bottom. Bake at 375° for 12 minutes or until lightly browned. Cool on a wire rack.

Sprinkle walnuts evenly in bottom of tart shell. Combine brown sugar, ¼ cup butter, corn syrup, and 2 tablespoons whipping cream in a saucepan; bring to a boil over medium heat, stirring constantly. Boil 1 minute, stirring constantly. Pour over walnuts. Bake at 375° for 13 minutes or until bubbly. Cool completely in pan on wire rack.

To serve, carefully remove sides of pan. Beat remaining whipping cream until stiff peaks form. Serve tart with whipped cream. Yield: one 9-inch tart.

Joanne Sebring

Heavenly Hosts
Bryn Mawr Presbyterian Church
Bryn Mawr, Pennsylvania

Chocolate-Almond Tassies

¼ cup butter or margarine, softened
1½ ounces cream cheese, softened
½ cup all-purpose flour
⅓ cup firmly packed brown sugar

1 large egg, lightly beaten
¼ cup chopped blanched almonds
¼ cup semisweet chocolate mini-morsels
½ teaspoon amaretto

Beat softened butter and cream cheese at medium speed of an electric mixer until creamy. Gradually add flour, beating well. Shape pastry into 12 (1-inch) balls. Press balls into a lightly greased minia-ture (1¾-inch) muffin pan; set aside.

Combine sugar and egg in a bowl. Add almonds, mini-morsels, and amaretto; stir well. Spoon 1 tablespoon mixture into each pastry shell. Bake at 350° for 20 to 25 minutes or until set and lightly browned. Cool in pan on a wire rack 10 minutes. Remove from pan, and let cool completely on wire rack. Yield: 1 dozen.   Mary O'Hara

Newcomers' Favorites, International and Regional Recipes
Aiken Newcomers' Club
Aiken, South Carolina

Lemon Tassies

For a little something to serve with coffee or tea, try these dainty cream cheese pastry cups that have a tangy lemon filling.

½ cup butter or margarine,
  softened
1 (3-ounce) package cream
  cheese, softened
1¼ cups all-purpose flour
Vegetable cooking spray

⅔ cup sugar
2 large eggs, beaten
3 tablespoons butter or
  margarine, melted
3 tablespoons fresh lemon juice
Garnish: whipped cream

Beat ½ cup butter and cream cheese at medium speed of an electric mixer until creamy. Gradually add flour, beating well. Shape pastry into 20 (1-inch) balls. Press balls into miniature (1¾-inch) muffin pans coated with cooking spray; set aside.

Combine sugar and next 3 ingredients; stir well. Spoon mixture evenly into pastry shells. Bake at 350° for 40 minutes. Cool in pans on wire racks 10 minutes. Remove from pans, and let cool completely on wire racks. Garnish, if desired. Yield: 20 tassies.

Among the Lilies
Women in Missions, First Baptist Church of Atlanta
Atlanta, Georgia

Strudelettes

A savory mixture of ground walnuts comprises the filling in these petite strudels.

1¼ cups all-purpose flour	1 tablespoon fresh lemon juice
½ cup butter or margarine	½ cup sugar
3 large eggs, divided	1 cup ground walnuts
1 teaspoon grated lemon rind	Powdered sugar

Place flour in a medium bowl; cut in butter with pastry blender until mixture is crumbly. Add beaten egg yolks, lemon rind, and lemon juice, stirring until dry ingredients are moistened. Divide pastry into 24 equal portions; chill at least 4 hours.

Beat egg whites at high speed of an electric mixer until foamy. Gradually add sugar, 1 tablespoon at a time, beating until stiff peaks form and sugar dissolves (2 to 4 minutes). Gently fold in walnuts.

Roll each portion of pastry into a 4-inch round on a lightly floured surface. Spread 2 tablespoons walnut mixture over each pastry round. Roll up, jellyroll fashion, slightly pushing in ends of pastry. Arrange pastry rolls, seam side down, on an ungreased baking sheet. Bake at 350° for 15 minutes or until lightly browned. Cool completely on wire racks. Cut each roll diagonally into thirds. Sprinkle with powdered sugar. Yield: 2 dozen.

Frances Koshinz

Cross-Town Cooking
Women's Group of Assumption and Sacred Heart Parishes
Bellingham, Washington

Pear Dumplings with Cream Custard

Garnish these dumplings with fresh mint leaves, positioning the leaves at the top of each pear to resemble its leaves.

1 egg yolk
2 cups whipping cream
1 tablespoon plus 1 teaspoon
    cornstarch
¼ cup sugar
¼ teaspoon salt
½ teaspoon vanilla extract
½ cup butter or margarine,
    softened

4 ounces cream cheese,
    softened
1½ cups all-purpose flour
3 medium-size firm ripe pears
1½ teaspoons sugar
½ teaspoon ground cinnamon
1 egg white, lightly beaten
Garnish: fresh mint leaves

Combine first 5 ingredients in a medium saucepan. Cook over medium heat, stirring constantly, until mixture thickens. Remove from heat; stir in vanilla. Set aside, and let cool.

Beat butter and cream cheese at medium speed of an electric mixer until creamy. Add flour, and beat at low speed just until blended. Divide pastry into 6 equal portions; shape each portion into a ball.

Roll each ball to a ⅛-inch thickness on a lightly floured surface; trim into a 7-inch circle.

Peel and core pears. Cut pears in half lengthwise. Combine 1½ teaspoons sugar and cinnamon; stir well. Sprinkle evenly over pastry circles. Place 1 pear half, cut side up, in center of each pastry circle. Fold pastry around pear halves; place, seam side down, on an ungreased baking sheet. Brush with egg white. Bake at 375° for 30 to 35 minutes or until golden.

To serve, spoon custard evenly onto 6 dessert plates. Top with dumplings. Garnish, if desired. Serve immediately. Yield: 6 servings.

Rogue River Rendezvous
The Junior Service League of Jackson County
Medford, Oregon

Apple Squares

2½ cups all-purpose flour
½ teaspoon baking powder
½ teaspoon salt
¾ cup shortening
1 large egg, lightly beaten
¼ cup cold water
1 tablespoon white vinegar
¾ cup sugar
3 tablespoons all-purpose flour
½ teaspoon salt
½ teaspoon ground cinnamon
¼ teaspoon ground nutmeg
8 large cooking apples, peeled and chopped
1 cup sifted powdered sugar
1 to 2 tablespoons warm water or milk
½ teaspoon vanilla extract or fresh lemon juice

Combine 2½ cups flour, baking powder, and ½ teaspoon salt in a medium bowl; cut in shortening with pastry blender until mixture is crumbly. Stir in egg. Sprinkle cold water and vinegar (1 tablespoon at a time) evenly over surface; stir with a fork until dry ingredients are moistened. Shape into a ball; chill.

Roll half of pastry to ⅛-inch thickness on a lightly floured surface. Place in a greased 15- x 10- x 1-inch jellyroll pan; trim off excess pastry along edges. Combine ¾ cup sugar and next 4 ingredients in a large bowl; stir well. Add chopped apple, and toss to coat. Spoon apple mixture into prepared pastry shell.

Roll remaining pastry to ⅛-inch thickness on a lightly floured surface. Transfer to top of apple mixture. Fold edges under, and crimp. Cut slits in top of pastry to allow steam to escape. Bake at 375° for 45 to 50 minutes or until lightly browned. Cool completely in pan on a wire rack.

Combine powdered sugar and remaining ingredients in a small bowl, stirring well. Drizzle on top of pastry. Cut into squares. Yield: 15 servings.

Anne Couch

Sharing Our Best
Neighborhood Ministries Auxiliary
Campbell and Youngstown, Ohio

Blackberry Pinwheels

Decorative pastry pinwheels create a shapely alternative for cobbler. Serve them warm for brunch or as a dessert topped with vanilla ice cream.

¼ cup plus 2 tablespoons butter
  or margarine
1 cup sugar
1 cup water
1½ cups all-purpose flour
2¼ teaspoons baking powder
¼ teaspoon salt
½ cup butter or margarine
⅓ cup milk

2 cups fresh or frozen
  blackberries, thawed and
  drained
½ to 1 teaspoon ground
  cinnamon
2 tablespoons butter or
  margarine, melted
2 tablespoons sugar

Melt ¼ cup plus 2 tablespoons butter in a medium saucepan over medium heat; add 1 cup sugar and water. Cook, stirring constantly, until sugar dissolves. Set syrup aside.

Combine flour, baking powder, and salt; cut in ½ cup butter with pastry blender until mixture is crumbly. Add milk; stir with a fork until dry ingredients are moistened. Turn out onto a lightly floured surface; knead 3 or 4 times.

Roll pastry into an 11- x 9-inch rectangle. Spoon blackberries on top of pastry; sprinkle with cinnamon. Roll up pastry, starting at long side; pinch seam to seal. Cut roll into 1¼-inch slices. Pour 2 tablespoons melted butter into a 2½-quart round or oval baking dish. Place slices, cut side up, in baking dish. Pour syrup evenly over slices. Bake at 350° for 35 minutes. Sprinkle with 2 tablespoons sugar; bake 15 additional minutes or until lightly browned. Serve warm, or let cool to room temperature. Yield: 10 servings.

Above & Beyond Parsley
The Junior League of Kansas City, Missouri

Peach Crisp with Bourbon Sauce

Here's a Bourbon Sauce with a definite kick to it. You can adjust the amount of bourbon to suit your taste.

7 large fresh ripe peaches (about 3 pounds)
1 teaspoon grated lemon rind
2 tablespoons fresh lemon juice
¼ teaspoon ground nutmeg
1 cup all-purpose flour
1 cup firmly packed brown sugar

¾ cup regular oats, uncooked
⅓ cup unsalted butter or margarine
½ cup coarsely chopped pecans or walnuts
Bourbon Sauce

Dip peaches in boiling water for 30 seconds. Remove skin; thinly slice peaches. Place peach slices in a buttered 9-inch square baking dish. Sprinkle with lemon rind, lemon juice, and nutmeg.

Combine flour, brown sugar, and oats; stir well. Cut in butter with pastry blender until mixture is crumbly. Stir in pecans. Sprinkle evenly over peach mixture. Bake at 325° for 30 minutes or until peaches are tender. Let cool in dish on a wire rack. Serve with Bourbon Sauce. Yield: 8 servings.

Bourbon Sauce

½ cup unsalted butter or margarine
1 cup superfine sugar

1 large egg, lightly beaten
½ cup bourbon

Place butter in top of a double boiler; bring water to a boil. Reduce heat to low; cook until butter melts.

Combine sugar and egg, stirring well. Add sugar mixture to butter; cook 15 minutes or until mixture reaches 160°, stirring occasionally. Remove from heat, and let cool. Stir in bourbon. Yield: 1¾ cups.

Specialties of the House
Kenmore Association
Fredericksburg, Virginia

Poultry

Father George's Quail Supreme, page 256

Flat Dumplings with Chicken

Parsley, green onion, and carrot add flavor and flecks of color to these dumplings. Kneading the dumplings four or five times gives them a pleasing texture and helps them hold together during the cooking process.

1 (5-pound) hen
3 quarts water
1½ teaspoons salt
½ teaspoon pepper
2 cups all-purpose flour
½ teaspoon baking powder
½ teaspoon salt

1 large egg, lightly beaten
1 tablespoon dried parsley flakes
1 tablespoon grated carrot
1 tablespoon minced green onion
1 tablespoon grated onion

Remove giblets, and rinse hen with cold water; pat dry. Combine hen and next 3 ingredients in a Dutch oven; bring to a boil. Cover, reduce heat, and simmer 3 hours or until hen is tender. Remove hen, reserving broth in pan. Let hen cool; skin, bone and, coarsely chop meat. Set meat aside; reserve ¾ cup broth. Bring remaining broth to a boil.

Combine flour, baking powder, and ½ teaspoon salt in a medium bowl; stir well. Add reserved ¾ cup broth, egg, and next 4 ingredients, stirring with a fork until dry ingredients are moistened. Turn dough out onto a heavily floured surface, and knead lightly 4 or 5 times. Roll dough to ⅛-inch thickness. Cut into 1½-inch squares, and drop into boiling broth. Reduce heat to medium; cook 15 minutes or until dumplings are tender, stirring occasionally. Stir in meat, and cook until thoroughly heated. Yield: 8 servings.   Ione Berry

Angel Food: Recipes and Reflections from Great Catholic Kitchens
The Sacred Heart Program
St. Louis, Missouri

Chicken Normandy

This recipe title refers to chicken that is cooked in the style of the Normandy region of northern France. Whipping cream, apples, and brandy are used in abundance in the region.

1 (3½-pound) broiler-fryer
½ teaspoon salt
¼ teaspoon pepper
1¼ cups apple juice
3 tablespoons brandy (optional)
1 medium onion, chopped
1 cup peeled and sliced cooking
  apple
1 cup sliced fresh mushrooms
¼ cup butter or margarine,
  melted
½ cup whipping cream
1 tablespoon cornstarch
¼ cup cold water

Remove giblets, and rinse chicken with cold water; pat dry. Sprinkle with salt and pepper. Place chicken, breast side up, on a lightly greased rack in a shallow roasting pan. Insert meat thermometer into meaty portion of thigh, making sure it does not touch bone. Combine apple juice and brandy, if desired; pour into pan. Bake, uncovered, at 350° for 1 hour or until meat thermometer registers 180°, basting every 15 minutes with apple juice mixture.

Remove chicken to a serving platter, reserving drippings in pan; set chicken aside, and keep warm. Pour drippings through a wire-mesh strainer into a medium saucepan; discard solids. Set drippings aside.

Cook onion, apple, and mushrooms in butter in a large skillet over medium-high heat, stirring constantly, until tender.

Add whipping cream to drippings in saucepan; bring to a boil over medium heat. Combine cornstarch and water, stirring until smooth. Stir into whipping cream mixture; return to a boil, and boil 1 minute, stirring constantly. Stir in apple mixture; cook over medium heat, stirring constantly, until thoroughly heated. Serve chicken with warm sauce. Yield: 4 servings.

Larry Brown

The Company's Cookin'
Employees of the Rouse Company
Columbia, Maryland

Rip's Barbecued Chicken

1 (5-ounce) bottle
  Worcestershire sauce
½ cup plus 2 tablespoons water
½ cup plus 2 tablespoons cider
  vinegar
2 tablespoons butter
2 to 3 slices bacon, chopped
1 clove garlic, crushed
1 teaspoon grated lemon rind

½ teaspoon salt
½ teaspoon pepper
½ teaspoon celery salt
½ tablespoon prepared mustard
⅛ teaspoon hot sauce
3 (1½-pound) broiler-fryers,
  halved
½ teaspoon salt
¼ teaspoon pepper

Combine first 12 ingredients in a medium saucepan; bring to a boil. Reduce heat, and simmer, uncovered, 30 minutes.

Sprinkle chicken with ½ teaspoon salt and ¼ teaspoon pepper. Grill, covered, over medium-hot coals (350° to 400°) 15 minutes, turning occasionally. Baste chicken with sauce. Grill, covered, 40 to 45 additional minutes or until chicken is done, turning and basting occasionally. Yield: 6 servings.   Roberta Torn

M.D. Anderson Volunteers Cooking for Fun
University of Texas M.D. Anderson Cancer Center
Houston, Texas

Oven-Fried Chicken with Honey-Butter Sauce

A basting mixture of honey, butter, and lemon juice gives this chicken a golden color and sweet flavor.

1 cup all-purpose flour
2 tablespoons paprika
2 teaspoons salt
¼ teaspoon pepper
1 (3½- to 4-pound) broiler-fryer,
  cut up

¾ cup butter or margarine,
  melted and divided
¼ cup lemon juice
¼ cup honey

Combine first 4 ingredients; dredge chicken in flour mixture. Place ½ cup butter in a shallow roasting pan. Add chicken, turning to coat. Bake, uncovered, skin side down, at 400° for 30 minutes.

Combine remaining ¼ cup butter, lemon juice, and honey. Turn chicken; pour honey mixture over chicken. Bake, uncovered, 20 additional minutes or until chicken is done, basting frequently with honey mixture. Yield: 4 servings.   Lu Ann Forsyth

Fiddlers Canyon Ward Cookbook
Fiddlers Canyon Ward Relief Society
Cedar City, Utah

Spiced Chicken

1 cup chopped onion	1 ripe papaya, peeled, seeded,
2 cloves garlic, minced	and cubed
3 tablespoons vegetable oil,	1 tablespoon cornstarch
divided	2 tablespoons cold water
1 (2½- to 3-pound) broiler-fryer,	Salt to taste
cut up	1 ripe avocado, peeled and
1½ cups orange juice	sliced
2 tablespoons sliced ripe olives	¼ cup slivered almonds, toasted
1½ teaspoons ground ginger	

Cook onion and garlic in 1 tablespoon oil in a large skillet over medium-high heat, stirring constantly, until tender. Remove onion mixture from skillet, and set aside.

Brown chicken pieces in remaining 2 tablespoons oil in skillet over medium-high heat; drain.

Return onion mixture and chicken to skillet. Add orange juice, olives, and ginger; stir well. Place papaya on top of chicken mixture. Bring to a boil; cover, reduce heat, and simmer 25 minutes. Remove chicken and papaya to a serving platter, reserving onion mixture and drippings in skillet.

Combine cornstarch and water, stirring until smooth. Stir into mixture in skillet. Bring to a boil; cook, stirring constantly, until thickened. Stir in salt to taste. Pour sauce over chicken and papaya; arrange avocado slices around chicken mixture. Sprinkle with almonds. Yield: 4 servings.   Joanne DeFiore

Flavors of Cape Henlopen
Village Improvement Association
Rehoboth Beach, Delaware

Maine Maple Chicken

The sweetness of real maple syrup is balanced by the tanginess of the tomato paste, white vinegar, and Dijon mustard mixture in this unique version of sweet-and-sour chicken.

5 chicken breast quarters
1 large onion, sliced
½ cup water
1 (6-ounce) can tomato paste
½ cup maple syrup
¼ cup white vinegar

¼ cup olive oil
2 tablespoons Dijon mustard
Salt and freshly ground pepper
   to taste
Garnish: fresh parsley sprigs

Place chicken, skin side up, in a lightly greased 13- x 9- x 2-inch baking dish. Place onion slices between chicken pieces. Pour water over chicken and onion. Bake, uncovered, at 375° for 30 minutes.

Combine tomato paste and next 4 ingredients. Stir in salt and pepper to taste, and pour over chicken. Bake 20 additional minutes or until chicken is done, basting frequently with tomato paste mixture. Garnish, if desired. Yield: 5 servings.

Brenda Curley

The Maine Collection
Portland Museum of Art
Portland, Maine

Chicken with Tarragon-Caper Sauce

The rich cream and caper sauce disguises the quick and easy nature of this elegant chicken entrée.

4 skinned and boned chicken
   breast halves
3 tablespoons vegetable oil
½ cup whipping cream
1 tablespoon capers

1 teaspoon lemon juice
1 tablespoon butter or
   margarine
½ teaspoon dried tarragon

Place chicken between 2 sheets of heavy-duty plastic wrap, and flatten to ¼-inch thickness, using a meat mallet or rolling pin.

Cook chicken in oil in a large skillet over medium heat 5 minutes on each side or until done. Remove chicken to a serving platter, reserving drippings in skillet. Set chicken aside, and keep warm.

Add whipping cream, capers, and lemon juice to drippings in skillet; bring to a boil. Remove from heat; add butter and tarragon, stirring until butter melts. Spoon sauce over chicken. Serve immediately. Yield: 4 servings.

Southwest Seasons Cookbook
Casa Angelica Auxiliary
Albuquerque, New Mexico*

Chicken Diane

4 (4-ounce) skinned and boned chicken breast halves	3 tablespoons chopped fresh chives
½ teaspoon salt	3 tablespoons chopped fresh parsley
½ teaspoon pepper	2 tablespoons brandy
2 tablespoons vegetable oil, divided	1 tablespoon fresh lime juice
2 tablespoons butter or margarine, melted and divided	2 teaspoons Dijon mustard
	¼ cup chicken broth

Place chicken between 2 sheets of heavy-duty plastic wrap, and flatten to ¼-inch thickness, using a meat mallet or rolling pin. Sprinkle with salt and pepper.

Cook chicken in 1 tablespoon oil and 1 tablespoon butter in a large skillet over medium-high heat 5 minutes on each side. Remove chicken to a serving platter, reserving drippings in skillet. Set chicken aside, and keep warm.

Add chives and next 4 ingredients to drippings in skillet; cook 15 seconds, stirring constantly. Add chicken broth, and cook, stirring constantly, until smooth. Stir in remaining 1 tablespoon oil and 1 tablespoon butter. Pour sauce over chicken. Serve immediately. Yield: 4 servings.

Carla Carter

Champions: Favorite Foods of Indy Car Racing
Championship Auto Racing Auxiliary
Indianapolis, Indiana*

Garden Chicken

Raid your vegetable garden or local produce market to find everything you need to create this vegetable-packed meal.

6 skinned and boned chicken breast halves
3 tablespoons all-purpose flour
3 tablespoons olive oil
½ pound fresh mushrooms, sliced
½ cup chopped celery
2 carrots, scraped and diagonally sliced
1 small eggplant, peeled and cubed
1 medium-size green pepper, cut into ½-inch strips
1 medium-size sweet red pepper, cut into ½-inch strips
1 small onion, chopped
2 cloves garlic, thinly sliced
1 chicken-flavored bouillon cube
¾ cup hot water
1 (15-ounce) can tomato sauce
½ cup Marsala
1 teaspoon dried oregano
½ teaspoon dried basil
Dash of dried thyme
Dash of black pepper
8 ounces rotini, uncooked

Dredge chicken in flour; brown chicken in oil in a large skillet over medium-high heat 4 to 5 minutes on each side. Remove chicken, reserving drippings in skillet. Set chicken aside, and keep warm. Cook mushrooms and next 7 ingredients in drippings in skillet, stirring constantly, 3 minutes or until carrot and celery are crisp-tender.

Dissolve bouillon cube in hot water; add to vegetable mixture. Stir in tomato sauce and next 5 ingredients; place chicken on top of sauce. Bring to a boil; cover, reduce heat, and simmer 25 minutes or until chicken is done.

Cook pasta according to package directions; drain well. Arrange pasta on a serving platter; spoon sauce over pasta, and top with chicken. Serve immediately. Yield: 6 servings.   Carrie Lee Davis

Celebrated South Carolinians!
American Cancer Society
Columbia, South Carolina

Hudson Valley Chicken

1 large cooking apple, peeled, cored, and chopped
¼ cup plus 3 tablespoons butter or margarine, melted and divided
1 teaspoon honey
1 teaspoon fresh lemon juice
3 tablespoons all-purpose flour
½ teaspoon salt
¼ teaspoon pepper
4 skinned and boned chicken breast halves
1 cup chicken broth
1 cup apple juice
½ cup cranberry juice cocktail
¼ cup apple brandy (optional)
1 (1-inch) stick cinnamon
Chopped fresh chives

Cook apple in 2 tablespoons butter, honey, and lemon juice in a large skillet over medium-high heat, stirring constantly, until apple is golden. Remove apple, reserving butter mixture in skillet; set apple aside.

Combine flour, salt, and pepper; dredge chicken in flour mixture. Cook chicken in reserved butter mixture and 2 tablespoons butter in skillet over medium heat 4 to 5 minutes on each side or until chicken is done. Remove chicken to a serving platter, reserving drippings in skillet. Set chicken aside, and keep warm.

Add chicken broth, apple juice, cranberry juice cocktail, brandy, if desired, and cinnamon stick to skillet. Bring to a boil; boil 13 minutes or until mixture is reduced to ⅔ cup, stirring occasionally. Stir in apple and remaining 3 tablespoons butter. Remove and discard cinnamon stick. Spoon sauce over chicken; sprinkle with chives. Yield: 4 servings.

Nancy Kloppenborg

Feeding the Flock
Holy Family Parish
Davenport, Iowa

Chicken Joseph Monroe

A touch of nutmeg brings out the flavor of the blue cheese and Swiss cheese balls nestled in these fancy chicken bundles.

¼ cup butter
6½ ounces cream cheese, softened
⅓ cup crumbled blue cheese
¼ cup plus 1 tablespoon butter or margarine, softened
¼ teaspoon ground nutmeg
¾ cup (3 ounces) shredded Swiss cheese

6 (4-ounce) skinned and boned chicken breast halves
1 tablespoon Dijon mustard
⅓ cup all-purpose flour
1 large egg, beaten
½ cup fine, dry breadcrumbs

Melt ¼ cup butter over low heat. The fat will rise to the top, and the milk solids will sink to the bottom. Skim off the white froth that appears on top. Then strain off the clear, yellow clarified butter, keeping back the sediment of milk solids. Set clarified butter aside.

Combine cream cheese and next 3 ingredients in a large mixing bowl; beat at medium speed of an electric mixer until creamy. Shape mixture into 6 balls; roll in Swiss cheese. Cover and chill 1 hour.

Place chicken between 2 sheets of heavy-duty plastic wrap, and flatten to ¼-inch thickness, using a meat mallet or rolling pin. Spread mustard evenly over each chicken breast half. Top each with a chilled cheese ball. Fold long sides of chicken over cheese ball; fold ends over, and secure with wooden picks. Dredge chicken in flour; dip in egg, and roll in breadcrumbs. Cover and chill 1 hour.

Brown chicken in clarified butter in a large ovenproof skillet over high heat 2 to 3 minutes. Place skillet in oven; bake, uncovered, at 400° for 7 minutes or until chicken is done. Remove and discard wooden picks. Yield: 6 servings.   Millie Martinus

Our Favorite Recipes
Unity Truth Center
Port Richey, Florida

Chicken Marbella

You can prepare this chicken dish with assorted chicken pieces instead of breasts. Skin the chicken pieces before marinating.

⅓ cup capers, undrained
1 cup pitted prunes
¾ cup firmly packed brown
  sugar
¾ cup dry white wine
½ cup pimiento-stuffed olives
⅓ cup red wine vinegar
⅓ cup olive oil
¼ cup dried oregano

9 cloves garlic, minced
3 or 4 bay leaves
½ teaspoon kosher salt
½ teaspoon freshly ground
  pepper
16 skinned and boned chicken
  breast halves
¼ cup chopped fresh parsley

Drain capers, reserving 1 tablespoon juice. Combine capers, reserved caper juice, and next 11 ingredients in a large shallow dish, stirring until blended. Add chicken, turning to coat. Cover and marinate in refrigerator 8 hours.

Remove chicken from marinade, reserving marinade. Arrange chicken in 2 ungreased 13- x 9- x 2-inch baking dishes. Spoon marinade evenly over chicken. Bake, uncovered, at 350° for 45 minutes or until chicken is done, basting frequently with marinade.

Remove chicken and prune mixture to a serving platter; sprinkle with parsley. Serve with marinade. Yield: 8 servings.   Joe Alber

CAP-tivating Cooking
YWCA of Peoria, Children and Parents Support
Peoria, Illinois

Marinated Chicken Breasts

1½ cups sour cream
1 clove garlic, minced
2 tablespoons lemon juice
1 teaspoon salt
1 teaspoon seasoned salt
1 teaspoon paprika

¼ teaspoon hot sauce
3 pounds skinned and boned
  chicken breast halves
1¼ cups fine, dry breadcrumbs
½ cup butter or margarine,
  melted

Combine first 7 ingredients in a large bowl; add chicken. Cover and marinate in refrigerator 8 hours. Remove chicken from marinade, discarding marinade.

Dredge chicken in breadcrumbs. Place in a single layer in 2 ungreased 13- x 9- x 2-inch baking dishes. Drizzle butter over chicken. Bake, uncovered, at 350° for 40 to 50 minutes or until chicken is done. Yield: 6 servings.   Sue A. Bauer

Lawtons Progressors, 50 Years and Still Cookin'
Lawtons Progressors 4-H Club
North Collins, New York

Crunchy Pecan Chicken

Buttermilk biscuit mix, Creole seasoning, and finely chopped pecans join forces to make a crispy and flavorful coating for these chicken breast halves.

1 cup buttermilk biscuit and
  baking mix
½ cup finely chopped pecans
1 teaspoon paprika
½ teaspoon salt
½ teaspoon Creole seasoning

4 skinned and boned chicken
  breast halves
½ cup buttermilk
½ cup unsalted butter or
  margarine, melted

Combine first 5 ingredients in a medium bowl; stir well. Dip chicken in buttermilk; dredge in pecan mixture. Place chicken in an ungreased 13- x 9- x 2-inch pan. Drizzle butter over chicken. Bake, uncovered, at 350° for 50 minutes or until chicken is done. Yield: 4 servings.

Come On In!
The Junior League of Jackson, Mississippi

Chicken Stroganoff

1 cup finely chopped onion
3 cloves garlic, minced
1 tablespoon sweet Hungarian paprika
1 teaspoon salt
¼ cup butter or margarine, melted
6 skinned and boned chicken breast halves, cut into 1-inch pieces
1½ cups chopped fresh mushrooms
2 tablespoons butter or margarine
3 tablespoons all-purpose flour
½ cup half-and-half
1 cup dry white wine
1 (8-ounce) carton sour cream
2 (9-ounce) packages refrigerated fettuccine

Cook first 4 ingredients in ¼ cup melted butter in a large skillet over medium-high heat, stirring constantly, until onion is tender. Add chicken, and cook 5 to 10 minutes or until chicken is done. Stir in mushrooms; cover, reduce heat, and simmer 3 minutes.

Melt 2 tablespoons butter in a heavy saucepan over low heat; add flour, stirring until smooth. Cook 1 minute, stirring constantly. Gradually add half-and-half; cook over medium heat, stirring constantly, until mixture is thickened and bubbly. Stir in wine. Pour over chicken mixture. Cook, uncovered, over low heat 7 minutes. Remove from heat; stir in sour cream.

Cook fettuccine according to package directions; drain well.

Combine chicken mixture and fettuccine; toss gently. Serve immediately. Yield: 6 servings. Esther Engemoen

Idalia Community Cookbook
Women's Fellowship of St. John United Church of Christ
Idalia, Colorado

Szechuan Chicken with Peppers and Cashews

Dried crushed red pepper adds a spicy kick to this Szechuan stir-fry.

¼ cup vegetable oil
½ to 1 teaspoon dried crushed red pepper
4 skinned and boned chicken breast halves, cut into ¾-inch pieces
1 medium-size green pepper, cut into thin strips
1 medium-size sweet red pepper, cut into thin strips

1 medium-size sweet yellow pepper, cut into thin strips
Ginger-Sherry Sauce
4 green onions, sliced diagonally
2½ tablespoons cornstarch
¼ cup cold water
½ cup unsalted cashews, toasted
Hot cooked rice

Pour oil around top of a preheated wok, coating sides; heat at medium-high (375°) for 2 minutes. Add crushed red pepper, and stir-fry 30 seconds. Add chicken, and stir-fry 2 minutes. Remove chicken from wok, and set aside. Add pepper strips to wok, and stir-fry 1 minute. Add Ginger-Sherry Sauce, chicken, and green onions to wok. Combine cornstarch and water, stirring until smooth. Stir into mixture in wok; cook, stirring constantly, until thickened. Stir in cashews. Serve over rice. Yield: 4 servings.

Ginger-Sherry Sauce

⅓ cup water
¼ cup soy sauce
1 tablespoon plus 1 teaspoon sugar

2 tablespoons dry sherry
1 tablespoon grated fresh ginger
2½ teaspoons white vinegar

Combine all ingredients in a small bowl, stirring well. Yield: ¾ cup.

Heard in the Kitchen
The Heard Museum Guild
Phoenix, Arizona

Chicken in Phyllo

Delicate, paper-thin sheets of crisp phyllo pastry encase this savory mixture of chicken and spinach.

2 (10-ounce) packages frozen chopped spinach
3 cups chopped cooked chicken
½ teaspoon dried oregano
¼ teaspoon salt
¼ teaspoon pepper
1 medium onion, chopped
1 tablespoon vegetable oil
3 large eggs, lightly beaten
⅛ teaspoon ground cumin
⅛ teaspoon ground nutmeg
⅛ teaspoon ground cardamom

⅛ teaspoon ground cinnamon
16 sheets frozen phyllo pastry, thawed in refrigerator
½ cup butter or margarine, melted
1 (28-ounce) can Italian-style tomatoes, drained and chopped
2 cups (8 ounces) shredded Swiss cheese
1 cup pine nuts, toasted

Cook chopped spinach according to package directions; drain well, and set aside.

Sprinkle chicken with oregano, salt, and pepper; set aside.

Cook onion in oil in a large skillet over medium-high heat, stirring constantly, until tender. Stir in spinach, beaten eggs, and next 4 ingredients; set aside.

Brush 1 sheet of phyllo with melted butter (keeping remaining phyllo sheets covered with a slightly damp towel). Place in a lightly greased 15- x 10- x 1-inch jellyroll pan. Repeat procedure with 7 additional phyllo sheets and butter.

Spoon chicken over phyllo in pan. Spoon spinach mixture over chicken; sprinkle with tomatoes, cheese, and pine nuts. Top with remaining 8 sheets of phyllo, brushing each sheet with melted butter. Trim pastry; moisten edges of pastry with water, and press together to seal. Bake, uncovered, at 350° for 1 hour or until golden. Cut into squares. Yield: 10 servings.

Nothin' Finer
Chapel Hill Service League
Chapel Hill, North Carolina

Turkey Baked in White Wine with Oyster Dressing

1 (12-pound) turkey
½ teaspoon garlic salt
½ teaspoon salt
½ teaspoon pepper
2 tablespoons butter or margarine

1 tablespoon all-purpose flour
2 cups dry white wine
1 cup water
1 tablespoon dried thyme
1 tablespoon dried basil
Oyster Dressing

Remove giblets, and rinse turkey thoroughly with cold water; pat dry. Sprinkle cavity with garlic salt, salt, and pepper. Tie ends of legs together with string. Lift wingtips up and over back, and tuck under bird. Rub outside of turkey with butter.

Shake flour in a large oven cooking bag, and place in a large roasting pan. Place turkey in bag. Combine wine and water. Pour 2 cups wine mixture into cavity of turkey. Combine remaining 1 cup wine mixture, thyme, and basil; pour over turkey. Close cooking bag, and seal. Make 6 (½-inch) slits in top of bag, following package directions. Insert meat thermometer through bag into meaty portion of thigh, making sure it does not touch bone. Bake at 325° until meat thermometer registers 180° (about 2 hours).

Remove roasting pan from oven; carefully cut a large slit in top of cooking bag. Remove turkey from bag, reserving ½ cup drippings for dressing. Let stand 15 minutes before carving. Serve with Oyster Dressing. Yield: 12 servings.

Oyster Dressing

1 cup chopped onion
1 cup chopped celery with leaves
½ cup butter or margarine, melted
8 cups torn day-old white bread
2 tablespoons chopped fresh parsley
½ teaspoon salt

½ teaspoon poultry seasoning
½ teaspoon hot sauce
¾ cup dry white wine
½ cup turkey drippings
1 (12-ounce) container fresh Standard oysters, drained and chopped
½ cup sliced fresh mushrooms

Cook onion and celery in butter in a large skillet over medium-high heat, stirring constantly, until tender. Combine vegetable mixture, bread, and next 4 ingredients in a large bowl. Add wine and turkey drippings, tossing gently. Add oysters and mushrooms; toss well. Spoon into a lightly greased 11- x 7- x 1½-inch baking dish. Cover and bake at 325° for 45 minutes. Uncover and bake 15 additional minutes or until lightly browned. Yield: 12 servings.

Still Gathering: A Centennial Celebration
Auxiliary to the American Osteopathic Association
Chicago, Illinois

Turkey Breast with Orange and Rosemary

A few distinctive ingredients such as balsamic vinegar, honey, and rosemary, turn a simple grilled turkey breast into a spectacular entrée.

1 (1½- to 2-pound) skinned and boned turkey breast	2 teaspoons dried rosemary, crushed
½ cup fresh orange juice	1 teaspoon salt
3 tablespoons olive oil	⅛ teaspoon dried crushed red pepper
2 tablespoons balsamic vinegar	
1 tablespoon honey	

Place turkey breast between 2 sheets of heavy-duty plastic wrap, and flatten to 1-inch thickness, using a meat mallet or rolling pin. Place turkey in a large heavy-duty, zip-top plastic bag.

Combine orange juice and next 6 ingredients in a jar. Cover tightly, and shake vigorously. Pour marinade mixture over turkey; seal bag securely. Marinate in refrigerator 8 hours, turning occasionally.

Remove turkey from marinade, reserving marinade. Bring marinade to a boil in a small saucepan; set aside.

Grill turkey, covered, over medium-hot coals (350° to 400°) 24 minutes or until done, turning and basting occasionally with marinade. Yield: 6 servings.

Back Home Again
The Junior League of Indianapolis, Indiana

Ground Turkey Gourmet

What's gourmet about ground turkey patties? These are laced with capers, cilantro, and sage and topped with a sauce of mushrooms, shallots, and wine. They're a sure bet to please the most discriminating palate.

1 pound fresh ground turkey
2 tablespoons capers, chopped
2 tablespoons chopped green onions
1 large egg, lightly beaten
1 tablespoon chopped fresh cilantro
1 tablespoon Worcestershire sauce
½ teaspoon salt
½ teaspoon ground sage
Dash of pepper
1 tablespoon plus 1 teaspoon olive oil, divided
1 cup quartered fresh mushrooms
2 tablespoons minced shallots
¼ cup dry white wine

Combine first 9 ingredients in a large bowl; stir well. Shape mixture into 4 (¾-inch-thick) patties.

Cook patties in 1 tablespoon olive oil in large skillet over medium-high heat 4 to 5 minutes on each side or until done. Remove patties to a serving platter, reserving drippings in skillet; set patties aside, and keep warm.

Cook mushrooms and shallot in drippings and remaining 1 teaspoon oil in skillet over medium-high heat, stirring constantly, until vegetables are tender. Add wine; bring to a boil. Cover, reduce heat, and simmer 2 minutes. Top patties with sauce. Serve immediately. Yield: 4 servings.

Helen L. Schmidt

Heavenly Hosts
Bryn Mawr Presbyterian Church
Bryn Mawr, Pennsylvania

Dijon Cornish Game Hens

4 (1½-pound) Cornish hens
1 (8-ounce) carton sour cream
½ cup Dijon mustard
⅔ cup fine, dry breadcrumbs
¼ cup chopped fresh parsley

Remove giblets, and rinse hens thoroughly with cold water; pat dry. Lift wingtips up and over back of hens, tucking wingtips under hens. Place, breast side up, in an ungreased 13- x 9- x 2-inch baking dish.

Combine sour cream and mustard; brush over entire surface of hens. Combine breadcrumbs and parsley; sprinkle evenly over hens. Bake, uncovered, at 425° for 45 minutes or until hens are done. Yield: 4 servings.   Rita Knox

Cookin' with Fire
Milford Permanent Firefighters Association
Milford, Massachusetts

Happy Holiday Hens

Happy hens are hens stuffed with rice, pecans, and apricots. Coat them with a glaze of apricot preserves, and they're absolutely giddy!

4 (1½-pound) Cornish hens
½ cup apricot preserves
⅓ cup soy sauce
½ teaspoon ground nutmeg
2 cups cooked rice
1 tablespoon plus 1 teaspoon
    soy sauce

½ cup minced green onions
½ cup pecan pieces, toasted
⅓ cup chopped dried apricot
    halves

Remove giblets, and rinse hens thoroughly with cold water; pat dry. Lift wingtips up and over back of hens, tucking wingtips under hens.

Combine preserves, ⅓ cup soy sauce, and nutmeg. Brush cavities of hens lightly with preserve mixture.

Combine rice and 1 tablespoon plus 1 teaspoon soy sauce, stirring well. Add green onions, pecans, and apricot; stir well. Stuff hens evenly with rice mixture, and close cavities. Secure with wooden picks, and tie leg ends together with string.

Place hens, breast side up, on a lightly greased rack in a shallow roasting pan. Brush lightly with preserve mixture. Bake, uncovered, at 375° for 45 minutes. Cover and bake 45 additional minutes or until done, basting with remaining preserve mixture. Yield: 4 servings.

From Generation to Generation
Sisterhood of Temple Emanu-El
Dallas, Texas

Father George's Quail Supreme

8 quail
¾ cup all-purpose flour
1 teaspoon salt
½ teaspoon pepper
¼ cup plus 2 tablespoons butter,
  melted and divided
½ cup dry white wine
½ cup chopped onion

½ cup chopped fresh
  mushrooms
¼ cup dry sherry
2 tablespoons butter, softened
Salt and pepper to taste
8 (½-inch) slices French bread,
  lightly toasted
Plum Sauce

Split quail lengthwise to, but not through, the breast bone; spread quail open, and pat dry. Combine flour, 1 teaspoon salt, and ½ teaspoon pepper; dredge quail in flour mixture.

Brown quail in ¼ cup butter in a large skillet over medium heat. Remove quail to an ungreased 13- x 9- x 2-inch baking dish, reserving drippings in skillet. Add wine to drippings; bring to a boil, deglazing pan by scraping particles that cling to bottom. Pour over quail. Bake, uncovered, at 350° for 30 minutes.

Cook onion and mushrooms in remaining 2 tablespoons melted butter in skillet over medium-high heat, stirring constantly, until tender. Cool. Combine vegetables, sherry, 2 tablespoons butter, and salt and pepper to taste; stir well. Spread evenly over bread slices. Broil 5½ inches from heat (with electric oven door partially opened) 2 minutes or until hot and bubbly. Place bread on a serving platter; top with quail. Serve with warm Plum Sauce. Yield: 4 servings.

Plum Sauce

1 cup red plum jam
1 tablespoon grated orange rind
½ cup fresh orange juice
1 tablespoon grated lemon rind

2 tablespoons fresh lemon juice
1 tablespoon cornstarch
½ teaspoon dry mustard

Combine first 5 ingredients in a small saucepan; add cornstarch and mustard, stirring well. Cook over medium heat, stirring constantly, until thickened and bubbly. Yield: 1½ cups.

Gracious Goodness, Charleston!
Bishop England High School Endowment Fund
Charleston, South Carolina

Salads

Ketchup Salad Dressing, page 272

Frozen Banana Salad

If you'd like to prepare these individual salads ahead, you can store them in heavy-duty, zip-top plastic bags in the freezer up to 1 month.

1 (16-ounce) carton sour cream
¾ cup sugar
2 tablespoons lemon juice
Dash of salt
2 medium-size ripe bananas,
  mashed

1 (8-ounce) can crushed
  pineapple, drained
⅓ cup chopped pecans
4 maraschino cherries, drained
  and chopped
Lettuce leaves (optional)

Combine first 4 ingredients in a large bowl; stir well. Fold in mashed banana and next 3 ingredients. Spoon evenly into paper-lined muffin pans. Freeze 3 hours or until firm. Unmold onto lettuce leaves, if desired. Serve immediately. Yield: 16 servings.   Ruth Shraga

Phi Bete's Best
Theta Alpha Gamma Chapter
Bedford, Indiana

Orange-Date Salad with Peanut Butter Dressing

½ cup sour cream
½ cup creamy peanut
  butter
¼ cup plus 2 tablespoons milk
¼ teaspoon salt
Dash of garlic powder
6 cups mixed salad greens

1 (8-ounce) package pitted
  dates, chopped
6 oranges, peeled, sectioned,
  and coarsely chopped
¼ cup chopped unsalted dry
  roasted peanuts
½ cup flaked coconut, toasted

Combine first 5 ingredients in a bowl; stir well. Cover and chill. Place greens in a bowl. Combine dates, oranges, and peanuts; spoon over greens. Drizzle with ¼ cup dressing. Sprinkle with coconut. Serve with remaining dressing. Yield: 6 servings.   Ileane Haas

Home Cookin'
Volunteer Services Council for Abilene State School
Abilene, Texas

Company Salad

Consider this make-ahead gelatin salad for your next potluck dinner. Cut it into squares when you get to your destination.

1 (3-ounce) package lemon-
    flavored gelatin
1½ cups boiling water
1½ cups miniature
    marshmallows
1 (20-ounce) can crushed
    pineapple, undrained
3 medium-size ripe bananas,
    sliced

½ cup sugar
1½ tablespoons all-purpose
    flour
1 large egg, lightly beaten
1 cup whipping cream
½ cup (2 ounces) shredded
    sharp Cheddar cheese

Place gelatin in a medium bowl; add boiling water, and stir 2 minutes or until gelatin dissolves. Add marshmallows, stirring gently until marshmallows dissolve. Let cool 30 minutes.

Drain pineapple, reserving liquid. Stir pineapple and banana into gelatin mixture. Pour into an ungreased 11- x 7- x 1½-inch dish. Cover and chill 3 hours or until firm.

Combine pineapple liquid, sugar, flour, and egg in a small saucepan; stir well. Cook over medium heat, stirring constantly, until mixture is thickened. Let cool.

Beat whipping cream until soft peaks form. Fold whipped cream into egg mixture. Spread evenly over gelatin mixture; sprinkle with Cheddar cheese. Cover and chill thoroughly. Cut into squares. Yield: 8 servings.

Kathy Huffman

Holiday Sampler
Welcome Wagon Club of the Mid Ohio Valley
Parkersburg, West Virginia

Festive Raspberry Salad

This chilled rice salad is pretty and sweet enough to do double-duty as a dessert—it's drizzled with a bright-red raspberry sauce.

1 (10-ounce) package frozen
   raspberries, thawed
½ cup red currant jelly
1½ teaspoons cornstarch
1 tablespoon cold water
2 cups milk
½ cup long-grain rice, uncooked

½ teaspoon salt
1 envelope unflavored gelatin
¼ cup cold water
1 cup whipping cream
⅓ cup sugar
¼ teaspoon almond extract

Combine raspberries and jelly in a small saucepan; stir well, and bring to a boil. Combine cornstarch and 1 tablespoon cold water, stirring until smooth. Gradually stir into hot raspberry mixture. Cook over medium heat, stirring constantly, 5 minutes or until sauce is thickened. Cover and chill.

Combine milk, rice, and salt in a medium saucepan. Bring to a boil; cover, reduce heat, and simmer 25 minutes or until liquid is absorbed and rice is tender.

Sprinkle gelatin over ¼ cup cold water; stir and let stand 1 minute. Add gelatin mixture to rice mixture, stirring well. Cover and chill 1 hour or until slightly thickened.

Beat whipping cream until foamy; gradually add sugar, beating until soft peaks form. Stir in almond extract. Gently fold whipped cream mixture into chilled rice mixture. Spoon into a lightly oiled 4-cup mold. Cover and chill until firm. Unmold salad onto a serving plate; drizzle with ¼ cup sauce. Serve salad with remaining sauce. Yield: 8 servings.

Florence Roth

Sisseton Centennial Cookbook
Sisseton Centennial Committee
Sisseton, South Dakota

Basil-Scented White Bean Salad with Olive Croutons

The olive paste used on these croutons is available at specialty food stores. You can make your own olive paste by processing pitted kalamata olives in your food processor until a paste forms.

2 cups dried navy beans
2 quarts water
4 bay leaves
1 large onion, coarsely chopped
1 large purple onion, coarsely chopped
4 shallots, sliced
4 cloves garlic, sliced

2 tablespoons olive oil, divided
4 tomatoes, seeded and coarsely chopped
¼ cup tightly packed fresh basil leaves, cut into thin strips
¼ cup fresh lemon juice
Salt and pepper to taste
Olive Croutons

Wash and sort beans. Bring water to a boil in a Dutch oven; add beans and bay leaves. Cover and remove from heat. Let stand 1 hour. Bring to a boil; cover, reduce heat, and simmer 1 hour or until beans are tender. Drain; remove and discard bay leaves.

Cook onions, shallot, and garlic in 1 tablespoon oil in a large skillet over medium heat 40 minutes or until onions are lightly browned, stirring often.

Combine beans and onion mixture; stir gently, and let cool 30 minutes. Add remaining 1 tablespoon oil, tomato, basil, and lemon juice; toss gently. Add salt and pepper to taste. Serve immediately with Olive Croutons. Yield: 6 servings.

Olive Croutons

12 (½-inch) French baguette slices

1 tablespoon olive oil
½ cup olive paste

Place bread slices on an ungreased baking sheet; brush lightly with olive oil. Bake at 350° for 10 minutes or until lightly browned. Spread evenly with olive paste. Yield: 12 croutons.

Taste Without Waist
The Service League of Hickory, North Carolina

Herbed Garden Vegetable Salad

Pour the dressing for this salad over the vegetables while they're still warm. They'll absorb the maximum amount of the dressing if it's on them as they cool.

6 cups sliced red potatoes (about 2 pounds)
3 cups fresh cut green beans (about ¾ pound)
2 cups sliced carrots
¾ cup vegetable oil
⅓ cup cider vinegar

1 tablespoon dried parsley flakes
1½ teaspoons dried basil
½ teaspoon salt
½ teaspoon garlic powder
¼ teaspoon pepper
Chopped fresh chives

Arrange potato, green beans, and carrot in a vegetable steamer over boiling water. Cover and steam 14 minutes or until tender. Transfer vegetables to a large bowl. Set aside, and keep warm.

Combine oil and next 6 ingredients in a jar. Cover tightly, and shake vigorously. Pour ¾ cup dressing over warm vegetables; toss gently. Cover and chill thoroughly, tossing occasionally.

To serve, pour remaining dressing over vegetables, and toss gently. Sprinkle with chopped chives, and serve with a slotted spoon. Yield: 8 servings.

Eunice Boeckenhauer

A Flock of Good Recipes
Shepherd of the Bay Lutheran Church
Ellison Bay and Sister Bay, Wisconsin

South-of-the-Border Potato Salad

1¾ pounds new potatoes, unpeeled
1 large tomato, peeled and chopped
¼ cup chopped purple onion
¼ cup chopped green onions
¼ cup chopped fresh cilantro
¼ cup canned chopped green chiles, drained

2 cups mayonnaise
2 tablespoons lime juice
2 tablespoons Dijon mustard
1 clove garlic, crushed
¼ teaspoon ground red pepper
Garnishes: chopped tomato, chopped green onions

Cook potatoes in boiling water to cover 20 minutes or until tender; drain and let cool slightly. Cut into ½-inch pieces.

Combine potato, tomato, and next 4 ingredients in a large bowl; toss gently. Combine mayonnaise and next 4 ingredients; stir well. Pour dressing over potato mixture; toss. Cover and chill thoroughly. Garnish, if desired. Yield: 12 servings.   Tammy McHargue

Essence of Kansas: 4-H Cookbook, Taste Two
Kansas 4-H Foundation
Manhattan, Kansas

Bibb Salad with Raspberry-Maple Dressing

Sweet maple syrup balances the tanginess of raspberry vinegar in the 3-ingredient dressing for this upscale green salad.

8　cups loosely packed torn Bibb
　　lettuce
1　small purple onion, sliced and
　　separated into rings

½　cup crumbled goat cheese or
　　blue cheese
½　cup sunflower kernels
　　Raspberry-Maple Dressing

Combine lettuce and onion in a large bowl; toss gently. Divide lettuce mixture among 6 individual salad plates. Sprinkle evenly with cheese and sunflower kernels. Drizzle with Raspberry-Maple Dressing. Yield: 6 servings.

Raspberry-Maple Dressing

⅔　cup vegetable oil
¼　cup raspberry vinegar

2　tablespoons maple syrup

Combine oil, vinegar, and maple syrup in a jar. Cover tightly, and shake vigorously. Yield: 1 cup.   Cathy Perry

Ridgefield Cooks
Women's Committee of the Ridgefield Community Center
Ridgefield, Connecticut

Mixed Greens and Pear Salad with Walnut Vinaigrette

Walnut oil adds a decidedly nutty flavor and fragrance to this vinaigrette. Walnut oil is expensive, so be sure to store it in the refrigerator to maximize its shelf life.

½ cup walnuts
1 tablespoon walnut oil
10 cups loosely packed torn mixed greens

1 large firm ripe pear, unpeeled
Walnut Vinaigrette

Cook walnuts in oil in a small skillet over medium heat, stirring constantly, until golden. Remove walnuts with a slotted spoon; set aside, and let cool.

Place greens in a large bowl. Core pear, and cut in half lengthwise. Cut pear lengthwise into ¼-inch slices; place in a small bowl. Pour Walnut Vinaigrette over pear slices; toss gently. Remove pear slices with a slotted spoon, reserving vinaigrette; set pear slices aside. Pour vinaigrette over greens; toss gently.

Divide greens among 4 individual salad plates. Top evenly with pear slices, overlapping slightly. Sprinkle with walnuts. Serve immediately. Yield: 4 servings.

Walnut Vinaigrette

1 shallot
½ cup extra virgin olive oil
2 tablespoons walnut oil
2 tablespoons red wine vinegar
1 tablespoon Dijon mustard

½ teaspoon sugar
¼ teaspoon salt
⅛ teaspoon freshly ground pepper

Position knife blade in food processor bowl; add shallot. Process until minced; add olive oil and remaining ingredients. Process until blended, stopping once to scrape down sides. Yield: ¾ cup.

A Cleveland Collection
The Junior League of Cleveland, Ohio

Southwestern Layered Salad with Cilantro-Jalapeño Dressing

1 (15-ounce) can black beans, rinsed and drained
2 tablespoons vegetable oil
2 tablespoons white wine vinegar
½ teaspoon salt
½ cup chopped purple onion
2 cups loosely packed shredded iceberg lettuce
1½ cups peeled, seeded, and chopped tomato

1 (15-ounce) can white corn, drained
½ cup chopped green pepper
1 cup (4 ounces) shredded Monterey Jack cheese
1 ripe avocado, peeled and cut into 6 wedges
4 slices bacon, cooked and crumbled
Garnish: fresh cilantro sprig
Cilantro-Jalapeño Dressing

Combine first 4 ingredients in a bowl; cover and marinate in the refrigerator 2 hours. Drain beans, discarding marinade. Reserve 2 tablespoons beans. Toss remaining beans with onion. Place lettuce in a bowl; spoon bean mixture over lettuce. Reserve 1 tablespoon tomato. Sprinkle remaining tomato over bean layer. Combine corn and green pepper; reserve 2 tablespoons corn mixture. Spoon remaining corn mixture over tomato layer. Sprinkle with cheese; cover and chill.

To serve, arrange avocado slices on top of salad in spoke fashion. Spoon reserved beans, tomato, and corn mixture between slices. Sprinkle bacon between slices. Garnish, if desired. Serve with Cilantro-Jalapeño Dressing. Yield: 6 servings.

Cilantro-Jalapeño Dressing

½ cup white wine vinegar
4 pickled jalapeño peppers, seeded

1 teaspoon salt
⅔ cup olive oil
½ cup packed fresh cilantro

Combine first 3 ingredients in container of an electric blender; cover and process until smooth. With blender on high, gradually add oil in a slow, steady stream. Process until thick and smooth, stopping once to scrape down sides. Add cilantro, and blend until finely chopped. Cover and chill. Yield: 1¼ cups.

Sensational Seasons: A Taste & Tour of Arkansas
The Junior League of Fort Smith, Arkansas

Spinach, Basil, and Pine Nut Salad

Fresh basil leaves act as part of the salad greens in this aromatic spinach salad.

6 cups loosely packed torn fresh
  spinach
2 cups loosely packed torn fresh
  basil
½ cup pine nuts
3 cloves garlic, minced

½ cup olive oil
4 ounces cooked ham, cut into
  very thin strips
1 cup freshly grated Parmesan
  cheese

Combine spinach and basil in a large bowl; toss gently.

Cook pine nuts and garlic in oil in a large skillet over medium-high heat, stirring constantly, just until pine nuts begin to brown. Add ham, and cook 1 minute, stirring constantly. Immediately pour pine nut mixture over spinach mixture; sprinkle with cheese. Toss gently, and serve immediately. Yield: 4 servings.

Back Home Again
The Junior League of Indianapolis, Indiana

Barbecue Slaw

Move over ordinary coleslaw—this easy barbecue-flavored variation, made with ketchup, is sure to become a favorite in your family. Try a hot ketchup for a spicier slaw.

⅓ cup sugar
⅓ cup ketchup
⅓ cup white vinegar

11 cups shredded cabbage
  (about 1 medium cabbage)

Combine first 3 ingredients in a small saucepan; bring to a boil, stirring until sugar dissolves. Pour hot vinegar mixture over cabbage; toss well. Cover and chill at least 3 hours. Yield: 8 servings.

Nothin' Finer
Chapel Hill Service League
Chapel Hill, North Carolina

Fancy Rice

2 cups cooked rice
1 cup golden raisins
½ cup chopped walnuts
1 apple, unpeeled and diced
2 tablespoons brown sugar
3 tablespoons butter or
  margarine, melted

¼ cup vegetable oil
2 tablespoons low-sodium
  soy sauce
2 tablespoons rice vinegar
2 teaspoons sugar
1 teaspoon dry mustard
½ teaspoon garlic salt

Combine first 6 ingredients in a bowl; stir well. Combine oil and next 5 ingredients; stir with a wire whisk. Pour dressing over rice mixture; toss. Cover and chill. Yield: 8 servings.   Robbie Noreen

Recipes from the End of the Road
Homer Special Olympics
Homer, Alaska

Black Bean and Rice Salad

1 (16-ounce) package long-grain
  rice
2 (14½-ounce) cans ready-to-
  serve chicken broth
½ cup water
2 bay leaves
2 (15-ounce) cans black beans,
  rinsed and drained
1 medium-size sweet red
  pepper, diced

1 medium-size green pepper,
  diced
1 medium onion, diced
½ cup olive oil
½ cup chopped fresh cilantro
3 tablespoons orange juice
2 tablespoons red wine vinegar
2 teaspoons ground cumin
1⅛ teaspoons chili powder
Lettuce leaves

Combine first 4 ingredients in a medium saucepan. Bring to a boil; cover, reduce heat, and simmer 25 minutes or until liquid is absorbed and rice is tender. Remove and discard bay leaves. Remove rice to a bowl. Stir in beans and next 9 ingredients. Cover and chill. Serve on lettuce. Yield: 10 servings.   Florence Lee D. Wellons

Fabulous Foods
St. John's Hospital and Southern Illinois
University School of Medicine
Springfield, Illinois

Saffron-Orzo Salad

Saffron is the world's most expensive spice. Luckily, a little bit goes a long way towards adding pungent flavor and a beautiful golden color to this salad.

½ cup currants
1 cup boiling water
1 (16-ounce) package orzo
½ cup olive oil
¼ teaspoon ground saffron
2 cloves garlic, minced
3 tablespoons fresh lemon juice
2 teaspoons ground turmeric
1 teaspoon sugar

½ teaspoon salt
¼ teaspoon ground cumin
¼ teaspoon pepper
⅔ cup pine nuts, toasted
¼ cup chopped fresh mint
¼ cup chopped fresh parsley
3 tablespoons chopped fresh cilantro

Combine currants and boiling water; let stand 5 minutes. Drain; set aside. Cook orzo according to package directions; drain. Set aside, and keep warm.

Combine oil and saffron in a bowl. Let stand 15 minutes. Stir in garlic and next 6 ingredients. Add orzo; toss. Let cool. Add currants, pine nuts, and remaining ingredients; toss. Yield: 10 servings.

Quilted Quisine
Paoli Memorial Hospital Auxiliary
Paoli, Pennsylvania

Pasta Salad with Chicken and Basil

2 cups chicken broth
3 skinned and boned chicken breast halves
½ pound bacon, chopped
6 ounces rotini, uncooked
4 ounces mozzarella cheese, cut into ½-inch cubes
½ cup cherry tomatoes, halved
½ cup chopped fresh basil

3 tablespoons red wine vinegar
2 teaspoons salt-free herb-and-spice seasoning
1 teaspoon Dijon mustard
½ teaspoon salt
½ teaspoon freshly ground pepper
½ cup olive oil
½ cup sour cream

Bring chicken broth to a boil in a medium skillet. Add chicken; cover, reduce heat, and simmer until chicken is done. Remove chicken, discarding broth. Let chicken cool, and coarsely chop meat. Set aside.

Cook bacon in a large skillet until crisp; remove bacon, discarding drippings. Drain bacon on paper towels; set aside.

Cook pasta according to package directions; drain. Rinse pasta with cold water; drain well, and place in a bowl. Add chicken, bacon, cheese, tomato, and basil; toss gently.

Combine vinegar and next 4 ingredients in a small bowl, stirring with a wire whisk. Gradually add oil, beating until blended. Stir in sour cream. Pour dressing over pasta mixture; toss gently. Cover and chill at least 2 hours. Yield: 6 servings.

Gracious Goodness, Charleston!
Bishop England High School Endowment Fund
Charleston, South Carolina

Santa Fe Turkey and Rice Salad

Chiles and cilantro are two of the feisty-flavored ingredients in this colorful southwestern salad.

4 cups water
2 cups long-grain rice, uncooked
4 cups cubed cooked turkey
2 large tomatoes, chopped
2 cups diced green pepper
2 cups fresh or frozen whole kernel corn, thawed
⅔ cup chopped purple onion
1 cup olive oil
½ cup finely chopped fresh cilantro
¼ cup plus 2 tablespoons white wine vinegar
1 (4½-ounce) can chopped green chiles, drained
2 tablespoons Dijon mustard
2½ teaspoons ground cumin
1 teaspoon salt
1 teaspoon pepper
Red leaf lettuce
Garnish: sliced ripe avocado

Bring water to a boil in a large saucepan; stir in rice. Cover, reduce heat, and simmer 20 minutes or until water is absorbed and rice is tender. Let cool.

Combine rice, turkey, and next 4 ingredients in a bowl; toss. Combine oil and next 7 ingredients; stir well. Pour dressing over rice mixture; toss. Serve immediately, or cover and chill. To serve, spoon onto a lettuce-lined platter. Garnish, if desired. Yield: 12 servings.

Desert Treasures
The Junior League of Phoenix, Arizona

Roast Beef Niçoise

You can serve this beef interpretation of Niçoise salad at room temperature or, if you prefer, chill the salad and the tangy Mustard Dressing.

1 pound fresh green beans
Mustard Dressing, divided
2 pounds small red potatoes, unpeeled
¼ cup minced shallots
¼ cup beef broth
2 medium-size purple onions, thinly sliced and separated into rings

2 pounds ¼-inch-thick slices cooked roast beef, cut into 2-inch pieces
Garnishes: purple onion rings, chopped fresh parsley, chopped fresh chives

Wash beans; remove ends. Cook in boiling water to cover 8 minutes or until crisp-tender; drain. Rinse with cold water, and drain well.

Combine beans and ½ cup Mustard Dressing in a medium bowl; toss gently. Set aside.

Cook potatoes in boiling water to cover 15 to 20 minutes or until tender; drain. Rinse potatoes with cold water, and drain well. Thinly slice potatoes. Combine sliced potatoes and shallot in a medium bowl; set aside.

Cook beef broth in a small saucepan over medium heat until thoroughly heated. Pour over potato mixture; add ½ cup Mustard Dressing, and toss gently.

Arrange bean mixture, potato mixture, onion rings, and roast beef in concentric circles on a large serving platter. Garnish, if desired. Serve salad with remaining Mustard Dressing. Yield: 8 servings.

Mustard Dressing

1 cup olive oil
¼ cup white vinegar
2 tablespoons Dijon mustard

1 teaspoon salt
Pepper to taste

Combine all ingredients in a small bowl; stir well with a wire whisk until blended. Yield: 1⅓ cups.

For Goodness Taste
The Junior League of Rochester, New York

Fruit Salad Dressing

½ cup sugar
2 tablespoons cornstarch
¼ cup plus 2 tablespoons
   pineapple juice
¼ cup boiling water

3 tablespoons orange juice
3 tablespoons lemon juice
2 large eggs, beaten
½ teaspoon salt

Combine sugar and cornstarch in a medium saucepan, stirring well. Combine pineapple juice and next 3 ingredients; gradually stir juice mixture into sugar mixture. Cook over medium heat, stirring constantly, until thickened and bubbly.

Gradually stir about one-fourth of hot mixture into beaten eggs; add to remaining hot mixture, stirring constantly with a wire whisk. Cook over medium-low heat, stirring constantly, 2 minutes or until mixture is thickened and smooth. Remove from heat; stir in salt. Let cool slightly. Cover and chill thoroughly. Serve dressing over fresh fruit. Yield: 1 cup.

Margaret Sullivan Berg

The Heritage Collection
Western Kentucky University Home Economics
Alumni Association
Bowling Green, Kentucky

Julie's Fresh Italian Dressing

This vinaigrette separates upon standing, so shake it just before serving.

¾ cup extra virgin olive oil
3 tablespoons red wine vinegar
1 clove garlic, minced
1 tablespoon minced onion
¾ teaspoon salt

½ teaspoon freshly ground
   pepper
½ teaspoon dried Italian
   seasoning

Combine all ingredients in a jar. Cover tightly, and shake vigorously. Chill at least 8 hours. Shake well just before serving. Serve dressing over salad greens. Yield: 1 cup.

Good Food, Good Company
The Junior Service League of Thomasville, Georgia

Ketchup Salad Dressing

½ cup sugar
½ cup white vinegar
½ cup vegetable oil
½ cup hot ketchup
1 tablespoon chopped fresh
  chives

1 clove garlic, halved
¼ teaspoon celery salt
¼ teaspoon salt
⅛ teaspoon pepper

Combine all ingredients in a bowl; beat with a wire whisk until blended. Cover and chill at least 8 hours. Remove and discard garlic. Store in an airtight container in refrigerator up to 2 weeks. Serve dressing over salad greens. Yield: 2 cups.

Almost Chefs, A Cookbook for Kids
The Palm Beach Guild for the Children's Home Society
Palm Beach, Florida

Parmesan Cheese Dressing

The white wine vinegar in this dressing has a milder, less pungent flavor than regular white vinegar.

⅔ cup mayonnaise
⅓ cup grated Parmesan cheese
⅓ cup milk

1 tablespoon white wine vinegar
¼ teaspoon Worcestershire
  sauce

Combine all ingredients in a small bowl, beating with a wire whisk until blended. Cover and chill thoroughly. Serve dressing over salad greens. Yield: 1 cup.
                                                              Karen Ellis

Treasured Favorites
Morton County Hospital Auxiliary
Elkhart, Kansas

Sauces & Condiments

Peach of the Old South Barbecue Sauce for Ribs, page 276

Brandied Date and Walnut Sauce

2 cups firmly packed brown
  sugar
1 cup water
1 (8-ounce) package pitted,
  chopped dates

1 cup chopped walnuts
¼ cup brandy

Combine sugar and water in a medium saucepan. Bring to a boil; reduce heat, and simmer 20 minutes, stirring occasionally. Remove from heat; stir in dates and remaining ingredients. Serve warm over ice cream. Store in refrigerator up to 2 weeks. Yield: 3¼ cups.

Ridgefield Cooks
Women's Committee of the Ridgefield Community Center
Ridgefield, Connecticut

Fabulous Fudge Sauce

The title of this thick, rich fudge sauce tells all—except maybe how quick and easy it is to make.

1 (12-ounce) package semisweet
  chocolate morsels
1 (14-ounce) can sweetened
  condensed milk

1 cup miniature marshmallows
½ cup milk
1 teaspoon vanilla extract

Combine all ingredients in a medium saucepan, and cook over medium-low heat until chocolate morsels and marshmallows melt, stirring occasionally. Serve warm over ice cream. Store in refrigerator. Yield: 3¼ cups. Jo Simmons

Dundee Presbyterian Church Cookbook
Dundee Presbyterian Church
Omaha, Nebraska

Kinderhaus's Famous Hot Fudge Sauce

4 (1-ounce) squares
   unsweetened chocolate
½ cup unsalted butter or
   margarine
1 cup whipping cream

¾ cup sugar
½ cup firmly packed brown
   sugar
1 teaspoon vanilla extract

Combine chocolate and butter in top of a double boiler; bring water to a boil. Reduce heat to low, and cook until chocolate and butter melt, stirring occasionally. Add whipping cream and remaining ingredients; cook, stirring constantly, until brown sugar dissolves and mixture is smooth. Serve warm sauce over ice cream. Store in refrigerator. Yield: 2½ cups.

June Varricchione

The Kinderhaus Cookbook
Kinderhaus Children's Center
Williston, Vermont

Toasted Pecan Sauce

Be sure to toast the pecans before adding them to this buttery dessert sauce. Toasting them will bring out their nutty flavor and help keep them crunchy.

½ cup butter or margarine
1¼ cups firmly packed brown
   sugar

2 tablespoons light corn syrup
½ cup whipping cream
1 cup chopped pecans, toasted

Melt butter in a saucepan over medium heat; add brown sugar and corn syrup, stirring until smooth. Bring to a boil; reduce heat, and simmer 1 minute, stirring constantly. Stir in whipping cream; bring to a boil, stirring constantly. Remove from heat, and stir in chopped pecans. Serve warm over ice cream. Store in refrigerator up to 2 weeks. Yield: 2¼ cups.

Linda Levy

Cookin' with C.L.A.S.S.
Citizens League for Adult Special Services
Lawrence, Massachusetts

A Sauce with Character!

Horseradish gives this simple sour cream sauce its distinctive "character."

1 (8-ounce) carton sour cream
3 tablespoons finely chopped
   onion
1 teaspoon sugar
½ teaspoon celery seeds

¼ teaspoon salt
2 teaspoons white vinegar
1 teaspoon prepared
   horseradish

Combine all ingredients in a small bowl; stir well. Cover and chill thoroughly. Serve over hot cooked vegetables, roast beef, or pork. Yield: 1 cup.   Sue Fowler

888 Favorite Recipes
Boy Scout Troop 888
Maryville, Tennessee

Peach of the Old South Barbecue Sauce for Ribs

Bourbon lends a distinctive flavor to this peach-sweetened barbecue sauce.

2 cups tomato puree
½ cup fresh lemon juice
½ cup sweetened bourbon
   whiskey
½ cup peach preserves

½ cup Dijon mustard
¼ cup firmly packed light
   brown sugar
2 tablespoons hot sauce
1 teaspoon salt

Combine all ingredients in a saucepan; stir well. Bring to a boil; cover, reduce heat, and simmer 20 minutes, stirring occasionally. Use as a basting sauce for ribs. Yield: 4 cups.   Riedel's Restaurant

Golden Oldies Cook Book
Catholic Diocese of Belleville Ministry to Sick and Aged
Belleville, Illinois

Roasted Red Pepper Sauce

Drizzle this roasted pepper sauce over grilled fish or toss with your favorite pasta for a flavor sensation you won't forget. A touch of garlic, brandy, vinegar, and ground red pepper accents the flavor of the sweet red peppers.

3 **large sweet red peppers**
  (about 18 ounces)
2 **cloves garlic**
1½ **tablespoons brandy**
2 **teaspoons red wine vinegar**

½ **teaspoon salt**
⅛ **teaspoon ground red pepper**
3 **tablespoons unsalted butter or**
  margarine

Cut peppers in half lengthwise; remove and discard seeds and membranes. Place peppers, skin side up, on an ungreased baking sheet; flatten peppers with palm of hand.

Broil 5½ inches from heat (with electric oven door partially opened) 15 to 20 minutes or until skins of peppers are charred.

Place peppers in a heavy-duty, zip-top plastic bag; seal bag, and let stand 10 minutes. Peel and discard skins.

Combine peppers, garlic, and next 4 ingredients in container of an electric blender or food processor; cover and process until smooth, stopping once to scrape down sides.

Pour mixture through a wire-mesh strainer into a small saucepan, discarding pulp. Add butter; cook over low heat until butter melts, stirring often. Yield: 1 cup.

The Pasquotank Plate
Christ Episcopal Churchwomen
Elizabeth City, North Carolina

Sweet Yellow Pepper Puree

This basil-scented sweet pepper sauce cranks up the flavor of fish and beef. Serve the sauce warm or chilled.

6 large sweet yellow peppers, diced
2 cups chopped onion
2 cloves garlic, minced
¼ cup olive oil

2 tablespoons chopped fresh basil
Salt and freshly ground pepper to taste

Cook sweet yellow pepper, onion, and garlic in oil in a large skillet over medium-high heat 10 minutes, stirring constantly. Cover, reduce heat, and simmer 30 minutes.

Position knife blade in food processor bowl; add sweet yellow pepper mixture, basil, and salt and pepper to taste. Process until smooth.

Pour mixture into a medium saucepan; cook over medium-high heat 5 minutes or until thoroughly heated, stirring often. Serve warm, or cover and chill. Yield: 3 cups.
Christine Ford

Cooking in the Litchfield Hills
The Pratt Center
New Milford, Connecticut

Sun-Dried Tomato Cream Sauce

1 (7-ounce) jar oil-packed sun-dried tomatoes, undrained
½ pound fresh mushrooms, sliced

1 tablespoon olive oil
1½ cups half-and-half
1 tablespoon minced fresh basil

Drain tomatoes, reserving 1 tablespoon oil. Cut tomatoes into very thin strips; set aside.

Cook mushrooms in 1 tablespoon olive oil in a large skillet over medium heat, stirring constantly, until tender. Stir in reserved 1 tablespoon oil and tomato strips. Add half-and-half and basil; bring to a boil. Reduce heat, and simmer 5 minutes, stirring constantly, or until slightly thickened. Serve over pasta. Yield: 2 cups.

Tampa Treasures
The Junior League of Tampa, Florida

Florida Fruit Salsa

A colorful combination of fresh papaya, mango, and pineapple comprises this fruit salsa from Florida, while onion, cilantro, and jalapeño spike the flavor.

1 cup diced fresh papaya
1 cup diced fresh mango
¾ cup diced fresh pineapple
½ cup diced purple onion
⅓ cup peeled and diced tomato

¼ cup chopped fresh cilantro
2 jalapeño peppers, seeded and chopped
⅓ cup red wine vinegar
2 tablespoons olive oil

Combine all ingredients in a bowl; stir well. Serve at room temperature, or cover and chill. Yield: 3½ cups. Jill Shockett

Signature Cuisine
Miami Country Day School Parents' Association
Miami, Florida

Peach Salsa

Fresh Georgia peaches star in this mild golden salsa. Serve it with cooked ham, pork, poultry, or seafood.

5 medium-size fresh ripe peaches, peeled and chopped
½ teaspoon minced fresh ginger
¼ cup minced green onions
1½ tablespoons sugar

1½ tablespoons lime juice
½ teaspoon dry mustard
⅛ teaspoon salt
⅛ teaspoon ground white pepper

Position knife blade in food processor bowl. Add one-fourth of chopped peaches and ginger; process until smooth. Transfer puree to a bowl; stir in remaining chopped peaches, green onions, and remaining ingredients. Cover and chill up to 4 hours. Yield: 3⅓ cups.

Among the Lilies
Women in Missions, First Baptist Church of Atlanta
Atlanta, Georgia

Sun-Dried Tomato Salsa

15 sun-dried tomatoes
¾ cup olive oil
6 cloves garlic
¼ cup chopped fresh basil
2½ tablespoons chopped fresh
    parsley
1½ teaspoons chopped fresh
    cilantro
1½ teaspoons chopped fresh
    oregano
1½ teaspoons chopped fresh
    thyme
1 teaspoon salt
½ teaspoon pepper

Place tomatoes in a bowl; add boiling water to cover. Let stand 30 minutes.

Position knife blade in food processor bowl. Add tomato mixture, olive oil, and remaining ingredients; process until smooth, stopping once to scrape down sides. Serve salsa over hot cooked pasta or with fish. Yield: 1½ cups.   Rita Clark

Flatbush Feasts, First Edition
Flatbush Development Corporation
Brooklyn, New York

Mary's Chili Sauce

14 medium-size ripe tomatoes,
    peeled and chopped
2 cups sugar
3 cups finely chopped onion
1 cup chopped green pepper
1 cup chopped sweet red
    pepper
2 tablespoons salt
3 (3-inch) sticks cinnamon
1 tablespoon whole cloves
1 tablespoon mustard seeds
1 teaspoon ground red pepper
2 cups white vinegar
    (5% acidity)

Combine first 6 ingredients in a large Dutch oven; bring to a boil. Reduce heat to low, and cook, stirring constantly, until sugar dissolves. Cook, uncovered, 2 additional hours or until mixture is thickened, stirring occasionally.

Place cinnamon sticks, cloves, and mustard seeds on a piece of cheesecloth; tie ends of cheesecloth securely with string. Add cheesecloth bag and ground red pepper to tomato mixture; stir in vinegar. Bring to a boil; reduce heat, and simmer, uncovered, 3 to 4 hours or until very thick, stirring occasionally.

Pour hot chili sauce mixture into hot jars, filling to ½ inch from top. Remove air bubbles, and wipe jar rims. Cover at once with metal lids, and screw on bands. Process in boiling-water bath 15 minutes. Yield: 5 half pints.

Nancy K. Fuller

Bethel's Bounty
Bethel Presbyterian Women
Davidson, North Carolina

Red Bean Relish

You may never make plain cucumber relish again once you try this version with kidney beans.

10 cups chopped cucumbers
  (about 4 pounds)
3 cups chopped green pepper
2 cups chopped onion
8 cups water
½ cup pickling salt
2 (16-ounce) cans kidney beans,
  rinsed and drained
3 cups sugar

2 cups white vinegar
  (5% acidity)
1 cup water
3 tablespoons all-purpose flour
1 tablespoon dry mustard
1 tablespoon ground turmeric
1 teaspoon celery seeds
1 teaspoon ground ginger

Combine cucumber, green pepper, and onion in a large nonmetal container; add 8 cups water and pickling salt, stirring well. Cover and let stand at room temperature 4 hours. Drain well. Add kidney beans, and set aside.

Combine sugar and next 3 ingredients in a medium saucepan; bring to a boil. Stir in mustard, turmeric, celery seeds, and ginger.

Pack cucumber mixture into hot jars, filling to ½ inch from top. Cover cucumber mixture with hot vinegar mixture, filling to ½ inch from top. Remove air bubbles; wipe jar rims. Cover at once with metal lids, and screw on bands. Process in boiling-water bath 15 minutes. Yield: 6 pints.

Margie Terrell Walker Doolen

A Taste of Twin Pines
Twin Pines Alumni of Twin Pines Cooperative House
West Lafayette, Indiana

German-Style Pear Relish

Serve this bold and spicy relish on ham or hot dogs. Jalapeño peppers, mustard, and turmeric give the relish its color and kick.

11 pounds firm ripe pears,
   peeled, cored, and quartered
4 large onions, quartered
2 large green peppers,
   quartered
2 large sweet red peppers,
   quartered
16 jalapeño peppers, seeded
2 cups white vinegar
   (5% acidity)

1 cup sugar
1 (12-ounce) jar bold and spicy
   mustard
1 tablespoon plus 1 teaspoon
   salt
1 teaspoon ground allspice
1 teaspoon ground turmeric
1 teaspoon celery seeds

Position knife blade in food processor bowl; add first 5 ingredients in batches, and process until finely chopped, stopping occasionally to scrape down sides.

Combine vegetables, vinegar, and remaining ingredients in a large Dutch oven; bring to a boil. Reduce heat, and simmer, uncovered, 20 minutes, stirring occasionally.

Pack hot pear mixture into hot jars, filling to ½ inch from top. Remove air bubbles, and wipe jar rims. Cover at once with metal lids, and screw on bands. Process in boiling-water bath 15 minutes. Yield: 11 pints.

Sandra Grider

Home Cookin'
Volunteer Services Council for Abilene State School
Abilene, Texas

Rhubarb-Apple Chutney

6 cups chopped fresh rhubarb
2 large cooking apples, peeled and chopped
2 medium onions, chopped
1½ cups raisins
1¼ cups firmly packed brown sugar
1¼ cups white vinegar (5% acidity)
¾ teaspoon curry powder
½ teaspoon ground ginger
½ teaspoon ground cinnamon
¼ teaspoon ground mace
¼ teaspoon ground red pepper
¼ teaspoon ground cloves
Dash of garlic powder

Combine all ingredients in a Dutch oven. Bring to a boil; cover, reduce heat, and simmer 2 hours or until thickened, stirring occasionally. Spoon hot chutney into hot jars, filling to ½ inch from top. Remove air bubbles; wipe jar rims. Cover at once with metal lids; screw on bands. Process in boiling-water bath 15 minutes. Yield: 3 pints.   Jane Winge

Ritzy Rhubarb Secrets Cookbook
Litchville Committee 2,000
Litchville, North Dakota

Golden Apricot Jam

2½ cups water
8 ounces dried apricots
2 tablespoons finely grated carrot
2½ teaspoons grated lemon rind
3⅓ cups sugar
3 tablespoons fresh lemon juice

Combine first 4 ingredients in a saucepan; bring to a boil. Cover, reduce heat, and simmer 25 minutes, stirring occasionally. Add sugar and juice; return to a boil, stirring constantly. Reduce heat to low; cook, stirring constantly, 25 minutes or until thickened. Pour hot jam into hot, sterilized jars, filling to ¼ inch from top. Remove air bubbles; wipe jar rims. Cover at once with metal lids; screw on bands. Process in boiling-water bath 5 minutes. Yield: 4 half pints.   Ruth Edwards

Sharing Our Best
Neighborhood Ministries Auxiliary
Campbell and Youngstown, Ohio

Pink Grapefruit Jelly

Only three ingredients, but lots of flavor! Spread this tangy jelly on toast or English muffins.

1 (1¾-ounce) package powdered pectin	4 cups pink grapefruit juice
	5 cups sugar

Combine pectin and juice in a Dutch oven. Bring to a boil over high heat, stirring constantly. Stir in sugar; return to a boil. Boil 1 minute, stirring constantly. Remove from heat; skim off foam.

Pour hot grapefruit jelly into hot, sterilized jars, filling to ¼ inch from top. Remove air bubbles; wipe jar rims. Cover at once with metal lids, and screw on bands. Process in boiling-water bath 5 minutes. Yield: 8 half pints.   LouAnn Hanson

Padre Kino's Favorite Meatloaf and Other Recipes from Baja, Arizona
Tucson Community Food Bank
Tucson, Arizona

Honey and Fruit Spread

Try this dried fruit and nut spread as a chunky topper for biscuits or scones.

½ cup butter or margarine, softened	¼ cup chopped dried fruit
¼ cup honey	2 tablespoons chopped pecans
	½ teaspoon grated orange rind

Beat butter and honey at medium speed of an electric mixer until creamy. Stir in dried fruit and remaining ingredients. Store in refrigerator. Yield: 1 cup.

A Flock of Good Recipes
Shepherd of the Bay Lutheran Church
Ellison Bay and Sister Bay, Wisconsin

Soups & Stews

Country Veal Stew, page 297

Summer Honeydew Soup

You can tell if a honeydew melon is ripe if you feel a very slight wrinkling of the rind and the melon feels heavy for its size. Unripe melons will ripen if left at room temperature.

1 ripe honeydew melon
1¼ cups freshly squeezed lime juice
1 cup freshly squeezed orange juice

½ cup dry white wine
2 tablespoons honey
1 kiwifruit, sliced

Cut honeydew melon in half; remove and discard seeds and membranes. Carefully scoop out 1½ cups melon balls, and set aside. Peel remaining melon, and cut into chunks.

Place melon chunks in container of an electric blender or food processor; cover and process until smooth, stopping once to scrape down sides. Combine melon puree, lime juice, and next 3 ingredients in a large bowl, stirring well. Stir in reserved melon balls. Cover and chill at least 2 hours.

To serve, ladle soup into individual soup bowls. Top each serving with a kiwifruit slice. Yield: 6 cups.   Sima Spector

Today's Traditional: Jewish Cooking with a Lighter Touch
Congregation Beth Shalom
Carmichael, California

Shrimp Gazpacho

1½ cups water
½ pound unpeeled small fresh shrimp
1 large cucumber, peeled, seeded, and coarsely chopped
1 medium-size green pepper, coarsely chopped
1 small onion, coarsely chopped
2 cloves garlic

2 pounds tomatoes, peeled, seeded, and chopped
2 cups tomato juice
4 bay leaves
2 tablespoons cider vinegar
2 tablespoons sugar
½ teaspoon salt
½ teaspoon pepper
½ teaspoon dried oregano

Bring water to a boil; add shrimp, and cook 3 to 5 minutes or until shrimp turn pink. Drain well; rinse with cold water. Chill. Peel shrimp, and devein, if desired. Place shrimp in a medium bowl. Cover and chill thoroughly.

Position knife blade in food processor bowl; add cucumber and next 3 ingredients. Process until smooth, stopping once to scrape down sides.

Combine pureed vegetables, chopped tomato, and next 7 ingredients in a large bowl; cover and chill at least 8 hours. Remove and discard bay leaves. Stir shrimp into tomato mixture just before serving. Yield: 8 cups.

Steve Kish

Heart Choice Recipes from Charleston's Greatest Chefs
Medical University of South Carolina Heart Center
Charleston, South Carolina

Cream of Red Onion Soup

For an extra special topper for this soup, sprinkle the crumbled blue cheese and walnuts onto thin slices of French bread, and broil until lightly browned.

3 large purple onions, thinly sliced	½ cup dry red wine
¼ cup butter or margarine, melted	½ teaspoon sugar
¼ cup all-purpose flour	2 cups half-and-half
2 (14½-ounce) cans beef broth, undiluted	Salt and freshly ground pepper to taste
	Crumbled blue cheese
	Toasted chopped walnuts

Cook onion in butter in a Dutch oven over medium-high heat, stirring often, until almost caramel in color. Reduce heat to low. Add flour, stirring until blended. Cook 1 minute, stirring constantly. Gradually add beef broth, wine, and sugar; cook over medium heat, stirring constantly, until mixture is thickened and bubbly. Stir in half-and-half and salt and pepper to taste. Cook, stirring constantly, just until thoroughly heated (do not boil).

To serve, ladle soup into individual soup bowls; top each serving with cheese and walnuts. Yield: 8½ cups. Joanne Crawford

Good to the Core
The Apple Corps of the Weller Center for Health Education
Easton, Pennsylvania

Palm Valley Cream of Palm Soup

Hearts of palm are actually the edible inner portion of the stem of the cabbage palm tree. They have a delicate flavor that's similar to an artichoke. In this ivory-colored soup, Swiss cheese provides the dominant flavor note.

1 cup chopped onion
1 clove garlic, pressed
½ cup butter or margarine, melted
½ cup all-purpose flour
2 (14½-ounce) cans ready-to-serve chicken broth
1 (14¼-ounce) can hearts of palm, drained and cut into ½-inch slices

1 cup half-and-half
Salt and pepper to taste
1 cup (4 ounces) shredded Swiss cheese
⅓ cup finely chopped fresh parsley

Cook onion and garlic in butter in a large skillet over medium-high heat, stirring constantly, until tender. Reduce heat to low; add flour, stirring until blended. Cook 1 minute, stirring constantly. Gradually add chicken broth; cook over medium heat, stirring constantly, until mixture is thickened and bubbly. Add hearts of palm, half-and-half, and salt and pepper to taste; stir well. Cook just until thoroughly heated (do not boil).

To serve, ladle soup into individual soup bowls. Top each serving of soup evenly with shredded Swiss cheese and chopped parsley. Yield: 5¾ cups.

Gwen Holborn

American Buffet
General Federation of Women's Clubs
Washington, DC

Golden Autumn Soup

Crisp apples, tart apple cider, and winter squash herald the arrival of autumn in this colorful soup. Serve it warm or chilled.

1½ pounds buttercup, butternut, or acorn squash	¼ teaspoon ground cumin
1 large onion, chopped	¼ teaspoon ground nutmeg
1 stalk celery, chopped	¼ teaspoon dried rosemary, crushed
2 tablespoons butter or margarine, melted	2 tablespoons butter or margarine
3 medium carrots, scraped and diced	2 tablespoons all-purpose flour
2 medium-size cooking apples, peeled, cored, and diced	1½ cups apple cider
3 cups chicken broth	¼ teaspoon ground cinnamon
1 teaspoon rubbed sage	½ cup (2 ounces) shredded sharp Cheddar cheese
	½ cup chopped walnuts, toasted

Cut squash in half crosswise; remove and discard seeds and membranes. Place squash, cut side down, in a large shallow pan. Add hot water to pan to depth of ¼ inch. Cover and bake at 375° for 40 to 45 minutes or until tender. Remove from oven; drain well. Scoop out pulp, discarding shells; set pulp aside.

Cook onion and celery in 2 tablespoons butter in a Dutch oven over medium-high heat, stirring constantly, until tender. Add squash pulp, carrot, and next 6 ingredients. Bring to a boil; reduce heat, and simmer, uncovered, 30 minutes.

Transfer squash mixture in batches to container of an electric blender; cover and process until smooth, stopping once to scrape down sides. Return puree to pan.

Melt 2 tablespoons butter in a small saucepan over low heat; add flour, stirring until smooth. Cook 1 minute, stirring constantly. Gradually add apple cider and cinnamon; cook over medium heat, stirring constantly, until mixture is thickened and bubbly. Add to puree, and simmer 5 minutes or until thoroughly heated.

To serve, ladle soup into individual soup bowls. Top each serving with cheese and walnuts. Yield: 8 cups.

Cooking with Herb Scents
Western Reserve Herb Society
Bay Village, Ohio

Pizza Soup

No need to choose between a thin and thick crust—this pizza's a soup! Add a grilled cheese sandwich and your supper's complete.

1 (15-ounce) can stewed tomatoes, undrained
1 (8-ounce) can tomato sauce
½ cup water
¾ cup thinly sliced fresh mushrooms
3 ounces pepperoni, thinly sliced
2 cloves garlic, crushed
1 tablespoon chopped fresh basil

1 tablespoon chopped fresh oregano
⅛ teaspoon ground red pepper
1 (4-ounce) can sliced ripe olives, drained
¼ cup chopped green onions
¼ cup (1 ounce) shredded mozzarella cheese

Combine first 3 ingredients in a large saucepan; cook over medium heat 5 minutes, stirring occasionally. Reduce heat to low; add mushrooms and next 5 ingredients; cook, uncovered, 20 minutes, stirring often. Remove from heat; stir in olives and green onions.

To serve, ladle soup into individual soup bowls. Top each serving with cheese. Yield: 4 cups.   Barbara Jean Dezsi

It's Rainin' Recipes
Charles B. Hopkins Chapter, Telephone Pioneers of America
Seattle, Washington

Italian Spinach Soup with Meatballs

You'll need about 1½ slices of bread to make the ¾ cup of soft breadcrumbs for these meatballs.

3 quarts chicken broth
2 stalks celery, cut into ½-inch
   pieces
2 carrots, scraped and cut into
   ½-inch pieces
1 large onion, quartered
½ teaspoon salt
1 pound ground beef
¾ cup soft breadcrumbs
1 large egg, lightly beaten
2 tablespoons grated Parmesan
   cheese
1½ tablespoons chopped fresh
   parsley
½ teaspoon salt

¼ teaspoon ground white
   pepper
1 (14½-ounce) can Italian-style
   tomatoes, undrained and
   chopped
1 (10-ounce) package frozen
   chopped spinach, thawed
   and drained
4 cloves garlic, crushed
2 tablespoons grated Parmesan
   cheese
3 tablespoons olive oil
2 tablespoons lemon juice
2 teaspoons dried basil

Combine first 5 ingredients in a large Dutch oven. Bring to a boil; reduce heat, and simmer, uncovered, 30 minutes. Remove vegetables with a slotted spoon, and discard; set broth aside.

Combine ground beef and next 6 ingredients in a large bowl; stir well. Shape meat mixture into 1-inch meatballs. Brown meatballs in a large nonstick skillet over medium heat. Drain, discarding drippings.

Bring broth to a boil; add meatballs. Reduce heat, and simmer, uncovered, 10 minutes or until done. Add tomatoes and remaining ingredients; bring to a boil. Reduce heat; simmer, uncovered, 10 additional minutes. Yield: 13½ cups.   Susan Zoccola

Enough to Feed an Army
West Point Officers Wives' Club
West Point, New York

Oyster and Artichoke Soup

When purchasing the fresh, shucked oysters for this recipe, look for oysters that are plump, uniform in size, have good color, and smell fresh. The oyster liquid they're packed in should be clear, not cloudy.

6 shallots, finely chopped
½ cup chopped celery
2 cloves garlic, minced
½ cup butter or margarine, melted
2 tablespoons all-purpose flour
3 cups chicken broth
1 (14-ounce) can artichoke hearts, drained and chopped
2 tablespoons chopped fresh parsley
2 bay leaves
½ teaspoon salt
¼ teaspoon pepper
¼ teaspoon dried thyme
Dash of ground red pepper
2 (12-ounce) containers fresh Standard oysters, drained

Cook shallot, celery, and garlic in butter in a large saucepan over medium-high heat, stirring constantly, until tender. Reduce heat to low. Add flour, stirring until blended. Cook 1 minute, stirring constantly. Gradually add chicken broth; cook over medium heat, stirring constantly, until mixture is slightly thickened.

Add artichoke hearts and next 6 ingredients; cover and cook over low heat 30 minutes. Remove and discard bay leaves.

Add oysters; cook, uncovered, over medium heat 3 to 5 minutes or until oysters begin to curl. Yield: 6 cups.

Heart & Soul
The Junior League of Memphis, Tennessee

Scallop-Cream Soup

If you can't make this soup right away, store the fresh scallops in an airtight container in the refrigerator, covered with their own juices, up to two days.

3 medium leeks
8 cups water
4 medium baking potatoes, peeled and thinly sliced
1¼ cups chopped celery
1 medium onion, diced
5 cloves garlic
2 chicken-flavored bouillon cubes
2 bay leaves, divided
1½ teaspoons pepper
½ teaspoon paprika
⅛ teaspoon dry mustard
Dash of ground red pepper

Dash of dried basil
Dash of dried rosemary
Dash of dried tarragon
Salt to taste
3 tablespoons butter or margarine
2 cups water
Dash of dried crushed red pepper
1½ pounds fresh bay scallops
3 tablespoons dry sherry
2 cups half-and-half
Garnishes: paprika, fresh parsley sprigs

Remove and discard root, tough outer leaves, and top of leek to where dark green becomes pale. Chop leek. Combine leek, 8 cups water, and next 5 ingredients in a Dutch oven; bring to a boil. Reduce heat; simmer, uncovered, 15 minutes, stirring occasionally. Add 1 bay leaf and next 8 ingredients; cover and cook over low heat 20 minutes. Discard bay leaf. Stir in butter; let cool slightly. Transfer leek mixture in batches to container of an electric blender; cover and process until smooth. Return to pan. Set leek mixture aside, and keep warm.

Bring remaining bay leaf, 2 cups water, and crushed red pepper to a boil in a large skillet. Reduce heat to medium; add scallops. Cover and simmer 5 minutes or until scallops are opaque. Drain, reserving 3 tablespoons liquid.

Place scallops, liquid, and sherry in container of an electric blender; cover and process until scallops are minced, stopping often to scrape down sides. Add scallop mixture and half-and-half to leek mixture; bring to a boil. Reduce heat, and simmer, uncovered, 5 minutes or until thoroughly heated, stirring often. To serve, ladle into individual soup bowls. Garnish, if desired. Yield: 12 cups.   Marie Lewis

Chefs and Artists
Back Mountain Memorial Library
Dallas, Pennsylvania

Ham and Cheese Chowder

2 cups peeled, cubed baking potato
½ cup water
1 cup chopped onion
3 tablespoons butter or margarine, melted
3 tablespoons all-purpose flour
3 cups milk
1 (16½-ounce) can cream-style corn
1½ cups (6 ounces) shredded Cheddar cheese
1½ cups chopped cooked ham
¼ teaspoon pepper

Combine potato and water in a medium saucepan; bring to a boil. Cover, reduce heat, and simmer 15 minutes or until tender. Drain, reserving liquid. Set potato aside. Add water to reserved liquid to equal 1 cup.

Cook onion in butter in a large saucepan over medium-high heat, stirring constantly, until tender. Reduce heat to low. Add flour, stirring until blended. Cook 1 minute, stirring constantly. Gradually add reserved liquid and milk; cook over medium heat, stirring constantly, until mixture is thickened and bubbly. Add potato, corn, and remaining ingredients; cook until cheese melts, stirring constantly. Serve immediately. Yield: 8 cups.   Sharon Goecke

Here's What's Cooking at Standish Elementary
Standish Elementary PTK
Standish, Michigan

Parsnip Chowder

Sweet parsnips and hearty potatoes pair up in this chunky chowder.

1 cup chopped onion
2 tablespoons butter, melted
4 medium baking potatoes, peeled and diced
1 pound parsnips, scraped and diced
3 cups water
2 cups milk
3 tablespoons minced fresh parsley
1 tablespoon minced fresh dill
Salt and freshly ground pepper to taste

Cook onion in butter in a Dutch oven over medium-high heat, stirring constantly, until tender. Add potato, parsnip, and water; bring to a boil. Cover, reduce heat, and simmer 25 minutes or until tender.

Remove 2 cups vegetables with a slotted spoon. Position knife blade in food processor bowl. Add vegetables; process until smooth. Return to pan. Stir in milk and remaining ingredients; cook over low heat 10 minutes or until thoroughly heated. Yield: 10 cups.   Ethel Green

Beyond Brisket
Sisterhood of Temple Israel
Natick, Massachusetts

Fresh Vegetable Stew

1 (19-ounce) can chick-peas (garbanzo beans), undrained	1⅓ cups chopped unpeeled eggplant
1 (15-ounce) can cannellini beans, undrained	1⅓ cups chopped kale
1½ cups chopped onion	1⅓ cups sliced fresh mushrooms
1 cup sliced celery	1⅓ cups chopped green pepper
2 cloves garlic, crushed	1⅓ cups chopped sweet red pepper
2 tablespoons olive oil	
3 cups chopped fresh tomato	1⅓ cups peeled, cubed red potato
1 tablespoon dried Italian seasoning	1⅓ cups sliced yellow squash
2 teaspoons salt	1⅓ cups sliced zucchini
1⅓ cups cut fresh green beans	4 cups cooked brown rice
	Grated Parmesan cheese

Drain chick-peas and cannellini beans, reserving liquid. Add enough water to liquid to equal 3½ cups. Set beans and liquid aside.

Cook onion, celery, and garlic in oil in a large Dutch oven over medium-high heat, stirring constantly, until tender. Add reserved liquid, tomato, Italian seasoning, and salt; stir well. Bring to a boil; cover, reduce heat, and simmer 15 minutes. Add green beans and next 8 ingredients. Bring to a boil; cover, reduce heat to medium, and simmer 25 minutes or until vegetables are tender, stirring occasionally. Stir in chick-peas and cannellini beans, and cook until thoroughly heated.

To serve, ladle stew over rice into individual soup bowls. Top each serving with cheese. Yield: 14 cups.   Susan West

Country Cupboard Collection, Treasured Recipes from AT&T
AT&T/Western Electric Council, Telephone Pioneers of America
Ballwin, Missouri

Beef Stew with Walnuts and Feta Cheese

1 medium onion, chopped
2 tablespoons butter, melted
3 pounds boneless chuck roast, cut into 1-inch cubes
½ cup dry red wine
½ cup water
¼ cup plus 2 tablespoons tomato paste
2 tablespoons white vinegar
1 clove garlic, minced
1 bay leaf
¼ teaspoon salt
¼ teaspoon pepper
1 (10-ounce) jar pearl onions, drained
8 ounces feta cheese, crumbled
¾ cup walnuts
Hot cooked orzo

Cook onion in butter in a Dutch oven over medium-high heat, stirring constantly, until tender. Add beef and next 8 ingredients. Bring to a boil; cover, reduce heat, and simmer 1 hour. Add onions; cover and simmer 1 hour or until meat and vegetables are tender. Stir in cheese and walnuts; simmer 5 additional minutes. Discard bay leaf. To serve, ladle stew over orzo into individual soup bowls. Yield: 9 cups.

Cooks Incorporated
Miami Valley Health Foundation
Dayton, Ohio

Sheepherder's Stew

1 (16-ounce) can whole tomatoes, undrained
¼ cup all-purpose flour
1½ teaspoons seasoned salt
1 teaspoon garlic powder
¼ teaspoon pepper
2 pounds boneless lamb, cubed
3 tablespoons vegetable oil
1 (15-ounce) can tomato sauce
½ cup dry red wine
2 cloves garlic, pressed
1 bay leaf
1 beef-flavored bouillon cube
½ teaspoon dried thyme
4 medium-size red potatoes, cut into ½-inch pieces
4 carrots, scraped and cut into 1-inch pieces
2 small onions, quartered
1½ cups frozen cut green beans

Drain tomatoes, reserving liquid. Add enough water to reserved tomato liquid to equal 2 cups. Set aside. Chop tomatoes, and set aside.

Combine flour and next 3 ingredients in a large zip-top plastic bag; add lamb. Seal bag securely, and shake until lamb is coated.

Brown lamb in oil in a Dutch oven over medium heat. Add tomatoes, tomato liquid, tomato sauce, and next 5 ingredients; stir well. Bring to a boil; cover, reduce heat, and simmer 1 hour.

Add potato, carrot, onion, and green beans. Bring to a boil; cover, reduce heat, and simmer 1 hour and 15 minutes or until vegetables are tender, stirring occasionally. Discard bay leaf. Yield: 12 cups.

Havelock Recipes and Remembrances
Havelock Centennial
Lincoln, Nebraska

Country Veal Stew

Team this chunky stew with a tossed green salad and crusty bread for the ideal meal on a chilly evening.

2 tablespoons all-purpose flour	3 medium carrots, scraped and cut into very thin 2-inch strips
1 teaspoon salt	
½ teaspoon freshly ground pepper	1 large onion, coarsely chopped
	1 large clove garlic, minced
2 pounds boneless veal shoulder roast, cut into 1-inch pieces	½ pound fresh mushrooms, cut into ¼-inch slices
2 tablespoons butter, melted	½ pound zucchini, cut into ¼-inch slices
2 (16-ounce) cans whole tomatoes, undrained and chopped	1 large sweet red or yellow pepper, cut into 1-inch pieces
2 cups chicken broth	½ cup country Dijon mustard

Combine flour, salt, and freshly ground pepper in a large zip-top plastic bag; add veal. Seal bag securely, and shake until veal is coated.

Brown veal in butter in a large Dutch oven over medium heat. Add tomatoes and next 4 ingredients; bring to a boil. Cover, reduce heat, and simmer 1 hour, stirring occasionally. Add mushrooms, zucchini, and sweet red pepper. Bring to a boil; cover, reduce heat, and simmer 25 minutes or until vegetables are tender. Stir in mustard. Serve immediately. Yield: 12¾ cups.

Above & Beyond Parsley
The Junior League of Kansas City, Missouri

Pork and Beer Stew

¼ cup all-purpose flour
¼ teaspoon salt
¼ teaspoon pepper
2 pounds boneless pork, cut into 1-inch cubes
2 tablespoons vegetable oil
2 medium onions, sliced
1 (12-ounce) can beer

4 sprigs fresh parsley
1 bay leaf
¼ teaspoon dried thyme
1½ cups sliced carrot
Salt and pepper to taste
Hot cooked medium egg noodles
Garnish: fresh parsley sprigs

Combine flour, ¼ teaspoon salt, and ¼ teaspoon pepper in a large zip-top plastic bag; add pork. Seal bag securely; shake until coated.

Brown pork in oil in a Dutch oven over medium heat. Add onion; cook, stirring constantly, 5 minutes or until tender. Stir in beer.

Place 4 parsley sprigs and bay leaf on a 6-inch square of cheesecloth; tie with string. Add to pork mixture; stir in thyme. Bring to a boil; cover, reduce heat, and simmer 1½ hours, stirring occasionally. Add carrot and salt and pepper to taste; cover and cook 30 minutes or until carrot is tender. Remove and discard cheesecloth bag.

To serve, ladle stew over noodles into individual soup bowls. Garnish, if desired. Yield: 5 cups.   Mary Christiano

Intermission, Opera in the Ozarks
Springfield Regional Opera Guild
Springfield, Missouri

Hearty Turkey Stew

1¼ pounds turkey tenderloins, cubed
8 small red potatoes, unpeeled and quartered
4 medium carrots, scraped and cut into ½-inch slices
1 large onion, chopped
4 cloves garlic, minced
3 tablespoons olive oil

2 tablespoons all-purpose flour
1 (10½-ounce) can chicken broth, undiluted
1 cup dry red wine
1 teaspoon dried thyme
1 teaspoon pepper
½ pound fresh mushrooms
½ cup chopped fresh parsley

Cook first 5 ingredients in oil in a large Dutch oven over medium-high heat 10 minutes, stirring often. Reduce heat to low. Add flour, stirring well. Cook 1 minute, stirring constantly. Add chicken broth, wine, thyme, and pepper. Bring to a boil; add mushrooms.

Place pan in oven; bake, uncovered, at 350° for 45 to 50 minutes or until turkey and vegetables are tender, stirring occasionally. Stir in parsley. Yield: 7 cups. Anne Erickson

Food for Family, Friends and Fellowship
Covenant Women Ministries of Forest Park Covenant Church
Muskegon, Michigan

Black Beans 'n' Vegetable Chili

Looking for a nutritious and delicious meatless main dish? Look no further—this chunky chili fills the bill.

1 large onion, coarsely chopped
1 tablespoon vegetable oil
1 (28-ounce) can whole tomatoes, drained and coarsely chopped
⅔ cup picante sauce
1½ teaspoons ground cumin
1 teaspoon salt
½ teaspoon dried basil
1 (15-ounce) can black beans, rinsed and drained

1 medium-size green pepper, cut into ¾-inch pieces
1 medium-size sweet red pepper, cut into ¾-inch pieces
1 large yellow squash or zucchini, cut into ½-inch pieces
Hot cooked rice
Shredded Cheddar cheese
Sour cream
Chopped fresh cilantro
Picante sauce (optional)

Cook onion in oil in a Dutch oven over medium-high heat, stirring constantly, until tender. Add tomatoes and next 4 ingredients; stir well. Bring to a boil; cover, reduce heat, and simmer 5 minutes.

Stir in beans, peppers, and squash. Cover and cook over medium-low heat 25 minutes or until vegetables are tender, stirring mixture occasionally.

To serve, ladle chili over rice into individual soup bowls. Top each serving with cheese, sour cream, and cilantro. Serve with additional picante sauce, if desired. Yield: 6 cups. Michele Farris

"Show-me" Fine Dining
United Guardsman Foundation
St. Joseph, Missouri

White Bean Chili

For variety, you can substitute fresh ground turkey for the chicken in this chili.

1 pound dried Great Northern
  beans
2 medium onions, chopped
1 tablespoon olive oil
2 (4½-ounce) cans chopped
  green chiles, undrained
4 cloves garlic, minced
2 teaspoons ground cumin
1½ teaspoons dried oregano
Dash of ground red pepper

6 cups chicken broth
5 cups chopped cooked chicken
  breast
3 cups (12 ounces) shredded
  Monterey Jack cheese, divided
Salt and pepper to taste
Sour cream
Salsa
Garnish: chopped fresh parsley

Sort and wash beans; place in a large Dutch oven. Cover with water 2 inches above beans; let soak overnight. Drain; set beans aside.

Cook onion in oil in Dutch oven over medium-high heat, stirring constantly, until tender. Add green chiles and next 4 ingredients; cook 2 minutes, stirring constantly. Add beans and chicken broth. Bring to a boil; cover, reduce heat, and simmer 2 hours or until beans are tender, stirring occasionally. Add chicken, 1 cup cheese, and salt and pepper to taste. Bring to a boil; reduce heat, and simmer, uncovered, 10 minutes, stirring often.

To serve, ladle chili into individual soup bowls. Top each serving evenly with remaining 2 cups cheese, sour cream, and salsa. Garnish, if desired. Yield: 13 cups.   Mary Gartland

Immacolata Cookbook
Immacolata Church Ladies Society
St. Louis, Missouri

Vegetables

Autumn Stuffed Squash, page 314

Sesame-Glazed Asparagus

1 pound fresh asparagus
6 green onions, cut diagonally
  into ¼-inch pieces
¼ cup butter or margarine,
  melted
1¼ teaspoons grated lemon
  rind
1 tablespoon lemon juice

¼ teaspoon salt
¼ teaspoon black pepper
⅛ teaspoon ground red pepper
1 tablespoon sesame seeds,
  toasted
1 teaspoon sesame oil
Garnishes: lemon slices, fresh
  flat-leaf parsley sprigs

Snap off tough ends of asparagus. Remove scales from stalks with a knife or vegetable peeler, if desired. Cut asparagus diagonally into 1-inch pieces. Cook asparagus in boiling salted water to cover 6 to 8 minutes or until crisp-tender; drain.

Cook green onions in butter in a skillet over medium heat 1 minute, stirring constantly. Add asparagus, lemon rind, and juice; cook, stirring constantly, 2 minutes or until heated. Stir in salt and peppers. Sprinkle with seeds and oil. Garnish, if desired. Yield: 4 servings.

Savory Secrets: A Collection of St. Louis Recipes
The Greater St. Louis Alumnae Chapter of Sigma Sigma Sigma
St. Louis, Missouri

Hot Stuffed Avocados

These chicken- and cheese-stuffed avocado halves are hearty enough to be served as a main dish.

2 tablespoons butter or
  margarine
2 tablespoons all-purpose flour
1 cup half-and-half
2 cups chopped cooked chicken
2 tablespoons minced onion

2 tablespoons minced celery
½ teaspoon Worcestershire
  sauce
3 ripe avocados
½ cup (2 ounces) shredded
  Cheddar cheese

Melt butter in a heavy saucepan over low heat; add flour, stirring until smooth. Cook 1 minute, stirring constantly. Gradually add half-and-half; cook over medium heat, stirring constantly, until mixture is thickened and bubbly. Stir in chicken and next 3 ingredients; cook until thoroughly heated, stirring occasionally.

Peel avocados, and cut in half lengthwise; remove seeds. Spoon chicken mixture evenly into avocado halves. Place in an ungreased 11- x 7- x 1½-inch baking dish. Add water to dish to depth of ¼ inch. Bake, uncovered, at 350° for 15 minutes. Sprinkle evenly with cheese; bake 5 additional minutes or until cheese melts. Serve immediately. Yield: 6 servings.

The Wild Wild West
The Junior League of Odessa, Texas

Green Beans Supreme

5 cups frozen cut green beans	1 teaspoon salt
½ cup sliced onion	½ teaspoon grated lemon rind
1 tablespoon minced fresh parsley	¼ teaspoon pepper
¼ cup butter or margarine, melted and divided	1 (8-ounce) carton sour cream
2 tablespoons all-purpose flour	½ cup (2 ounces) shredded process American cheese
	½ cup fine, dry breadcrumbs

Cook green beans according to package directions; drain well, and set aside.

Cook onion and parsley in 2 tablespoons butter in a large skillet over medium-high heat, stirring constantly, until tender. Reduce heat to medium-low. Stir in flour, salt, lemon rind, and pepper. Add sour cream, stirring well. Add green beans; cook until thoroughly heated, stirring occasionally.

Spoon mixture into an ungreased 8-inch square baking dish; sprinkle with cheese. Combine breadcrumbs and remaining 2 tablespoons butter; sprinkle over cheese. Broil 8 inches from heat (with electric oven door partially opened) 5 minutes or until cheese melts and breadcrumbs are browned. Yield: 6 servings.

Thelma Wilson

Candlelight and Wisteria
Lee-Scott Academy
Auburn, Alabama

Old-Fashioned Vermont Beans

Maple syrup, a Vermont specialty, lends a sweet flavor note to these baked yellow-eyed beans.

1 (16-ounce) package dried
   yellow-eyed beans
½ teaspoon baking soda
1 medium onion
1 to 1½ cups maple syrup

2 tablespoons prepared mustard
½ teaspoon dry mustard
5 ounces salt pork
2 teaspoons salt

Sort and wash beans; place in a large Dutch oven. Cover with water 2 inches above beans; add baking soda, and let soak 8 hours.

Drain and rinse beans; return to pan. Add water to cover; bring to a boil. Cover, reduce heat, and cook 1 hour. Drain beans, reserving 4 cups liquid. Place onion in Dutch oven; add beans, syrup, and mustards, stirring gently.

Score fat on salt pork in a diamond design; add to bean mixture. Stir in reserved liquid and salt. Cover and bake at 325° for 4½ hours. Uncover and bake 1 additional hour or until beans are tender. Yield: 24 servings.

Chris Loso

Ronald McDonald House of Burlington, Vermont,
Anniversary Edition Cookbook
Ronald McDonald House of Burlington, Vermont

Ginger Beets

4 medium-size fresh beets
   (about ¾ pound)
1 small onion, thinly sliced
   and separated into
   rings
1 tablespoon sugar

1 tablespoon grated fresh
   ginger
Salt and pepper to taste
3 tablespoons butter or
   margarine
2 tablespoons water

Trim off roots and stems of beets; peel beets, and cut into ¼-inch-thick slices.

Layer one-third each of beets and onion in a greased 8-inch square baking dish. Repeat layers twice with remaining beets and onion.

Sprinkle mixture with sugar, ginger, and salt and pepper to taste; dot with butter, and add water. Cover and bake at 400° for 30 minutes, stirring mixture twice. (Add additional water to dish, if necessary.) Serve beets immediately. Yield: 4 servings.

Nothin' Finer
Chapel Hill Service League
Chapel Hill, North Carolina

Spicy Orange Broccoli

Chopped fresh chives would work nicely as a garnish instead of parsley, if your herb garden or local market offers the option.

1½ **pounds fresh broccoli**
1 **cup fresh orange juice**
1 **tablespoon cornstarch**
1 **teaspoon grated orange rind**
½ **teaspoon dried tarragon**

½ **teaspoon dry mustard**
2 **or 3 drops of hot sauce**
Garnishes: grated orange rind,
chopped fresh parsley

Remove broccoli leaves, and cut off tough ends of stalks; discard. Wash broccoli thoroughly, and cut into spears. Arrange broccoli in a steamer basket over boiling water. Cover and steam 5 minutes or until crisp-tender. Set aside, and keep warm.

Combine orange juice and cornstarch in a small saucepan; stir until smooth. Add orange rind and next 3 ingredients, stirring well. Cook over medium heat, stirring constantly, until thickened and bubbly. Pour sauce over broccoli. Garnish, if desired. Serve immediately. Yield: 4 servings.

Sallie Tillman

Enough to Feed an Army
West Point Officers Wives' Club
West Point, New York

Sassy Brussels Sprouts

Peanuts and lemon juice add a lively burst of flavor to brussels sprouts.

2 (10-ounce) packages frozen
  brussels sprouts
½ cup butter or margarine,
  melted
⅔ cup coarsely chopped salted
  roasted peanuts

½ to 1 teaspoon salt
Freshly ground pepper to taste
2 teaspoons fresh lemon juice
Garnish: grated lemon rind

Cook brussels sprouts according to package directions; drain well.
Cook brussels sprouts in butter in a large skillet over medium-high heat 1 minute, stirring constantly. Add peanuts, salt, and pepper to taste; cook 2 minutes, stirring constantly. Stir in lemon juice. Garnish, if desired. Serve immediately. Yield: 6 servings.

Sugar Snips & Asparagus Tips
Woman's Auxiliary of Infant Welfare Society of Chicago
Chicago, Illinois

Hunter's-Style Carrots

Porcini mushrooms, also called cèpes, have a meaty texture and woodsy flavor. The dried form of the mushroom that is called for in this recipe must be softened in liquid before using.

½ ounce dried porcini
  mushrooms
½ cup Madeira
1½ pounds small carrots,
  scraped and cut diagonally
  into ½-inch pieces
3 tablespoons olive oil
⅛ teaspoon salt

1 ounce prosciutto, cut into
  very thin strips
2 large cloves garlic, minced
3 tablespoons chopped fresh
  flat-leaf parsley
⅛ teaspoon freshly ground
  pepper

Rinse mushrooms thoroughly with cold water; drain well. Combine mushrooms and Madeira in a small bowl; let stand 2 hours. Drain, reserving liquid. Finely chop mushrooms, and set aside.
Cook carrot in oil in a large skillet over medium-high heat 15 minutes, stirring frequently. Add reserved liquid, mushrooms, and salt;

reduce heat to medium-low, and cook, stirring constantly, 8 minutes or until carrot is lightly browned. Add prosciutto and garlic, and cook 1 minute or until thoroughly heated. Stir in parsley and pepper. Serve immediately. Yield: 4 servings. Dana Frederickson

From Your Neighbor's Kitchen
Friends of Riverton Park
Riverton, New Jersey

Company Cauliflower with Herby Pecan Butter

1 large cauliflower
20 pecan halves
¼ cup butter or margarine, melted

¼ cup finely chopped pecans
1 teaspoon minced fresh thyme
Garnish: fresh thyme sprigs

Remove outer leaves and stalk of cauliflower, leaving head whole. Wash cauliflower. Place in a vegetable steamer over boiling water. Cover and steam 15 minutes or until tender. Place cauliflower on a serving plate; set aside, and keep warm.

Cook pecan halves in butter in a small skillet over medium heat, stirring constantly, until lightly toasted. Remove pecans with a slotted spoon, reserving butter in skillet. Cook chopped pecans in butter in skillet, stirring constantly, until lightly toasted. Stir in minced thyme.

Stud cauliflower with toasted pecan halves; pour chopped pecan mixture over cauliflower. Garnish, if desired. Serve immediately. Yield: 8 servings. Lane Furneaux

The Jubilee of Our Many Blessings Cookbook
United Methodist Women
Highland Park United Methodist Church
Dallas, Texas

Creamed Celery with Water Chestnuts

Consider this creamy, crunchy vegetable mixture when you want a new side dish for beef.

4 cups sliced celery
½ teaspoon salt
1 (2½-ounce) jar sliced
 mushrooms, drained
½ cup sliced water chestnuts
¼ cup slivered almonds
3 tablespoons butter or
 margarine

3 tablespoons all-purpose flour
½ cup milk
1 cup chicken broth
½ cup grated Parmesan cheese
½ cup crushed round buttery
 crackers
2 tablespoons butter or
 margarine, melted

Place celery in a saucepan; add water to cover. Stir in salt. Bring to a boil; reduce heat, and simmer 5 minutes. Drain well. Combine celery, mushrooms, water chestnuts, and almonds; set aside.

Melt 3 tablespoons butter in a heavy saucepan over low heat; add flour, stirring until smooth. Cook 1 minute, stirring constantly. Gradually add milk and chicken broth; cook over medium heat, stirring constantly, until mixture is thickened and bubbly. Add celery mixture; stir well.

Spoon into a greased 2-quart baking dish; sprinkle with cheese. Combine cracker crumbs and 2 tablespoons butter; sprinkle over cheese. Bake, uncovered, at 350° for 30 minutes. Yield: 8 servings.

Simply Heavenly
Woman's Synodical Union of the Associate Reformed
Presbyterian Church
Greenville, South Carolina

Celery Root and Parsley Puree

1 large celery root, peeled and
 cubed (about ¾ pound)
1 medium-size red potato,
 peeled and cubed
1½ cups water

½ cup whipping cream
¼ teaspoon salt
¼ teaspoon pepper
3 tablespoons chopped fresh
 parsley

Combine celery root, potato, and water in a medium saucepan; bring to a boil. Cover, reduce heat, and simmer 15 minutes or until vegetables are tender. Drain vegetables, discarding liquid. Let vegetables cool slightly.

Position knife blade in food processor bowl; add vegetables, whipping cream, salt, and pepper. Process until smooth, stopping once to scrape down sides; return mixture to pan. Add parsley; cook over medium heat, stirring constantly, until thoroughly heated. Serve immediately. Yield: 4 servings.   Audrey Patterson

Cooking in the Litchfield Hills
The Pratt Center
New Milford, Connecticut

Heavenly Corn

2 **cups frozen whole kernel corn, thawed**	½ **teaspoon salt**
1 **cup whipping cream**	¼ **teaspoon pepper**
3 **large eggs, beaten**	**Dash of ground nutmeg**
3 **tablespoons butter or margarine, melted**	3 **egg whites**
	¼ **cup (1 ounce) shredded Swiss cheese**

Combine first 7 ingredients in a medium bowl; stir well.

Beat egg whites at high speed of an electric mixer until stiff peaks form. Gently fold egg white into corn mixture; spoon into a buttered 2-quart baking dish. Top with cheese. Bake, uncovered, at 300° for 55 minutes. Increase oven temperature to 375°; bake 5 additional minutes. Serve immediately. Yield: 6 servings.   Jane Ryan

Favorite Recipes
National Association of Women in Construction
Tri-County Chapter #317
Vero Beach, Florida

Braised Lentils

It's important to use a skillet with a tight-fitting lid when braising the lentils. It will keep the liquid from evaporating during the lengthy cooking time.

6 slices bacon, chopped
½ cup chopped onion
1 carrot, scraped and chopped
3 cups chicken broth
1¼ cups dried lentils
2 tablespoons white wine
    vinegar

2 tablespoons butter or
    margarine
1 bay leaf
¼ teaspoon salt
⅛ teaspoon pepper

Cook bacon in a large skillet until crisp; remove bacon, reserving 2 tablespoons drippings in skillet. Set bacon aside.

Cook onion and carrot in drippings in skillet over medium-high heat, stirring constantly, until vegetables are tender. Stir in chicken broth, lentils, white wine vinegar, butter, and bay leaf; bring to a boil. Cover, reduce heat, and simmer 1 hour. Remove and discard bay leaf. Stir in salt and pepper; sprinkle with bacon. Serve immediately. Yield: 4 servings.

Great Recipes from Great Gardeners
The Pennsylvania Horticultural Society
Philadelphia, Pennsylvania

Creamed Mushroom Puff

½ pound fresh mushrooms,
    sliced
¼ cup butter or margarine,
    melted
½ cup all-purpose flour
1 cup milk

¼ cup whipping cream
2 tablespoons freshly grated
    Parmesan cheese
½ teaspoon salt
Pinch of ground red pepper
3 large eggs, separated

Cook mushrooms in butter in a medium saucepan over medium-low heat, stirring constantly, until tender. Add flour, stirring until blended. Cook 1 minute, stirring constantly. Gradually add milk and whipping cream; cook over medium heat, stirring constantly, until mixture is thickened and bubbly. Add cheese, salt, and pepper, stirring until cheese melts.

Beat egg yolks until thick and pale. Gradually stir beaten egg yolk into mushroom mixture.

Beat egg whites at high speed of an electric mixer until stiff peaks form. Gently fold one-fourth of egg white into mushroom mixture. Fold in remaining egg white. Spoon into a buttered 1-quart soufflé dish. Bake at 375° for 40 to 45 minutes or until puffed and set. Serve immediately. Yield: 4 servings. Carolyn Walker

The Company's Cookin'
Employees of the Rouse Company
Columbia, Maryland

Buttermilk Batter-Fried Onion Rings

Make a hamburger a happening with these jumbo fried onion rings.

1 **pound large Spanish onions**	1 **tablespoon sugar**
1 **cup all-purpose flour**	½ **teaspoon salt**
1 **cup buttermilk**	**Peanut oil**
1 **teaspoon baking powder**	

Cut onions into ½-inch slices, and separate into rings. Set aside.

Combine flour and next 4 ingredients in a medium bowl, stirring with a wire whisk until smooth.

Pour oil to depth of 2 inches into a Dutch oven; heat to 375°. Dip rings into batter. Fry, a few at a time, until golden, turning once. Drain well on paper towels. Serve immediately. Yield: 4 servings.

Family & Company
The Junior League of Binghamton, New York

Ginger Peas with Summer Squash

Fresh ginger and cilantro give an unexpected flavor twist to this green and yellow vegetable medley.

1 pound fresh snow pea pods
3 tablespoons thinly sliced green
   onions
2 teaspoons grated fresh ginger
1 clove garlic, minced
2 tablespoons olive oil

¾ pound yellow squash, thinly
   sliced
1 sweet yellow pepper, chopped
1 tablespoon chopped fresh
   cilantro or parsley
Salt and pepper to taste

Wash snow peas; trim ends, and remove strings. Cut snow peas lengthwise into thin strips, and set aside.

Cook green onions, ginger, and garlic in oil in a large skillet over medium-high heat 1 minute, stirring constantly. Add snow peas, squash, and chopped pepper; cook 9 to 10 minutes or until crisp-tender, stirring occasionally. Sprinkle with cilantro. Add salt and pepper to taste. Serve immediately. Yield: 8 servings.

From Portland's Palate
The Junior League of Portland, Oregon

Red Peppers Royale

4 large sweet red peppers
14 ounces fresh spinach
1 small onion, minced
1 clove garlic, minced
1 tablespoon extra virgin olive
   oil
1 (15-ounce) carton ricotta
   cheese

¼ cup freshly grated Parmesan
   cheese
2 large eggs, lightly beaten
½ to ¾ teaspoon salt
Freshly grated Parmesan cheese
Garnish: fresh parsley sprigs

Cut red peppers in half lengthwise. Remove and discard seeds and membranes; set peppers aside.

Remove stems from spinach; wash leaves thoroughly, and pat dry. Position knife blade in food processor bowl; add spinach. Process until finely chopped.

Cook spinach, onion, and garlic in oil in a large skillet over medium heat, stirring constantly, until onion is tender. Add ricotta cheese and next 3 ingredients; stir well. Spoon spinach mixture evenly into pepper halves. Place in a 13- x 9- x 2-inch baking dish; add water to dish to depth of ¼ inch. Bake, uncovered, at 350° for 30 minutes. Sprinkle with additional Parmesan cheese. Garnish, if desired. Serve immediately. Yield: 8 servings.

The William & Mary Cookbook
Society of the Alumni, College of William and Mary
Williamsburg, Virginia

Better than Grandma's Mashed Potatoes

Don't tell Grandma, but carrots, onion, and dillweed in these mashed potatoes rival her recipe.

3 **pounds baking potatoes, peeled**
2½ **quarts chicken broth**
4 **small carrots, scraped and cut into ½-inch pieces**
1 **small onion, chopped**
¼ **cup butter or margarine**
1 **teaspoon dried dillweed**

1½ **cups sour cream**
3 **tablespoons chopped fresh parsley**
1 **teaspoon salt**
¼ **teaspoon pepper**
1 **tablespoon butter or margarine**

Combine potatoes and chicken broth in a Dutch oven; bring to a boil. Reduce heat, and simmer 15 minutes. Add carrot and onion, and simmer 20 minutes or until potatoes are tender; drain.

Combine cooked vegetables, ¼ cup butter, and dillweed in a large bowl; mash. Add sour cream and next 3 ingredients, stirring well. Spoon potato mixture into a greased 11- x 7- x 1½-inch baking dish; dot with 1 tablespoon butter. Cover and bake at 325° for 1 hour. Yield: 8 servings.

Sharon Fowler

Kailua Cooks
Le Jardin Academy
Kailua, Hawaii

Four-Cheese Potatoes

Cheddar, mozzarella, ricotta, and Parmesan cheeses give this potato dish its full-bodied flavor.

12 medium-size red potatoes (about 4 pounds), unpeeled
3 cups (12 ounces) shredded Cheddar cheese, divided
2 cups (8 ounces) shredded mozzarella cheese
2 cups ricotta cheese
1 (8-ounce) carton sour cream
⅓ cup grated Parmesan cheese
¼ cup finely chopped green onions
3 tablespoons chopped fresh parsley
2 cloves garlic, crushed
1 teaspoon dried basil
¼ teaspoon pepper

Cut potatoes into 1-inch cubes. Cook in boiling water to cover 10 minutes. Drain well, and set aside.

Combine 1½ cups Cheddar cheese and next 9 ingredients in a large bowl; stir well. Gently stir in potato cubes. Spoon mixture into a greased 13- x 9- x 2-inch baking dish. Sprinkle with remaining 1½ cups Cheddar cheese. Bake, uncovered, at 350° for 30 minutes or until potato is tender. Yield: 8 to 10 servings.

Desert Treasures
The Junior League of Phoenix, Arizona

Autumn Stuffed Squash

A colorful medley of diced vegetables is snuggled inside each golden-colored acorn squash in this autumn-inspired recipe.

2 small acorn squash
¼ cup butter or margarine, melted and divided
½ cup diced onion
½ cup diced carrot
½ cup diced sweet red pepper
½ cup diced zucchini
½ cup diced fresh mushrooms
1 small clove garlic, minced

Cut acorn squash in half crosswise; remove and discard seeds and membranes. Brush cut sides of acorn squash with 1 tablespoon melted butter. Place squash, cut side down, in a 9-inch square baking dish. Add hot water to baking dish to depth of 1 inch. Cover and bake at 350° for 30 minutes.

Cook onion and next 5 ingredients in remaining 3 tablespoons butter in a large skillet over medium-high heat, stirring constantly, until tender. Spoon mixture evenly into squash halves. Cover and bake 35 additional minutes or until squash is tender. Serve immediately. Yield: 4 servings.

E. Hurrle

Country Cookin' of St. Augusta
St. Ann's Christian Women, St. Mary Help of Christian Church
St. Cloud, Minnesota

Zucchini in Dill Cream Sauce

6 **medium zucchini (about 2 pounds), cut into very thin strips**
½ **cup water**
¼ **cup finely chopped onion**
1 **teaspoon salt**
1 **teaspoon chicken-flavored bouillon granules**
½ **teaspoon dried dillweed**
2 **tablespoons butter or margarine, melted**
2 **teaspoons sugar**
1 **teaspoon lemon juice**
½ **cup sour cream**
2 **tablespoons all-purpose flour**

Combine first 6 ingredients in a large saucepan. Bring to a boil; cover, reduce heat, and simmer 5 minutes or until vegetables are crisp-tender. Remove zucchini and onion, reserving ½ cup liquid in pan. Set vegetables aside.

Add butter, sugar, and lemon juice to liquid in pan, stirring gently to combine. Combine sour cream and flour, stirring until smooth. Stir half of hot mixture into sour cream mixture; add to remaining hot mixture, stirring constantly. Cook over medium heat, stirring constantly, until mixture is thickened and bubbly. Add reserved vegetables, and cook 1 minute or until thoroughly heated. Serve immediately. Yield: 6 servings.

Ruth Lovell

Reflections of the West
Telephone Pioneers of America, Skyline Chapter No. 67
Helena, Montana

Thai Zucchini

The intriguing flavor combinations of Thai cuisine are taking this exotic fare mainstream. In this recipe, mild-flavored zucchini is the perfect partner for the stronger flavors of the ginger, red pepper, rice vinegar, soy sauce, and peanuts.

1 clove garlic, minced
1 teaspoon minced fresh ginger
⅛ teaspoon dried crushed red pepper
2 teaspoons olive oil
⅓ cup finely chopped unsalted roasted peanuts

3 tablespoons chicken broth
3 tablespoons rice vinegar
2 tablespoons soy sauce
⅛ teaspoon sugar
3 medium zucchini (about 1 pound), cut into very thin strips

Cook garlic, ginger, and red pepper in oil in a large skillet over medium-high heat 1 minute, stirring constantly. Add peanuts and next 4 ingredients; stir well. Add zucchini, and cook, stirring constantly, 5 minutes or until crisp-tender. Serve immediately. Yield: 4 servings.

Above & Beyond Parsley
The Junior League of Kansas City, Missouri

Tomatoes Pinehurst

Salad dressing, marinated artichoke hearts, Parmesan cheese, and fresh basil give these baked tomato halves an Italian accent. Serve them with fish or beef.

4 large tomatoes
1 cup Italian salad dressing
1 (6-ounce) jar marinated artichoke hearts, drained and sliced
1⅓ cups crushed round buttery crackers
½ cup unsalted butter or margarine, melted

⅓ cup freshly grated Parmesan cheese
1 tablespoon chopped fresh basil
2 tablespoons plus 2 teaspoons unsalted butter or margarine

Dip tomatoes into boiling water 20 seconds; remove with a slotted spoon, and plunge into ice water. Slip skins off, using a paring knife. Cut tomatoes in half; arrange tomato halves, cut side up, in an ungreased 13- x 9- x 2-inch baking dish. Pour Italian dressing evenly over tomato halves; cover and chill at least 8 hours.

Spoon sliced artichoke hearts evenly over tomato halves. Combine cracker crumbs and ½ cup melted butter; stir well. Sprinkle crumb mixture evenly over tomato halves. Sprinkle evenly with cheese and basil; dot with 2 tablespoons plus 2 teaspoons butter. Bake, uncovered, at 350° for 20 minutes or until golden. Serve immediately with a slotted spoon. Yield: 8 servings.

Come On In!
The Junior League of Jackson, Mississippi

Peacock Vegetables

Proudly serve this colorful vegetable blend at your next tailgate party or potluck dinner, and get ready for the raves.

2 **purple onions, cut into eighths**	4 **cloves garlic, thinly sliced**
2 **small yellow squash, cut into ½-inch strips**	2 **tablespoons minced fresh parsley**
2 **small zucchini, cut into ½-inch strips**	1 **tablespoon balsamic vinegar**
1 **sweet red pepper, cut into ½-inch strips**	1 **tablespoon olive oil**
	1 **teaspoon dried oregano**
1 **sweet yellow pepper, cut into ½-inch strips**	¼ **teaspoon salt**
	¼ **teaspoon pepper**
1 **green pepper, cut into ½-inch strips**	

Place first 7 ingredients in a large bowl. Combine parsley and next 5 ingredients in a jar; cover tightly, and shake vigorously. Pour over vegetables; toss well.

Spoon vegetable mixture into an ungreased 13- x 9- x 2-inch pan. Bake at 425° for 20 minutes, stirring every 5 minutes. Serve warm or at room temperature. Yield: 6 servings.

The Bess Collection
The Junior Service League of Independence, Missouri

Herbed Crêpes with Piperade Filling

1½ cups all-purpose flour
1 cup milk
1 cup water
¼ cup butter, melted
4 large eggs, lightly beaten
1 tablespoon chopped fresh
  parsley
1 teaspoon salt
½ teaspoon dried tarragon
½ teaspoon dried chives
Dash of ground white pepper
Vegetable cooking spray
Piperade Filling
Freshly grated Parmesan cheese

Combine first 10 ingredients in container of an electric blender; cover and process 1 minute. Cover and chill 2 hours.

Coat bottom of an 8-inch crêpe pan or nonstick skillet with cooking spray; place over medium heat until hot.

Pour ¼ cup batter into pan; quickly tilt pan in all directions so batter covers bottom of pan. Cook 1 minute or until crêpe can be shaken loose from pan. Turn crêpe over, and cook about 30 seconds. Place crêpe on a dish towel to cool. Repeat with remaining batter. Stack crêpes between sheets of wax paper to prevent sticking.

Spoon filling down center of spotty side of each crêpe; fold sides over. Place, seam side down, in 2 greased 13- x 9- x 2-inch baking dishes. Sprinkle with cheese. Bake, uncovered, at 400° for 8 minutes or until thoroughly heated. Serve immediately. Yield: 8 servings.

Piperade Filling

1 pound fresh mushrooms,
  sliced
2 tablespoons butter, melted
1 tablespoon vegetable oil
1 teaspoon lemon juice
Salt and pepper to taste
3 medium onions, thinly
  sliced
1 tablespoon butter, melted
1 tablespoon vegetable oil
2 large green peppers, cut into
  thin strips
1 large sweet red pepper, cut
  into thin strips
1 (28-ounce) can Italian-style
  tomatoes, drained
2 cloves garlic, minced
1 (10-ounce) package frozen
  artichoke hearts, thawed,
  drained, and chopped
¼ teaspoon dried oregano
2 tablespoons chopped fresh
  parsley

Cook mushrooms in 2 tablespoons butter and 1 tablespoon oil in a large skillet over medium-high heat, stirring constantly, until tender. Add lemon juice, and salt and pepper to taste; stir well. Set aside.

Cook onion in 1 tablespoon butter and 1 tablespoon oil in a large skillet over medium-high heat 5 minutes, stirring constantly. Add green and red peppers, and cook, stirring constantly, until tender. Add tomatoes and garlic; cook over medium-high heat 15 minutes or until liquid is evaporated, stirring occasionally. Stir in chopped artichoke hearts, oregano, and parsley. Add mushroom mixture; stir well. Yield: 8 cups.

The Elegant Cook
The Friends of the Eastern Christian School Association
North Haledon, New Jersey

Vegetable Strudel

In this savory version of strudel, phyllo pastry encases a cheese and vegetable mixture. Keep the phyllo covered with a slightly damp towel until you're ready for it, to keep the sheets from becoming dry and brittle.

1½ cups (6 ounces) shredded
    sharp Cheddar cheese
1½ cups chopped cooked
    broccoli
1 cup chopped cooked
    cauliflower
1 cup chopped cooked carrot
2 large eggs, lightly beaten

½ teaspoon salt
½ teaspoon dried basil
½ teaspoon dried tarragon
¼ teaspoon pepper
7 sheets frozen phyllo pastry,
    thawed in refrigerator
Melted butter or margarine

Combine first 9 ingredients in a large bowl; stir well.

Work with 1 sheet of phyllo at a time (keep remaining sheets covered with a slightly damp towel). Place 1 phyllo sheet on an ungreased baking sheet. Lightly brush with butter. Layer 5 more sheets of phyllo on top, brushing each sheet with butter. Spread vegetable mixture over phyllo to within 2 inches of edges. Place remaining sheet of phyllo over mixture. Fold edges over twice to seal. Fold in half lengthwise; brush with butter. Bake at 350° for 30 to 35 minutes or until golden. Cut into 1½-inch slices. Yield: 8 servings.
    Bethe Pilch

A Jewish Family Cookbook
Valley Beth Shalom Nursery School
Encino, California

Acknowledgments

Each of the community cookbooks listed is represented by recipes appearing in *America's Best Recipes*. Unless otherwise noted, the copyright is held by the sponsoring organization whose mailing address is included.

300th Anniversary Cookbook, All Hallows' Episcopal Church, 809 Central Ave., P.O. Box 235, Davidsonville, MD 21035

888 Favorite Recipes, Boy Scout Troop 888, Fairview United Methodist Church, 2505 Old Niles Ferry Pike, Maryville, TN 37803

Above & Beyond Parsley, Junior League of Kansas City, Inc., 9215 Ward Pkwy., Kansas City, MO 64114

Almost Chefs, A Cookbook for Kids, Palm Beach Guild for the Children's Home Society, 3600 Broadway, West Palm Beach, FL 33407

American Buffet, General Federation of Women's Clubs, 1734 North St. NW, Washington, DC 20036-2990

Among the Lilies, Women in Missions, First Baptist Church of Atlanta, 754 Peachtree St. NE, Atlanta, GA 30365

Anatolian Feast, Food of Türkiye, American Turkish Association, Inc., 1400 Hermann 4G, Houston, TX 77004

Angel Food: Recipes and Reflections from Great Catholic Kitchens, Sacred Heart Program, 3900 Westminster Pl., St. Louis, MO 63108

Angels & Friends Favorite Recipes II, Angels of Easter Seal, 299 Edwards St., Youngstown, OH 44502

Appalachian Appetites, Service League of Boone, P.O. Box 2651, Boone, NC 28607

Back Home Again, Junior League of Indianapolis, Inc./J.L.I. Publications, 3050 N. Meridian St., Indianapolis, IN 46208

Bay Leaves, Junior Service League of Panama City, Inc., P.O. Box 404, Panama City, FL 32402

The Bess Collection, Junior Service League of Independence, P.O. Box 1571, Independence, MO 64055

The Best of Sunset Boulevard, University Synagogue Sisterhood, 11960 Sunset Blvd., Los Angeles, CA 90049

Bethel's Bounty, Bethel Presbyterian Women, 19920 Bethel Church Rd., Davidson, NC 28036

Beyond Brisket, Sisterhood of Temple Israel, 145 Hartford St., Natick, MA 01760

By Special Request, Our Favorite Recipes, Piggly Wiggly Carolina Employees, 4401 Piggly Wiggly Dr., Charleston, SC 29405

California Sizzles, Junior League of Pasadena, Inc., 149 S. Madison Ave., Pasadena, CA 91101

Candlelight and Wisteria, Lee-Scott Academy, 2307 E. Glenn Ave., Auburn, AL 36830

CAP-tivating Cooking, YWCA of Peoria, Children and Parents Support, 301 N.E. Jefferson, Peoria, IL 61602

Carol & Friends, A Taste of North County, Carol & Friends Steering Committee of the Carol Cox Re-Entry Women's Scholarship Fund at CSU-San Marcos, California State University, San Marcos, San Marcos, CA 92096

Carolina Harvest: 20 Years of Culinary Heritage, American Cancer Society-South Carolina Division, 128 Stonemark Ln., Columbia, SC 29210

Celebrate!, Junior League of Sacramento, Inc., 778 University Ave., Sacramento, CA 95825

Celebrated South Carolinians!, American Cancer Society, 128 Stonemark Ln., Columbia, SC 29210

Celebration: Saint Andrew's School 30th Anniversary Book of Celebrated Recipes, St. Andrew's School Parents' Association, 3900 Jog Rd., Boca Raton, FL 33434

Champions: Favorite Foods of Indy Car Racing, Championship Auto Racing Auxiliary, 2915 N. High School Rd., Indianapolis, IN 46224

Chefs and Artists, Back Mountain Memorial Library, 96 Huntsville Rd., Dallas, PA 18612

A Cleveland Collection, Junior League of Cleveland, Inc., 10819 Magnolia Dr., Cleveland, OH 44106

Coastal Cuisine, Texas Style, Junior Service League of Brazosport, P.O. Box 163, Lake Jackson, TX 77566

Coe Hall Cooks!, Coe Hall, Planting Fields Rd., Planting Fields Arboretum, Oyster Bay, NY 11771

A Collection of Favorite Recipes, Po'okela Church, P.O. Box 365, Makawao, HI 96768

Come On In!, Junior League of Jackson, Inc., P.O. Box 4709, 805 Riverside Dr., Jackson,
    MS 39296-4709

Come Savor Swansea, First Christian Congregational Church, P.O. Box 76, Swansea, MA 02777

The Company's Cookin', Employees of the Rouse Company, 10275 Little Patuxent Pkwy., Columbia,
    MD 21044

Conflict-Free Cooking, National Court Reporters Foundation, 8224 Old Courthouse Rd.,Vienna,
    VA 22182-3808

Cookin' for the Kids, Wal-Mart Distribution Center #6011, 2200 Manufacturers Blvd., Brookhaven,
    MS 39601

Cooking in the Litchfield Hills, Pratt Center, 163 Papermill Rd., New Milford, CT 06776

Cooking Up a Storm, Florida Style, Brookwood Guild, 901 7th Ave. S, St. Petersburg,
    FL 33705-1998

Cooking with Christopher in Mind, Family and Friends of Christopher Lee Hamilton, 625 Simon Dr.,
    East Peoria, IL 61611

Cooking with Class, A Second Helping, Charlotte Latin School, P.O. Box 6143, Charlotte, NC 28277

Cooking with Herb Scents, Western Reserve Herb Society, 30531 Timber Ln., Bay Village, OH 44140

Cookin' with C.L.A.S.S., Citizens League for Adult Special Services, Inc., 1 Parker St., Lawrence,
    MA 01843

Cookin' with Fire, Milford Permanent Firefighters Association, 21 Birch St., Milford, MA 01757

Cooks Incorporated, Miami Valley Health Foundation, 31 Wyoming St., Dayton, OH 45409

A Cook's Tour of the Bayou Country, Churchwomen of the Southwest Deanery of the Episcopal
    Diocese of Louisiana, 214 Circle Dr., Franklin, LA 70538

Country Cookin' of St. Augusta, St. Anne's Christian Women, St. Mary Help of Christian Church,
    c/o Marilyn Hurrle, 24466 County Rd. 7, St. Cloud, MN 56301

Country Cupboard Collection, Treasured Recipes from AT&T, AT&T/Western Electric Council,
    Telephone Pioneers of America, 1111 Woods Mill Rd., Ballwin, MO 63011

Cranbrook Reflections: A Culinary Collection, Cranbrook House and Gardens Auxiliary, 380 Lone Pine
    Rd., Box 801, Bloomfield Hills, MI 48303

Cross-Town Cooking, Women's Group of Assumption and Sacred Heart Parishes, 1015 14th St.,
    Bellingham, WA 98225

Culinary Arts, Volume II, Society of the Arts of Allentown Art Museum, 5th and Court Sts.,
    P.O. Box 388, Allentown, PA 18105-0388

Culinary Classics, From Our Kitchens, Mountain State Apple Harvest Festival, Inc., P.O. Box 1362,
    Martinsburg, WV 25401

Culinary Masterpieces, Birmingham Museum of Art, 2000 8th Ave. N, Birmingham,
    AL 35203-2278

Derry Community Playground Cookbook, Derry Playground Committee, P.O. Box 228, East Derry,
    NH 03041

Desert Treasures, Junior League of Phoenix, Inc., P.O. Box 10377, Phoenix, AZ 85064

Dining with Southern Elegance, Terrebonne Association for Family and Community Education,
    P.O. Box 627, Houma, LA 70361-0627

Discover Oklahoma Cookin', Oklahoma 4-H Foundation, Inc., 205 Poultry Science, Stillwater,
    OK 74078

Dock 'n Dine in Dorchester, Long Wharf Lighthouse Committee, P.O. Box 643, Cambridge, MD 21613

Door County Cooking, Bay View Lutheran Church, 340 W. Maple St., Sturgeon Bay, WI 54235

Dundee Presbyterian Church Cook Book, Dundee Presbyterian Church, 5312 Underwood Ave., Omaha,
    NE 68132

Education That's Cooking, Our Favorite Recipes, Rowan-Cabarrus Community College, Phi Beta Lambda
    and Phi Theta Kappa, I-85 off Jake Alexander Blvd., Salisbury, NC 27145

The Elegant Cook, Friends of the Eastern Christian School Association, 50 Oakwood Ave., North
    Haledon, NJ 07508

Enough to Feed an Army, West Point Officers Wives' Club, P.O. Box 44, West Point, NY 10996

Essence of Kansas: 4-H Cookbook, Taste Two, Kansas 4-H Foundation, Inc., 116 Umberger Hall, Kansas State University, Manhattan, KS 66506

Exclusively Pumpkin Cookbook, Coventry Historical Society, Box 534, Coventry, CT 06238

Fabulous Foods, Children's Miracle Network, St. John's Hospital and Southern Illinois University School of Medicine, 800 E. Carpenter, Springfield, IL 62702

Family & Company, Junior League of Binghamton, Inc., 55 Main St., Binghamton, NY 13904

Family Style Cookbook, Northern Door Child Care Center, 340 Hwy. 57, Sister Bay, WI 54234

Favorite Recipes, St. Isaac Jogues Senior Guild, St. Mary's of the Hills Catholic Church, 2675 John R. Rd., Rochester Hills, MI 48307

Favorite Recipes National Association of Women in Construction, Tri-County Chapter #317, 2250 S. Old Dixie Hwy., Vero Beach, FL 32962

The Feast, St. Mary's Catholic Community, P.O. Box 399, 616 Dearborn St., Caldwell, ID 83606-0399

Feeding the Flock, Holy Family Parish, 1926 N. Marquette, Davenport, IA 52804

Fiddlers Canyon Ward Cookbook, Fiddlers Canyon Ward Relief Society, 760 E. Cobble Creek Dr., Cedar City, UT 84720

First United Methodist Church Centennial Cookbook, 1993, United Methodist Women of First United Methodist Church, 302 E. 2nd St., Casper, WY 28601

Five Star Sensations, Auxiliary of University Hospitals of Cleveland, 11100 Euclid Ave., Cleveland, OH 44106

Flatbush Feasts, First Edition, Flatbush Development Corporation, 1418 Corelyou Rd., Brooklyn, NY 11226

Flavors of Cape Henlopen, Village Improvement Association, P.O. Box 144, Boardwalk and Grenoble Pl., Rehoboth Beach, DE 19971

A Flock of Good Recipes, Shepherd of the Bay Lutheran Church, Hwy. 42, P.O. Box 27, Ellison Bay, WI 54210

Food for Family, Friends and Fellowship, Covenant Women Ministries of Forest Park Covenant Church, 3815 Henry St., Muskegon, MI 49441

Food for Thought, Indian Creek School Parent Teacher Organization, Evergreen Rd., Crownsville, MD 21032

For Goodness Taste, Junior League of Rochester, Inc., 110 Linden Oaks, Ste. A, Rochester, NY 14625

Franciscan Centennial Cookbook, Franciscan Sisters, 116 8th Ave. SE, Little Falls, MN 56345

From Generation to Generation, Sisterhood of Temple Emanu-El, 8500 Hillcrest Rd., Dallas, TX 75225

From Portland's Palate, Junior League of Portland, 4838 S.W. Scholls Ferry Rd., Portland, OR 97225

From the Hearts and Homes of Bellingham Covenant Church, Covenant Women's Ministries of Bellingham Covenant Church, 920 E. Sunset Dr., Bellingham, WA 98226

From Your Neighbor's Kitchen, Friends of Riverton Park, P.O. Box 47, Riverton, NJ 08077

The Gasparilla Cookbook, Junior League of Tampa, Inc., 87 Columbia Dr., Tampa, FL 33606

Georgia Land, Medical Association of Georgia Alliance, 938 Peachtree St. NE, Atlanta, GA 30309

The Global Gourmet, Concordia Language Villages, 901 S. 8th St., Moorhead, MN 56562

Golden Oldies Cook Book, Catholic Diocese of Belleville Ministry to Sick and Aged, 2620 Lebanon Ave., Belleville, IL 62221

Good Food, Good Company, Junior Service League of Thomasville, P.O. Box 279, Thomasville, GA 31799

Good to the Core, Apple Corps of the Weller Center for Health Education, 2009 Lehigh St., Easton, PA 18042

Gracious Goodness, Charleston!, Bishop England High School Endowment Fund, 203 Calhoun St., Charleston, SC 29401

Great Recipes from Great Gardeners, Pennsylvania Horticultural Society, 325 Walnut St., Philadelphia, PA 19106-2777

Harbor Hills Book Club's Lunch Bag, Harbor Hills Book Club, 683 Santa Maria Ln., Davidsonville, MD 21035

Havelock Recipes and Remembrances, Havelock Centennial, 6205 Havelock Ave., Lincoln, NE 68507

Hawaiian Medley, A Cookbook of Old Favorites, Volume IV, Kamehameha Band Booster Club, Kapalama Heights, Honolulu, HI 96817

Heard in the Kitchen, Heard Museum Guild, 22 E. Monte Vista Rd., Phoenix, AZ 85004-1480

Heart & Soul, Junior League of Memphis, Inc., 3475 Central Ave., Memphis, TN 38111

Heart Choice Recipes from Charleston's Greatest Chefs, Medical University of South Carolina Heart Center, 171 Ashley Ave., Charleston, SC 29425

Heavenly Hosts, Bryn Mawr Presbyterian Church, 625 Montgomery Ave., Bryn Mawr, PA 19010

Here's What's Cooking at Standish Elementary, Standish Elementary Parents and Teachers for Kids, 583 E. Cedar St., Standish, MI 48658

The Heritage Collection, Western Kentucky University Home Economics Alumni Association, 3341 Cemetery Rd., Bowling Green, KY 42103

Holiday Sampler, Welcome Wagon Club of the Mid Ohio Valley, P.O. Box 5365, Vienna, WV 26105

Holy Cow, Chicago's Cooking!, Church of the Holy Comforter, P.O. Box 168, Kenilworth, IL 60043

Home Cookin', Volunteer Services Council for Abilene State School, P.O. Box 451, S. 25th and Maple, Abilene, TX 79602

Hopeful Hearts Cookbook, Macoupin County Adopt-a-Pet Animal Shelter, 226 Maple, Benld, IL 62009

Idalia Community Cookbook, Women's Fellowship of St. John United Church of Christ, 28439 Co. Rd. 7, Idalia, CO 80735

Immacolata Cookbook, Immacolata Church Ladies Society, 8900 Clayton Rd., St. Louis, MO 63117

The Impossible Diet Cookbook, Recovery Alliance, Inc., P.O. Box 561, Milford, CT 06460

Intermission, Opera in the Ozarks, Springfield Regional Opera Guild, 109 Park Central, Springfield, MO 65806

It's Rainin' Recipes, Charles B. Hopkins Chapter, Telephone Pioneers of America, 1600 7th Ave., Rm. 2013, Seattle, WA 98191

A Jewish Family Cookbook, Valley Beth Shalom Nursery School, 15739 Ventura Blvd., Encino, CA 91436

The Jubilee of Our Many Blessings Cookbook, United Methodist Women, Highland Park United Methodist Church, Bethlehem Center, 6435 Malcolm Dr., Dallas, TX 75214-3187

June Fete Fare, Women's Board of Abington Memorial Hospital, Old York Rd., Abington, PA 19001

Kailua Cooks, Le Jardin Academy, 1110-A Kailua Rd., Kailua, HI 96734

The Kinderhaus Cookbook, Kinderhaus Children's Center, R.D. 2, Box 443, Williston, VT 05495

Lawtons Progressors, 50 Years and Still Cookin', Lawton Progressors 4-H Club, 2093 Shirley Rd., North Collins, NY 14111-9746

M.D. Anderson Volunteers Cooking for Fun, University of Texas M.D. Anderson Cancer Center, Volunteer Services, 1515 Holcombe, Houston, TX 77030

The Maine Collection, Portland Museum of Art, 7 Congress Sq., Portland, ME 04101

Meals by Mildred and Other Fine Methodist Cooks, First United Methodist Church, 311 3rd St. NE, Hickory, NC 28601

Mitten Bay Gourmet, Mitten Bay Girl Scout Council, 5470 Davis Rd., Saginaw, MI 48604

The Montauk Lighthouse Cookbook, Montauk Lighthouse Committee, R.F.D. #2, Box 112, Montauk, NY 11954

Mountain Measures, Junior League of Charleston, Inc., 1009 Bridge Rd., Charleston, WV 25314

Moveable Feasts, Mystic Seaport Museum Stores, 47 Greenmanville Ave., Mystic, CT 06355

The Nashville Cookbook, Nashville Area Home Economics Association, 1041 Hickory Hollow Rd., Nashville, TN 37221

New Additions and Old Favorites, Canterbury United Methodist Church, 350 Overbrook Rd., P.O. Box 130699, Birmingham, AL 35213

Newcomers' Favorites, International and Regional Recipes, Aiken Newcomers' Club, 712 Winged Foot Dr., Aiken, SC 29803

Nothin' Finer, Chapel Hill Service League, P.O. Box 3003, Chapel Hill, NC 27515

One of a Kind, Junior League of Mobile, Inc., Mobile Junior League Publications, P.O. Box 7091, Mobile, AL 36607

Our Cherished Recipes, Second Edition, First Presbyterian Church, P.O. Box 513, 5th and Main, Skagway, AK 99840

Our Daily Bread, Womens Club of Our Lady of Mt. Carmel, 1045 W. 146th St., Carmel, IN 46032

Our Favorite Recipes, Unity Truth Center, 5844 Pinehill Dr., Port Richey, FL 34668

Our Favorite Recipes, Seasoned with Love, Neighborhood Bible Studies, c/o Patti Moore, 1814 Silver Pines Rd., Houston, TX 77062

Out of Our League, Junior League of Greensboro, Inc., league address: 220 State St., Greensboro, NC 27408; book order address: *Out of Our League,* ABR, P.O. Box 2463, Birmingham, AL 35201

Padre Kino's Favorite Meatloaf and Other Recipes from Baja, Arizona, Tucson Community Food Bank, Inc., 827 S. Park Ave., P.O. Box 26727, Tucson, AZ 85726

Party Potpourri, Junior League of Memphis, Inc., 3475 Central Ave., Memphis, TN 38311

The Pasquotank Plate, Christ Episcopal Churchwomen, 200 McMorrine St., Elizabeth City, NC 27909

Pass the Plate, Episcopal Church Women of Christ Episcopal Church, P.O. Box 836, New Bern, NC 28563

Perfect Endings: The Art of Desserts, Friends of the Arts of the Tampa Museum of Art, 600 N. Ashley Dr., Tampa, FL 33602

Phi Bete's Best, Theta Alpha Gamma Chapter, 813 27th St., Bedford, IN 47421

Plain & Elegant: A Georgia Heritage, West Georgia Medical Center Auxiliary, 1514 Vernon Rd., LaGrange, GA 30240

Quilted Quisine, Paoli Memorial Hospital Auxiliary, 255 W. Lancaster Ave., Paoli, PA 19301

Recipes and Remembrances, Hospice at Grady Memorial Hospital, 561 W. Central Ave., Delaware, OH 43015

Recipes and Remembrances of Tolland, Tolland Historical Society, 52 Tolland Green, P.O. Box 107, Tolland, CT 06084

Recipes and Reminiscences of New Orleans, Parent's Club of Ursuline Academy, Inc., 2635 State St., New Orleans, LA 70118

Recipes from the End of the Road, Homer Special Olympics, P.O. Box 207, Anchor Point, AK 99556

Recipes from the Heart I, South Suburban Humane Society Auxiliary, 228 Monee Rd., Park Forest, IL 60466

Reflections of the West, Telephone Pioneers of America, Skyline Chapter No. 67, 441 N. Park Ave., Helena, MT 59601

Rhode Island Cooks, American Cancer Society, Rhode Island Division, Inc., 400 Main St., Pawtucket, RI 02860

Ridgefield Cooks, Women's Committee of the Ridgefield Community Center, 316 Main St., Ridgefield, CT 06877

Ritzy Rhubarb Secrets Cookbook, Litchville Committee 2000, P.O. Box 11-B, Litchville, ND 58461

Rogue River Rendezvous, Junior Service League of Jackson County, 526 E. Main St., Medford, OR 97504

Ronald McDonald House of Burlington, Vermont, Anniversary Edition Cookbook, Ronald McDonald House, 16 S. Winooski Ave., Burlington, VT 05401

Savannah Style, Junior League of Savannah, Inc., 330 Drayton St., Savannah, GA 31401

Savor the Brandywine Valley, A Collection of Recipes, Junior League of Wilmington, Inc., 1801 N. Market St., Wilmington, DE 19802

Savory Secrets: A Collection of St. Louis Recipes, Greater St. Louis Alumni Chapter of Sigma Sigma Sigma, 4710 Iroquois Trail, Godfrey, IL 62035

Seasoned Skillets & Silver Spoons, Columbus Museum Guild, 1251 Wynnton Rd., Columbus, GA 31906

Seasoned with Love, Woodbridge Lioness Club, 13220 Nassau Dr., Woodbridge, VA 22193

Sensational Seasons: A Taste & Tour of Arkansas, Junior League of Fort Smith, Inc., P.O. Box 3266, Fort Smith, AR 72913

Sharing Our Best, Neighborhood Ministries Auxiliary, 1402 Wright Dr., Youngstown, OH 44505

"Show-me" Fine Dining, United Guardsman Foundation, 705 Memorial Dr., St. Joseph, MO 64503

Signature Cuisine, Miami Country Day School Parents' Association, 601 N.E. 107th St., Miami, FL 33161

Simple Elegance, Our Lady of Perpetual Help Women's Guild, 8151 Poplar Ave., Germantown, TN 38138

Simply Heavenly, Woman's Synodical Union of the Associate Reformed Presbyterian Church, 1 Cleveland St., Greenville, SC 29601

Sisseton Centennial Cookbook, Sisseton Centennial Committee, 305 E. Walnut, Sisseton, SD 57262

Some Like It Hot, Bement School, The Street, Deerfield, MA 01342

Some Like It Hot, Junior League of McAllen, Inc., 2212-E Primrose, McAllen, TX 78504

Soroptimist Cooks, Soroptimist International of Dixon, c/o Jacqueline DuPratt, 910 Sievers Way, Dixon, CA 95620

Southern Accent, Junior League of Pine Bluff, Inc., 3 Elm Woods Cir., Pine Bluff, AR 71603

Southern Savoir Faire, Altamont School, 4801 Altamont Rd., Birmingham, AL 35222

Southern Sideboards, Junior League of Jackson, Inc., P.O. Box 4709, Jackson, MS 39296-4709

Southwest Seasons Cookbook, Casa Angelica Auxiliary, Inc., 5629 Isleta Blvd. SW, Albuquerque, NM 87105

Specialties of Indianapolis, Volume 2, Home Economists' Guild of Indianapolis, 7305 East 55th St., Indianapolis, IN 46226

Specialties of the House, Kenmore Association, Inc., 1201 Washington Ave., Fredericksburg, VA 22401

St. Catherine of Siena Celebration Cookbook, St. Catherine of Siena Church, 118 S. State St., DuBois, PA 15801

St. Stephen's Feast, St. Stephen Protomartyr Catholic Church, 3949 Wilmington Ave., St. Louis, MO 63116

Still Fiddling in the Kitchen, National Council of Jewish Women, 30233 Southfield Rd., #100, Southfield, MI 48076

Still Gathering: A Centennial Celebration, Auxiliary to the American Osteopathic Association, 142 E. Ontario St., Chicago, IL 60611

Sugar Snips & Asparagus Tips, Woman's Auxiliary of Infant Welfare Society of Chicago, 1931 N. Halsted, Chicago, IL 60614

The Summerhouse Sampler, Wynnton Elementary School PTA, 2303 Wynnton Rd., Columbus, GA 31906

Sweet Home Alabama Cooking, 44th National Square Dance Convention, 484 Planters Rd., Montgomery, AL 36109-1832

Tampa Treasures, Junior League of Tampa, Inc., 87 Columbia Dr., Tampa, FL 33613

Taste and Share the Goodness of Door County, St. Rosalia's Ladies Sodality of St. Rosalia's Catholic Church, Hwy. 42, Sister Bay, WI 54210

A Taste of Aloha, Junior League of Honolulu, Inc., 1802-A Keeaumoku St., Honolulu, HI 96822

A Taste of Georgia, Newnan Junior Service League, Inc., P.O. Box 1433, Newnan, GA 30264

A Taste of History, University of North Alabama Women's Club, Box 5366, Florence, AL 35632-0001

A Taste of Oregon, Junior League of Eugene, Inc., 2839 Willamette St., Eugene, OR 97405

A Taste of Reno, Food Bank of Northern Nevada, 994 Packer Way, Sparks, NV 89431

A Taste of South Central Pennsylvania, South Central Pennsylvania Food Bank, 3908 Corey Rd., Harrisburg, PA 17109

A Taste of Twin Pines, Twin Pines Alumni of Twin Pines Cooperative House, 321 Highland Dr., West Lafayette, IN 47906

Tastes and Traditions: The Sam Houston Heritage Cookbook, Study Club of Huntsville, P.O. Box 6404, Huntsville, TX 77342-6404

Taste the Good Life, Assistance League of Omaha, 3569 Leavenworth, Omaha, NE 68105

Taste Without Waist, Service League of Hickory, P.O. Box 1563, Hickory, NC 28603

Tempting Southern Treasures Cookbook, Riverchase Women's Club, 2166 Baneberry Dr., Hoover, AL 35244

The Texas Experience, Richardson Woman's Club, Inc., P.O. Box 831963, Richardson, TX 75082

Three Rivers Cookbook I, Child Health Association of Sewickley, Inc., 1108 Ohio River Blvd., Sewickley, PA 15143

Thru the Grapevine, Junior League of Greater Elmira-Corning, Inc., P.O. Box 3150, Elmira, NY 14905

Thymely Treasures, Hubbard Historical Society, 269 Hager St., Hubbard, OH 44425-2013

Today's Traditional: Jewish Cooking with a Lighter Touch, Congregation Beth Shalom, 4746 El Camino Ave., Carmichael, CA 95608

To Market, To Market, Junior League of Owensboro, Inc., P.O. Box 723, Owensboro, KY 42302

Treasured Favorites, Morton County Hospital Auxiliary, 455 Hilltop, Elkhart, KS 67950

Treasured Gems, Hiddenite Center Family, Inc., Church St., Hiddenite, NC 28636

A Treasure of Taste, Auxiliary to St. Joseph Hospital, 215 W. 4th St., Mishawaka, IN 46544

Trinity and Friends Finest, Women of Holy Trinity, P.O. Box 25, Churchville, MD 21028

Tri-State Center for the Arts Celebrity Cookbook, Tri-State Center for the Arts, P.O. Box 712, Pine Plains, NY 12567

Tropical Seasons, A Taste of Life in South Florida, Beaux Arts of the Lowe Art Museum of the University of Miami, Inc., 1301 Stanford Dr., Coral Gables, FL 33146

Virginia Celebrates, Council of the Virginia Museum of Fine Arts, 2600 Grove Ave., Richmond, VA 23221

Virginia Cookery, Past and Present, Episcopal Church Women of Olivet Episcopal Church, P.O. Box 10373, Alexandria, VA 22310

The Virginia Hostess, Junior Woman's Club of Manassas, Inc., P.O. Box 166, Manassas, VA 22110

What's Cookin', Montgomery County Humane Society, 14645 Rothgeb Dr., Rockville, MD 20850

The Wild Wild West, Junior League of Odessa, Inc., 2707 Kermit Hwy., Odessa, TX 79763

The William & Mary Cookbook, Society of the Alumni, College of William and Mary, P.O. Box 2100, Williamsburg, VA 23187-2100

Women Cook for a Cause, Women's Resource Center of Schoolcraft College, 18600 Haggerty Rd., Livonia, MI 48152

Women's Ministry Daily Bread, Word of Life Fellowship, 565 Lovers Ln., Steubenville, OH 43952

National Community Cookbook Award Winners

The editors salute the three national and six regional winners of the 1994 Tabasco® Community Cookbook Awards competition sponsored by McIlhenny Company, Avery Island, Louisiana.

- **First Place Winner:** *Cooking Then and Now*, Gulf Coast Heritage Association, Inc., Osprey, Florida
- **Second Place Winner:** *Heard in the Kitchen*, Heard Museum Guild, Phoenix, Arizona
- **Third Place Winner:** *River Road Recipes III*, Junior League of Baton Rouge, Inc., Baton Rouge, Louisiana
- **New England:** *Cooking with Fire*, Fairfield Historical Society, Fairfield, Connecticut
- **Mid-Atlantic:** *Queen Anne Goes to the Kitchen*, Episcopal Churchwomen of St. Paul's Parish, Centreville, Maryland
- **South:** *Tell Me More*, Junior League of Lafayette, Inc., Lafayette, Louisiana
- **Midwest:** *Madison County Cookbook*, St. Joseph Church, Winterset, Iowa
- **Southwest:** *Cafe Oklahoma*, Junior Service League of Midwest City, Midwest City, Oklahoma
- **West:** *Feast of Eden*, Junior League of Monterey County, Inc., Monterey, California

Index
